TESTING

This book is due for return on or before the last date shown below.

22. AUG. 1986

1 1 DEC 1994

Don Gresswell Ltd., London, N.21 Cat No. 1208

London & Sydney

© 1986 Douglas Shelley and David Cohen
Croom Helm Ltd, Provident House, Burrell Row,
Beckenham, Kent BR3 1AT
Croom Helm Australia Pty Ltd, Suite 4, 6th Floor
64–76 Kippax Street, Surry Hills, NSW 2010, Australia

British Library Cataloguing in Publication Data
Shelley, Douglas
  Testing psychological tests.
  1. Psychological tests
  I. Title   II. Cohen, David, 1946–
  150'.28'7   BF176
ISBN 0-7099-3384-3
ISBN 0-7099-3389-4 Pbk

Phototypeset by Sunrise Setting, Torquay, Devon
Printed and bound in Great Britain
by **Billing & Sons Limited, Worcester.**

CONTENTS

Introduction	1
1. Can Tests Test Without an Environment?	12
2. Are People Consistent or Inconsistent?	31
3. Psychometric Tests, Projective or a New Pattern?	47
4. How Much Individuality Can We Know?	65
5. Types of Validity	81
6. How Reliable Are Tests? How Variable Are People?	106
7. The Perfect Sample	123
8. Odder Techniques	134
9. Popular Testing	151
10. Playful Criteria	163
Bibliography	192
Index	199

60	**F**
36	**H P**
24	**N F U**
18	**T A Z X**
12	**A H X N T**
9	**Z U P T A D**
6	**X D F P N H Z**
5	**D X U N Z T F H**

INTRODUCTION

This is, of course, the optician's chart which hangs on many doctors' walls. It may not look like a psychological test, but it is one. It assesses perceptual and mental ability. The optician judges the vision of the subject according to the way he or she reads the letters on the chart. Despite looking so simple, the test suffers from many problems that afflict far more complex tests. Consider the following points. How well would someone whose first language was Arabic do? What would the consequences be on their score of usually reading from right to left, as opposed to left to right? Would people be able to guess what a letter was if they could only perceive half its shape, like the lower half of a 'B'? Middle-class Europeans would probably recognise the rules of the 'game' involved in reading the chart. People from a different culture might not know they had to read the letters as well as they could so that the optician would be better placed to help them. As they might misread the situation, they might get very nervous. Sensitive opticians might understand their anxiety and set them at their ease; insensitive opticians might get impatient and make their clients perform less well. Results of the test may depend on how well motivated people are, even on whether they want to have spectacles or not. Those who hate the idea of spectacles may well strain to the utmost to show they don't need them. The professional body that represents opticians in Britain, The Society of Opticians, recognises these difficulties.

Psychological tests have many added complications, but it is telling that an analysis of a test as simple as the optician's chart should reveal so many hazards in the way of making an accurate assessment. Recent work on the blind has shown that for decades, using such tests, opticians underestimated the residual sight many still had. Psychological tests are usually treated as frills. Courses in all aspects of psychology involve examining the evidence of test results, yet the topic remains something of an esoteric one. Only those who love statistics, understand the mysteries of factor analysis, and are not frightened by the idea of rotation of factors are likely to be interested.

We shall argue throughout that this is a short-sighted approach because psychological tests raise, and involve, many of the central issues in psychology today. Some, already noted when discussing sensitive opticians, include:

(1) How well we can use results from the laboratory or questionnaires to predict behaviour in the real world?
(2) What is the relationship between attitudes people claim to have and the way they actually behave?
(3) How consistent are individuals from situation to situation and across time?
(4) What is a fair test of a person's skills? Can individuals from different classes and cultures be tested in identical ways?
(5) What aspects of the environment affect performance?
(6) What constitutes a proper sample to base a psychological truth on? If all American undergraduates do X, what can this reveal about the whole human species, if anything?
(7) How complete a picture of a person can one ever get from his or her scores on a series of tests?

Testing also obliges psychologists to confront ethical and political dilemmas because tests are used to make judgements, allocate resources and decide who gets jobs or educational opportunities. The most obvious recent political controversy about testing has been the IQ debate where some have argued that blacks have a lower average IQ and the Japanese have a higher-than-average IQ. As Stephen Jay Gould (1981) has argued in his book, *The Mismeasurement of Man*, there is a long history of using psychological tests in order to justify the political *status quo*. If blacks are inferior, why bother to improve their educational opportunities? Psychological tests are at the heart of such controversies.

One reason why testing has remained rather an esoteric subject is that it seems to require mathematical aptitude. Psychologists do not like to admit publicly their students' feelings about statistics. Fear of statistics is widespread partly because the majority of psychology students in the UK have humanities rather than science A-levels. The good news is that reading this book requires no special mathematical skills. You will not be bombarded with equations for the good reason that statistics often confuse rather than clarify issues. The logical, and psychological, criticisms we offer do not depend on wielding clever mathematical analyses. Rather, our critique (which involves using a number of tests as 'case histories' to illustrate particular problems) focuses on the relationship between what a test claims to be doing and what, in practice, it can be doing. The case histories examine tests in some detail and place each one in a general context. The book is not an exhaustive guide to all tests, but a guide to issues in psychology raised by the use of tests. Like other enthusiasts, enthusiasts for tests often make too grand claims. The limits of any particular test are interesting in themselves. We would also argue the limits of psychological tests as a whole may well reveal the limits of certain approaches to psychology. Henry Murray, a student of personality, once said that all human beings were in some respects unique and like no other men, in some respects like some other men, and in some respects like all other men. At their best, psychological tests can offer comparative data about how we resemble some other men. I am as extravert as my friend George but far less so than Frederick. This is only one aspect of psychology, however. Tests will not explain why I have learned to play backgammon in a particularly aggressive way and why these games remind me of my father. Certain questions in psychology cannot begin to be answered through testing. By the end of this book the reader ought to have a better idea of what these might be.

The history of testing is longer than one might expect. Long before there were psychologists there were psychological tests. Michael Foucault (1973) has charted the development of scientific medicine and the way that doctors made growing use of scientific tools in the eighteenth century to legitimate their authority. By 1810 the idea of measuring mental abilities had been established. Today, we remember Gall and Spurzheim as the eccentric creators of phrenology, the science of the bumps. Decorative charts showed the relationship between bumps on the skull and personality. The outer bumps revealed the inner man. A big bump in one spot meant that you were gifted at 'amativeness'; a small bump here indicated lamentable extravagance. Feel the skull, know the man. By 1860 phrenology was largely discredited, but Gall and Spurzheim left conventional medicine with a model that compared different mental, and emotional, abilities. That proved to be a more valuable legacy than their sensational claims for the bumps.

The need to show that some people were superior became manifest in Victorian Britain. With the British Empire dominating much of the globe, Victorians were eager to prove that they deserved their power. The white man ruled not because he had more guns but because he had more brains. Intrepid explorers who set out to find the source of the Nile or the Zambesi also documented the lives and abilities, or lack of abilities, of the natives they encountered *en route*. The heathen was not just a savage but could be scientifically proved to be an idiot. Walvins (1984) has charted some of these enterprises. It is easy with hindsight to expose and mock such attitudes, but the scientific adventures of Victorians helped pave the way for psychological tests. Francis Galton, one of the fathers of testing, travelled in Africa with various measuring devices, and reported, as he expected, that the white sahib was indeed far more intelligent than any other creature.

Historians now generally reckon that the first psychological laboratory was set up by the German 'experimental philosopher' Willhelm Wundt in Leipzig in 1879. Wundt was more interested in experimenting than in testing individuals to establish differences between them, but he attracted a number of American students. These included James McKeen Cattell, who was to become an influential figure in the United States. Cattell held the chair of psychology at Colombia University, helped found the American Psychological Association, created the magazine *Popular Science*, and published one of the first accounts of psychological tests. His paper *Mental Tests and Measurements* (1896) described fifty different tests and offered individuals the chance to take ten of them.

The 1890s saw much energy devoted to the creation of psychological tests in America. Apart from Cattell, Jastrow had perfected thirteen psychological tests which he demonstrated in 1893 at an exhibition in Chicago. Hugo Munsterberg at Harvard had fourteen tests for school children by 1891. In 1893 Gilbert at Yale reported on the testing of some 1,200 school children. The American Psychological Association set up a committee so that different laboratories could know what others were doing. The American Association for the Advancement of Science decided to sponsor a survey to examine 'the abilities of the white race in the United States'. In the early fervour, the ugly political uses of testing were already hinted at.

In Europe it might have been expected that Britain would become a centre for testing. In 1882 the energetic Galton set up a laboratory in South Kensington to measure human faculties. Galton even had a mobile display which he toured round exhibitions. For a fee, the Victorian, on his or her day out, could be comprehensively measured. Galton offered to do head circumference, perceptual tests and a variety of intellectual exercises from mental arithmetic to anagrams against the clock.

Despite Britain's early lead, it was Paris that was to pave the way in the creation of tests. The French psychologist Alfred Binet, working together with Victor Henri, proposed a series of tests of the 'whole man'. In a paper they published in 1896, they suggested the need for tests of memory, imagery, imagination, aesthetic sense, attention, motor skills and even such elusive characteristics as strength of will and moral fibre. By 1903 Binet's aims were narrower. His book, *L'Étude Experimentale de L'Intelligence*, laid the groundwork for the first standardised intelligence tests. In 1905, with Theodore Simon, he produced the first intelligence scale for children. Binet saw that intelligence had to increase as children grew up, and he was the first to arrive at the concept of *mental age* as opposed to chronological age. Confidence abounded. By 1903 the American psychologist Thorndike was able to claim in his *Educational Psychology* that some tests were better than others in predicting educational success.

Today there are far more tests, far more psychology and far less confidence in either. To see the world as these early psychologists saw it requires an effort of the imagination. Binet believed that through his tests it would be possible to revolutionise the teaching of handicapped children; Freud thought that psychoanalysis would relieve centuries of human suffering; the behaviourist John B. Watson believed it would be possible to re-condition human beings to make them paragons of achievement and adjustment without a neurosis in sight. Terman adapted Binet's work to embark on his longitudinal study of children with a 'genius' IQ, hoping his findings might eventually suggest how to bring up more geniuses.

Soon, however, psychological tests were being used to reinforce the *status quo*. During the First World War the American military made considerable use of IQ tests. Humane psychologists like Robert Yerkes, a specialist in animal behaviour, used the results to argue that Jews ought to be kept out of the United States because they were so inferior that they would pollute the racial mix: blacks ought not to be allowed to breed at all. Intelligence testing can reinforce political and social prejudices, (Gould 1981; Kamin 1982).

Binet rapidly had to accept limitations. Originally, he hoped to develop a comprehensive set of tests, assessing far more than intelligence. It proved just too complex. He produced only norms of average performance at a particular age, norms against which to judge individual children. IQ scores are a child's mental age divided by his, or her, chronological age. Without norms for each group it is impossible to measure mental age. By the time he died in 1911, Binet had published one scale and two refinements of it. Terman, at Stanford University, continued the work which led to the publication in 1917 of the Stanford-Binet Test. It remains one of the two standard intelligence tests. After Binet's death his collaborator Theodore Simon hired the young Jean Piaget to study why children made mistakes on the test. One of the authors of this book has argued that many of the flaws in Piaget's work stem from these origins because his focus had to be on why children failed to be logical. The historically interesting point is that early efforts to refine intelligence tests were to influence the development of child psychology tremendously (Cohen 1983).

Despite the initial enthusiasm, by 1920 the only tests which could claim much reliability and validity were intelligence tests. No respectable tests of attitudes or personality existed. Paradoxically, there was great hunger for such tests — especially in America. The behaviourist Watson complained in 1927 that America was 'psychology mad'. It certainly had a passion for insight. Self-help magazines sprouted, and some had frank titles like *Self Help Psychology*. Large circulation glossies like *McCalls* and *Liberty* ran articles on psychology and, especially, on how the upwardly mobile American could use psychology. Topics covered included how to be a better parent, how to impress the boss and how to win friends and influence people. A witty book could be written on the early history of popular testing.

During the First World War, opposition to the use of tests hardly surfaced. Yerkes pushed faith in testing for the army, but by 1940 America was witnessing an early version of modern controversies about IQ and testing. Minton (1984) has studied the exchanges in the late 1930s between Terman's group at Stanford, by now firm believers in IQ tests and the role of heredity, and the Iowa Child Welfare Research Station, who had doubts about both of these. The Iowa group argued for the role of the environment and claimed that Terman's tests were inadequate. Terman commented: 'It appears characteristic of the Iowa group that they so often find difficulty reporting accurately the data of others or their own'. Minton points out that the exchanges between these groups were 'especially heated and derisive'. They were early versions of the rows that erupted in the late 1960s, when Arthur Jensen claimed his results showed that black Americans scored, on average, one standard deviation lower than whites on IQ tests. In practical terms that meant about 15 IQ points lower. Since then a vast amount of literature has argued the case for and against IQ tests, whether intelligence depends mostly on heredity, and what the true meaning of these results are, if indeed they were true in the first place.

Today psychological tests are widely used in Britain, the USA, Japan and continental Europe. Britain has only one regular producer of tests, the National Foundation for Educational Research (NFER) which allows only properly qualified individuals to buy most of its tests. America has a much larger test-creation industry. Educational Testing Service, Psychological Test Services, Western Psychological Services are among the leading manufacturers of tests. The American Psychological Association estimates that there are perhaps 8,000 tests in active service. A glance at the literature will reveal there are tests of everything ranging from the Quick Tests (which tests how clever you are as fast as possible) to the Intercollegiate Basketball Instrument (which tests how much team spirit you have). There are tests of leadership, creativity, attitudes to everything from addiction to zoology, capacity for moral judgement and, one of our favourites, a test of how well you can drive which does not require you to do anything as banal as get in a car. Education, medicine and industry consume tests. All aspects of human activity are covered. We have not yet traced a paper-and-pencil test of sexual prowess, but no doubt some ambitious psychologist is creating the Orgasmic Potential Test which depends entirely on answers in the head rather than in the bed. Buros, the leading manual of testing, lists over 2,000 tests created from 1971 to 1977 with this activity, it is surprising there are so few general books on testing. Manuals explain how to use particular tests, and there is extensive literature on intelligence testing but no general critical guide to the issues that surround testing, often issues at the heart of psychology.

We have drawn extensively on a regular feature of our magazine *Psychology News*, 'This Month the Test we Test . . .', written each month by Douglas Shelley. Since 1979 some 40 tests have been reviewed. We have expanded these critical pieces and used many as 'case histories' to illustrate problems that arise out of testing, and in some chapters have analysed a number of tests that bear crucially on a certain theme.

Chapter 1 looks at a very basic issue in testing. Can one create an effective test in a neutral environment? One of the ideals of testing, an ideal that would show off how scientific it is, is to find tasks or questions which can be set in the controlled environment of the laboratory and yet will predict how someone will perform in the uncontrolled arena of real life. This noble aim seems to be highly elusive even with rather less complex creatures than human beings. Dogs will not perform thus, it seems, even when they are tested on tasks which specific breeds were bred for! Chapter 2 expands on this theme by looking at how consistent people are. When we say someone is anxious, do we mean that they are anxious all the time or that they are more likely to reveal anxiety in particular situations? Tests often make assumptions about the consistency of behaviour because there is no point in showing that I am ambitious and well motivated today if tomorrow, when I go for a major interview, I flop in my chair like a tramp and start singing punk songs. Will I do that if I become managing director? An analysis of three tests suggests that we are far from arriving at a way of judging the consistency of behaviour. Chapter 3 compares different methods of testing and looks in particular at tests like the Thematic Apperception Test and Rorschachs, which claim to give a much deeper understanding of individual motives than anything so crude as a questionnaire where one must tick 'yes', 'no' or 'maybe' to complex questions. Chapter 4 expands on this debate by examining a number of tests which appear to allow for individual complexities. These include tests of personal interests and those that tap what view of the world an individual prefers. There has been a long debate in psychology about the use of *idiographic* methods, techniques which allow both for some exact measurement and some degree of individuality. A recent book (Runyan 1984) is devoted to looking at such techniques, and covers such novelties as *assisted autobiography*, where the subject collaborates with a psychologist. Their mutual aim is a picture of the 'whole man' that is not completely flawed by egomania. How well can tests get to the depth of a person? Is there much point in using tests not to compare people against each other but to deepen the understanding of an individual?

Those who use tests assume that they have some validity. Chapter 5 examines a number of instances where tests seem to have no obvious validity. What is the use of giving a driving test with a pencil and paper? Even motoring morons (such as one of the authors of this book, who failed his driving test on every item) appear to do well on this test because there is no link between the skills it requires and the skills it purports to test. A number of other cases of tests, which bear no relationship to the realities they claim to be assessing, are examined. Chapter 6 considers how reliable tests are, given how unreliable human beings can be. Performance on quite simple tasks fluctuates from day to day. The chapter takes a critical look at four tests — one used on Down's Syndrome children, one used on old people, one used on scientists themselves — to delve into how tests cope with the variability of our behaviour.

One perennial problem of all psychological studies is sampling. Freud was criticised because it was pointed out that psychoanalysis might work for neurotic Viennese ladies who had nothing better to do than have an interesting complex in between shopping and the opera, but ordinary people were too poor to indulge in such delicious crises. Freud's sample was far too specialised to allow him to make universal claims. Today the most studied specimen is the American college undergraduate, who usually has to participate in a number of experiments in order to get through his course. (Psychology cares about freedom!) Chapter 7 is devoted to some of the problems of sampling mice and men. The sample that an experiment or test is performed on is critical. We examine the sampling of a test of menstrual symptoms, of one of attitudes to work and one of family conversations. Few samples are impeccable.

Chapter 8 looks at some unusual forms of assessment. As a result of our criticisms in Chapters 2 to 7, we argue there is a need to develop more diverse kinds of tests, some aiming to use quite new approaches. We examine some examples. Despite much scepticism concerning tests, the media continue to use them. Chapter 9 is a survey of how the press in the UK uses testing and the extent (very small) to which they warn readers not to take their tests too seriously. The last chapter, 10, returns to some of the political and ethical questions raised in this introduction. If testing is used to select people against each other, for jobs or scarce education, how fair are those tests? It is not just that few tests are culture-free or culture-fair, but that most make assumptions about society, usually conventional assumptions. These include the notion that the dominant culture has the right to impose its standards on minorities, that those who conform will do well in school, that academic skills are worth more than practical skills. Only when we have a leak do we rate the plumber superior to the philosopher.

In the final chapter we also try to suggest some new criteria for judging tests, criteria which we hope will lead to the development of some new tests. In the early chapters of this book we show how hard it is to construct tests which are reliable, valid, based on a proper sample, and usefully able to predict how people will behave in the real world. Attaching numbers to people is not hard; attaching *meaningful* numbers is very problematic. The conventional criteria for judging tests come from one tradition in psychology, the tough scientific one. If only people were quarks, all would be quantified — and well. Even tests that emerged from the 'softer' tradition of clinical psychology, like the Rorschach Ink Blot test, accept these conventional criteria as correct.

These conventional criteria can be divided into two sorts; *numerical* criteria and *reality* criteria. Numerical criteria deal with the relationship of test scores to each other. Individuals when re-tested on a test ought to score much the same as before; tests ought to be internally consistent; the correct answer should not always be *yes*; pilot studies ought to ensure that people understand the questions and that there is a balance of questions on different aspects of a topic. We often criticise tests for failing to meet these rigorous criteria, but they are manifestly useful — though there are occasions when psychologists stick to them too rigidly.

Reality criteria are more complicated. Issues such as how representative a sample ought to be and how well a test predicts raise more complex problems. We shall argue that these criteria are both too narrow and not narrow enough. They are not narrow enough because there is an insidious trend for psychologists to compare performance on one test with performance on another. How well I solve anagrams may nicely predict how well I will solve crossword puzzles, but it will reveal little about how well I speak when trying to chat up a girl. In textbooks, these criteria often appear rigorous, but they are often not used rigorously. More rigour is needed, though, if we are to continue to use tests to predict behaviour. The conventional criteria, paradoxically, are also too narrow. The emphasis on prediction means that those who devise tests have tended to ignore other potential criteria. Some of these involve issues such as what subjects think of the tests they are taking, how they can exploit taking the tests to develop themselves, and what kind of tests they believe would be more useful to them. As Sternberg (1981) noted, the agenda for testing is very much set by psychologists. New criteria ought to explore these kinds of issues. One suggestion put forward is that one should judge tests by the extent to which people recognise themselves in the results. This is appealing, partially useful, but also limiting. We try in the final chapter to outline some new criteria to improve technical standards and, also, to protect test-takers.

This is not the 'Michelin Guide to Good Testing'. We have not given each test a number of forks for reliability and a number of stars for validity. We have tried to select tests which raise important and interesting issues so the emphasis we place on different aspects of tests varies. We normally comment on reliability, validity and sampling, but not necessarily to the same extent for each test as we would be obliged to do were this the psychometric Michelin. Also, as a result of our emphasis, though we do cover many central tests like the Wechsler, other intelligence tests, the TAT, the Eysenck Personality Inventory and Kelly's Repertory Grid, we do not pretend this is an exhaustive manual of all tests. Rather, the tests we have chosen raise central issues. By focusing on them we hope to show that testing is not an esoteric adjunct to psychology. It is a vital tool even if the tool is not perfect. Certainly, using some tests is rather like trying to bang in a nail with a corkscrew. It can be done, but the nail won't quite fit, your thumb will be damaged, and the corkscrew is out of true. Knowing what psychological tests can, and can't do, seems crucial in deciding what psychology can, and can't, do. We would like to thank Chris Brand and, especially, Professor Alan Smithers for their testing comments.

1 CAN TESTS TEST WITHOUT AN ENVIRONMENT?

If tests are to assess individuals fairly, then results on them should not be influenced by the environment. The rules that surround many formal examinations recognise this ideal. All candidates enter the examination hall on equal terms. They are not allowed to bring in books, or advisers; they are not allowed to talk to the invigilator or others in the room. The aim is to create a vacuum, and in that vacuum candidates will be able to concentrate totally to do their best. The only variable reflected in their answers will be their different abilities. To protect candidates from any distractions, most authorities make the hall in which an examination is held almost a quarantined space. Imagine trying to get an urgent phone message through to someone sitting an A-level! It would be virtually impossible.

Psychologists have gone even further, they have tried to devise what seems to be 'an ideal testing environment'. There the influence of all variables, other than the subjects' skill, could be eliminated. As it happens, there is much evidence from personality research to suggest that people will respond very differently either to examination conditions or to the psychologists' utopian, neutral environment. Different personality types respond very differently. To create an environment that is 'equal for all' may require divine intervention, and, so far at least, God seems uninterested in psychological tests.

In this chapter we look at three case studies that reflect basic problems about the environment in which a test is given. The first case study looks at work on dogs. Enthusiasts for tests like the IQ test argue that it is a neutral test and the best predictor of subsequent performance out in the real world. With an IQ test under 110 you are unlikely to get to university: with an IQ of over 140 you are unlikely to end up a dustman. Terman's longitudinal study of high-IQ children did show that many went on to do very well. Many grew up into politicians and lawyers, doctors and businessmen; others, however, ended up with nothing more to their intellectual credit than a very high IQ. Endless debates agonise on whether IQ does predict adequately. The first case study suggests a more radical thesis. It is based on tests of dog intelligence. Scott and Fuller (1965) found, against their preconceptions, that they could not construct tests for dogs which allowed specific breeds to show off the special abilities they had been bred for. Outside the relevant and natural environment, the dogs just did not perform. What is true for a dog is likely to be even more true for human beings, who, even in dog-loving Britain, are more complicated creatures.

Our next two case studies develop points about the environment. The second case study examines the family environment. The Parental Bonding Instrument sounds fearsome, but is, in fact, an attempt to assess what makes families stay together. Developed in Australia, the test is odd in largely neglecting issues of class and socio-economic factors. The test presumes a neutral environment in all continents, too. The third case study looks at what subjects think of questionnaires and the factors that they know influence their answers. Just as psychologists dream of a neutral environment, so they dream of a perfect subject. The perfect subject responds freely and naturally but without any self-awareness. He or she never thinks about the demands filling in a questionnaire imposes, let alone any flaws in the questions. It would be impertinent for a rat to quibble at the design of the maze he was being made to run. The human subject should be as uncritical. This may be a psychologist's fantasy. Subjects think about questionnaires and even have feelings and opinions about them! Whyte (1956) and Packard (1959) gave hints on how to outwit the questionnaire-laden psychologists, but did not study how the subject might feel about the exercise.

Scott and Fuller (1965), in their work on dogs, do not replace more conventional critiques of testing which suggest that class, culture and motivation affect performance. Their study raises more basic issues.

Case Study One

Test tested: Performance of Dogs
Example of questions: Get food from top of obstacles
Form of answer: Correct solution
Our focus: Environment

Perhaps dog breeds represent the ultimate in artificial selection for sameness and diversity within the same species: the poodle, St

Bernard, spaniel and alsatian seem so different and yet they can usually successfully interbreed. Scott and Fuller began research into the genetics of the social behaviour of dogs in the late 1940s at Jackson Laboratory in Maine, USA. They compared the behaviour of pure-bred animals and several breeds, when reared by their own mothers and when cross-fostered with mothers of other strains, and between pure and cross-bred animals: fox terrier, Shetland sheepdog, beagle, American cocker spaniel and basenji. On various tests the most obvious overall differences were between the wary, independent and quiet basenjis and the lively, sociable cocker spaniels. These two breeds were crossed for the genetic experiments. The reciprocal cross — a male of one breed by female of the other, and vice versa — tests possible effects of sex-linked inheritance and maternal environment. The first generation hybrid males are crossed back to their pure-bred mothers, so that the backcross and first generations are raised in the same maternal environment, and all differences ought to be due to heredity. The second generation hybrids should show maximum variability due to heredity. Scott's and Fuller's results are so mortifying that we quote them at length:

> We found that it was extremely difficult to set up a test which would measure only one ability. Basenjis are excellent jumpers and climbers and we invented a box-climbing test to measure this. Food was placed on the top of boxes of varying heights, and the Basenjis had to climb or jump to get it. However, they were quite wary of strange objects in their pens and were not strongly interested in food. They approached the boxes rather hesitantly and did not make unusually good scores. By contrast, cockers are not naturally gifted in jumping or climbing . . . they were not wary of the boxes and were strongly interested in food. They would back off at a distance, run full tilt at the boxes, and scramble up with such energy that they often got the food quicker than did the Basenjis with their superior ability.

Many dog owners ask which breed is the most intelligent and the answer is 'all breeds would do equally well provided they could be equally motivated, did not show emotional reactions that interfered with the test and did not have sensory or motor defects that interfered with performance'. The authors found that, at one time, many of the dogs were doing either well or badly in all the problem-solving tests (similar to IQ tests), but it turned out that this correlation was caused by the fact that the basenjis, and some of their descendants, showed a fear of strange apparatus. That made them relatively poor performers.

If a test is set up so that one dog cannot do it and another can barely succeed, the initial difference in hereditary ability may not be great. However, the dog which fails soon stops trying (perhaps with teacher's 'help') while the one which succeeds becomes more highly motivated with each success (perhaps these dogs have 'middle-class' parents). Work at more and more complicated problems can considerably magnify the original hereditary difference (again with teacher's 'help' about expectations of success and failure). Motivation also leads to practice. A beagle in a field is excited by the new smells and sights, whether there is game present or not, and travels over every yard of ground. A fox terrier is completely bored unless it can hear something or see a moving object which it can chase. So the beagle practices his hunting, which reinforces the difference in original ability.

Finally, the different breeds of dogs seem to differ in their range of general adaptability. In the standard environments which were set up, most of the tests were done by the dogs on their own to avoid the possibility of receiving unconscious help from the experimenters. The hunting breeds, like the cockers and beagles, were excellent performers; working dogs like the Shetland sheepdog bred to work with human beings and obey orders did relatively badly. They did not develop confidence, and often seemed to be waiting for someone to tell them what to do rather than going ahead and solving the problem by themselves.

Scott's and Fuller's work suggests that when testers have employed that hallowed god, a standard testing situation, they may well have controlled out most of the environmental influences on test performance, especially those that are positive. Their own imposed devices have led them to a genetic interpretation of their findings; as it were, they overestimate the independent beagle and underestimate the sociable sheepdog.

The intelligence of dogs may appear esoteric, but Scott's and Fuller's research has implications in the classroom. Stott (1981) looked at behaviour disturbance and failure to learn in 'a study of cause and effect'. Many studies show that children who have learning difficulties also suffer from behavioural and emotional problems such as being too aggressive, too passive, too dependent and too defensive. Stott reasoned that the only way to find out whether such behaviour difficulties caused learning difficulties or vice versa was to start before children went off to school.

Stott studied 1,292 Canadian children from Guelph, Ontario. He asked teachers to screen them for behaviour problems within three months of their entering kindergarten at an average age of 5.7 years. They had had no formal instruction in reading or writing and, Stott believed, no experience of failure. Teachers were given six questions to answer:

(1) Is he/she timid, lacking confidence, fearful of joining in activities?
(2) Does he/she seem unconcerned about being in the teacher's 'good books', never greeting or smiling or showing work for approval?
(3) Does he/she have phases of lethargy and unresponsiveness to what is going on around him?
(4) Is it difficult to make him/her settle to any activity or keep seated?
(5) Does he/she react impulsively to everything — grabbing things out of turn, continually pestering, meddling, getting into tempers when frustrated, and not heeding correction for more than a moment?
(6) Does he/she seem to go out of his/her way to be naughty, to annoy the teacher or other children, to make provocatively rude, or nasty remarks?

No contact was made with the schools until the cohort were near the end of their third school year. The teachers at that time, who were not the same as those who had carried out the kindergarten screening, were asked to check the same six questions for each of the original pupils still attending the same schools. Each child was given a score from 0 to 3 for each question, and a total score for all six. The children were divided into low, medium and high groups. Written group tests of reading and arithmetic were also given to the children, who were subsequently divided into three equal groups.

The six questions typify general ways in which children cope with their human and material environment. A child who is timid (Question 1) will be afraid to commit himself to any strange task and so will deprive himself of the experiences needed for the development of problem-solving skills. They could be labelled 'basenji-type children'. Stott claims this form of behaviour disturbance has been little emphasised, compared with hyperactivity, as a cause of academic failure because such children seem dull, so they don't bother the teacher. Their poor performance in IQ tests, full of just the sorts of strange and difficult problems from which they withdraw, confirms their 'dullness'.

The emotional disturbance typified by Question 2 suggests a state of affairs in which the child is deprived of the 'cognitively stimulating atmosphere where the teacher was rated at least as moderately warm'. They could be labelled 'fox terrier children'. Shipman and her co-workers (1976) found that to be a prerequisite for academic success in young children. Low-achieving children showed less than average enjoyment of talking, listening and verbal interaction. Question 3 (lethargy and unresponsiveness to environmental stimuli) tapped such lethargy and gave the highest correlation with poor academic performance.

Question 4 concerns hyperactivity. Here one of the physical differences between our dogs and our pupils emerges: we don't expect our dog to sit down and read books about how to become super-dogs. Much schooling relies on physical passivity designed to torture the overactive child.

Question 5 identifies temperamental impulsivity which interferes with learning because the child does not give himself time to perceive the relevant features of the task, to relate them to his earlier experiences, or to reflect upon his present perceptions in order to organise them into concepts. This sounds very similar to Kagan's 'Reflectivity-Impulsivity' dimension. Kagan's impulsive child is more concerned with giving any quick, immediate response rather than with its actual content.

Question 6 identifies the hostile child who not only does not seek approval but actively seeks disapproval. As teacher wants all children to do well, they, of course, will go out of their way to do badly.

Stott notes that 'first-hand observations of low-achieving children [indicate] that the coping styles typified by the six screening questions are likely to engender cognitive styles which are inimical to learning'. Later he adds,

> The strategy for non-involvement which the failing child chooses depends on his temperament and his cultural tradition. If he is apprehensive by nature he will be tempted to retreat into a pose

of dullness . . . at least 20 per cent of young children, even in a moderately well-to-do locality suffer from handicaps of motivation and behaviour which impair spontaneous learning. . . . The advice of certain linguists assumes that all children possess positive motivation, the confidence and the skills of attention and reflectivity which would enable them to acquire reading without anything more than stand by help from the teacher.

Usually, tests of children presume such interest and motivation, reflecting perhaps middle-class values.

Historically, psychology has had an uneasy relationship with class, which is, after all, a sociological concept. Studies do, of course, point to the different success rates of working-class and middle-class children, but there has been rather little study of how class is reflected in behaviour or attitudes. This is, perhaps, especially true of American psychology since one of the powerful myths of American society is that it is relatively classless. Anyone can make it to the White House or to the board of General Motors. Psychological tests do often reveal class differences, but it is surprising how easily the whole issue can be relegated. Our second case study tries to explore two separate issues — that of class and that of studying, not the individual, but the whole family. Psychology pays much lip-service to the importance of families. Ever since Freud, it has been acknowledged that the family makes or breaks individuals, but its dynamics are notoriously hard to study. An Australian team, led by Parker, created the Parental Bonding Instrument (not as homage to the Marquis de Sade!) to see how parents bonded their children to them.

Case Study Two

Test tested: The Parental Bonding Instrument
Example of questions: 'Think back to when you were 16. As you remember your Mother and Father which of the following is true:'
Spoke to me with a warm and friendly voice.
Tended to baby me.
Did not want me to grow up.

Form of answer: 4-point scale
Our focus: Class

By the time Parker, Tupling and Brown came to create their test, they could draw on a vast literature to tell them what made good parents. Dr Spock has had many predecessors. Pollock (1983) in her book *Forgotten Children* has traced guides on good parenting back to the seventeenth century. Parker *et al.* (1979) also used studies which looked at how parents behaved. Given psychology's bias to study the abnormal, such studies focus most on parents whose children had psychiatric problems. This led the authors to a two-dimensional model in which *care* and *psychological control* were the crucial variables. They believed that the notion of 'psychological control' was unclear and so, while also examining 'care', they said they wanted to concentrate on 'psychological control'. The literature suggested affection, sensitivity, co-operation, indifference, strictness, punitiveness, rejection, control, overprotection and encouragement of independence and of autonomy were all variables to study. Honing in on *psychological control*, the authors left out *physical control*. Some research has suggested that working-class parents are more likely to slap or clout their children to discipline them though it may also be that working-class parents admit that more readily. In Britain, the upper middle classes prefer to cart their children off to boarding school where teachers and prefects wield the cane. One of the oddities of this test is that it was devised in Australia and published in Britain. Parker *et al.* do not comment on this fact even though Australia is an immigrant society with a far less rigid class structure. A test, they assume, can cross oceans without too much difficulty. From their analysis of the literature the authors got a list of 114 items. These were reduced to 99 and factor analysed with a limitation of four factors. The first factor, which accounted for 52 per cent of the variance, was strongly bipolar, and labelled 'care/involvement versus indifference/rejection'. The second factor took up 29 per cent of the variance and was called 'control/overprotection/intrusion versus encouragement of independence'. The third factor was bipolar, accounted for 11 per cent of the variance, and contained 'overprotection' and 'encouragement of autonomy'. The authors found the fourth factor difficult to interpret because of its diverse content. The items which did not clearly contribute to one of the first three factors were culled, leaving 48 items for the main study.

To validate the test 79 female and 71 male respondents aged from 17 to 40 (mean age 25) completed forms, so data were collected for 150 mothers and 148 fathers. Validation consisted of comparing scale scores with responses to a subset of the Thematic Apperception Test and also interviewing 65 of the sample. It is noted that 'the responses consistently showed the expectation or stereotype that mothers are controlling whether directly or indirectly'. In the interviews each subject was asked to discuss the 'emotional relationship' they had with each parent, and the likelihood that each parent would let them 'do their own thing'. Two raters independently assessed the content of these interviews, and assigned a score from 5 to 1 for each parent's 'care' and 'overprotectiveness'.

A factor analysis of the total samples' responses to the 48 items was performed, and it was decided that the final scales of a two-dimensional model would consist of 25 items: 12 'care' items and 13 'overprotection' items. Using a Likert scaling from 0 to 3, the 12 items of the 'care' scale allow a maximum score of 36, and the 13 items of the 'overprotection' scale allow a maximum score of 39.

As the scales were developed on an unrepresentative group, mainly of nurses, a sample of 500 patients attending three general practitioners in Sydney (Australia) gave normative data. The general findings were: mothers are experienced as more caring and somewhat more overprotective than fathers, but the sex of the child does not influence a parent's capacity to 'care' or to be 'overprotective'.

There was a weak positive association between higher social class and a greater maternal care score, but no clear association between social class and parental care and overprotection. Australia is much less of a class-ridden society than Britain. The Newsons' (1970) research is especially relevant when considering the cross-cultural applicability of the Parker *et al.* data. The Newsons found that working-class children are taught to be independent in the sense that they learn to fend for themselves *among other children* in a variety of situations where adult supervision is likely to be minimal. They are allowed to wander much further than their middle-class counterparts to recreation grounds where there are large groups of unsupervised children. By contrast, the middle-class parents exerted control over their children's choice of friends and location of play, and encouraged them to be independent by learning to rely on *other adults* for support. Middle-class children could stay a night away from home with a friend, but it had to be fully understood that the friend's mother was in charge. Thus, the Newsons concluded that the middle-class child is introduced to independence by degrees and in a *highly protected* context.

No doubt the Newsons' findings are generally true of British children, but would this be borne out if validation of the Parental Bonding Instrument was attempted in Britain? The reason for doubt is the allegedly unobtrusive nature of middle-class control, and the successful 'brainwashing' of children into thinking that they are autonomous when in fact their movements are more closely monitored than the punter's favourite horse in the 3.30. This may be the reason why 'psychological control of children' appears to be such an ambiguous dimension, and also why the Thematic Appercention Test revealed 'direct' or 'indirect' control rather than no control at all. A 'sense of autonomy' may mean nothing more than controlling elements being successfully hidden (e.g. a 'reasoned' no, rather than a definitive no without reasons). As questions are answered retrospectively an effect for the 'golden age' of childhood cannot be ruled out.

Parker sees the scales as allowing five types of parental bonding to be examined: average (defined statistically); high care/low over protection (which might be conceptualised as optimal bonding); low care/low overprotection (conceptualised as absent or weak bonding); high care/high overprotection (conceptualised as affectionate constraint); and low care/high overprotection (conceptualised as affectionless control).

Although it would be very unwise to use the test's normative data in Britain, the instrument itself could be a most useful research tool in foster care. For decades social workers have been exhorted to 'match' foster parents with foster children, and sometimes foster parents' own children with foster children, and yet 'how to match what with whom' has never been answered. Parker's two-dimensional model is limited, but it does assess very important aspects of family relationships. Many local authorities have adopted schemes for the short-term fostering of adolescents who are expected to fit into a particular family pattern. The test could be used to create a typology of foster families and hopefully, one could be developed for children in care. The questionnaire is short, easily scored, and might be an acceptable substitute for some of the voluminous case material that social workers are expected to compile. It would be absurd to think that this instrument by itself would be a panacea for foster-care problems, but any improvement on the 50 per cent breakdown rate can only be an improvement. To make it effective, though, would require it to be amplified with proper concern for how different social classes may think it correct to bring their children up. To do that successfully would require a different perception of class. Instead of the familiar assumption of 'middle class good — working class bad', a new Bonding Instrument would look at the ways individuals of different classes tried to express both their care, love and protectiveness. For all its merits, the Parental Bonding Instrument is a symptom of how psychology, with its focus on the individual, would rather ignore class.

A rather less serious instance of this fantasy of the neutral environmental is the way psychological tests ignore the weather. Howarth and Hoffman (1984), in a small but useful study, have just shown that the weather affects both our mood and our competence. Sunny days do make us feel, yes, sunnier. And when it is hot, we concentrate less well.

The neutral environment also demands that the subject taking psychological tests be not too self-aware. He or she should not understand the rules of the game and grasp too clearly the significance of the questions the psychologist is asking. Bannister (1981) argued that, here, personal construct theory had much to offer test and research design, a point to which we shall come later. Doing so he noted wryly:

> Curiously psychologists are most likely to acknowledge the humanity of their subjects when they begin to fear that subjects are somehow tricking and confusing them. Hence the rush to embed lie scales into questionnaires (deceiving the subject in order that the subject shall not deceive the scientist); the search for the naïve subject who will be too stupid to realise the point of the experiment (a search which ultimately carries many psychologists into the land of the rat, the cat and the wood louse) . . .

To be studied properly, the subject must remain fairly naïve. America has seen much research into the design of questionnaires and 'experimenter effects' where subjects seem to please those who study them. Surprisingly, though, it is Polish psychology which has produced one of the most subversive studies. Usually, psychologists explain behaviour in terms of the past experience of the subject. If young Johnny is depressed, was it because he was badly potty-trained (à la Freud), or because he learned bad emotional habits (à la behaviourists)?

Yet if a psychologist asks young Johnny to fill in a questionnaire, Johnny's history becomes irrelevant because the whole focus is on how Johnny responds to a question instead of why. This would be highly eccentric in another context. Imagine going to a doctor with a heavy cold and being asked only how forcefully you coughed, whether mucus was more concentrated in the left or right nostril and being measured for the amount of gunk streaming from your eyes. After which, you were never asked how you actually came to be in this state or offered any remedy. Personality questionnaires have never held out any hope for a cure of anything — unless they are specifically clinical — but have suffered from the other faults. Maria Nowakowska of the Research Centre for Praxiology, Polish Academy of Sciences, offers a useful analysis of 'a Model for Answering a Questionnaire Item'. What are the precise reasons why individuals tick one answer to a question rather than another?

Case Study Three: A Question of Questionnaires

Test tested: Model for Answering a Questionnaire Item
Example of Questions: Do you often feel depressed? (Subjects were then asked about a series of questions about how they reacted to this item)
Form of answer: 7-point scale
Our focus: The self-awareness of subjects.

Nowakowska's work suggests that psychologists cannot treat subjects as naïve. In the past there have been studies of how people answer questionnaires, but these focus on mistakes of design which seduce the subject into slack, repetitive or untrue answers. For example, psychologists have tried to assess the effects of response style, response set and match (that is, whether the subject's interpretation of questions 'matches' that of the psychologist).

Militants and liberals often comprise the 'response set', and will endorse most politically 'left' items (no benefit cuts; free National Health Service and anti-capital punishment). The trouble with the 'response set' is that they may support contradictory actions:

freedom of expression, but outlaw the National Front and British Movement. 'Response style' is concerned with a preference for a certain type of answer. The authoritarian personality who sees everything in 'black-and-white' terms will opt for extremes. If asked to rate their opinions on a 7-point scale, this group will always use the ends, either agreeing or disagreeing violently. Finally, the subject's interpretation of the question has come under scrutiny. A Welsh Nationalist may affirm 'Patriotism towards your country' if his belief is that the question is about Wales, but not if the question is believed to be about, or includes, England. A recent legal wrangle over intelligence tests highlighted the differences between testers' and testees' expectations of what constitutes the correct answer. Is 'winter' defined as 'a season', 'cold season', 'the coldest season of the year', or 'in the northern hemisphere, the period between December to February'? Dispute!

Nowakowska selected 28 items from Cattell's 16-Personality Factors Questionnaire. 56 subjects answered 17 questions about each of the 28 items. All the questions ranged from positive ('This item was important for you') to negative ('This item was trivial for you') and were scored on 7-point scales. The following list gives an example from either the positive or the negative end of each question:

1. this item was trivial for you
2. this item clearly defined the situation
3. this item clearly defined your reaction to the presented situation
4. this item did not demand long bringing to mind of facts and experiences
5. this item was difficult to understand because of the choice of words
6. you rarely think about the subject of this item
7. you prefer that someone who makes a difference to you does not know your answer to this item
8. this item was difficult to understand because of the intricate structure of the sentence
9. you reacted rarely this way
10. you like to think about the subject of this item
11. you have never been in the situation described in this item
12. this item was unpleasant for you

13. your answer to this item would be approved by your social environment
14. this item aroused anxiety in you
15. you could not change your answer
16. this item reminded you of some previously experienced failure or threat
17. you had no difficulty in sincerely answering this item

A factor analysis produced 4 common and 3 specific factors and were interpreted as follows:

(1) *Emotional and motivational attitude* was made up of unpleasant or pleasant content of the question (scale 12); presence or lack of anxiety (scale 14): and seeing answering as a threat. This factor covers the very act of answering as well as the content of the question. Some people may see all questions as a threat: if I say that I like to take the lead then I will be seen as bossy, but I will look as though I cannot think for myself if I say I do not like to take the lead. Neither option sounds good.

(2) *Past (specific) experience* is whether the topic of the question was interesting or not (scale 10) and the frequency of reactions. This tries to compare a new situation presented in a question with an old experience of something we think would be similar. If someone felt very embarrassed when speaking at a parent/teacher association, a job requiring public performance might be seen as threatening. On the other hand, a farmer could well have no anxieties about performing in public no experience of doing so, and no interest in doing so. While Factor 1 helps to determine the subject's emotional reaction to the question, Factor 2 is a system of combining information to arrive at possible decisions.

(3) *Intellectual evaluation of question and answer* is concerned with the vagueness or clarity of the question (scales 2 and 3), whether it takes a short or long time to answer (scale 4), if an item is easy or difficult to understand (scales 5 and 8), whether or not a person thinks they are likely to change an answer (scale 15), and the trouble people had in making a sincere appraisal of themselves (scale 17). This Factor 3 has important implications for construct validity. One cannot draw conclusions from data when subjects are guessing the answers because they cannot understand the questions. Reliability is also affected. The subject may interpret the meaning of a question in different ways at different times.

(4) *Value of question* is measured by the importance of the question (scale 1), strong or weak relationships between its content and subject's own problems (scale 6), and whether it was associated with any traumatic experience (scale 16). This Factor 4 enables a subject to distinguish his, or her, own significant issues, but outside the context of this research, it does nothing for anybody trying to interpret test scores. Pets can be a very major consideration in people's lives. Elizabeth Taylor chose to stay on a boat rather than subject her pets to Britain's stringent quarantine regulations and James Herriot, the very wealthy novelist-cum-vet, never took a holiday abroad because he would have been separated from his dogs. Yet the rarity of questions about pets, rather than 'pet' questions, can mean only that either psychologists do not like pets or that their captive college samples do not have the facilities to keep pets. This factor must be the strongest argument in favour of methods like Kelly's Repertory Grid, where subjects have to generate their own values and preferences, and set the agenda for testing.

(5) *Social desirability* is a specific factor about consistency or inconsistency with the opinion of the subject's social group. Caution, though, is required. The late Robert McKenzie (who used to appear on television at every British election with his old-fashioned swingometer) researched the political statements of policy endorsed by political activists and found that those endorsed by active members of the Labour Party were more in agreement with those issued by the Conservative Party Central office! This factor can be interpreted as a specific component of the more general Factor 4, measuring the value of the question.

(6) *Specific emotional context* is a specific factor where there is either a strong or weak connection of the content of the question with traumatic experiences (scale 16). A person might be afraid of enclosed spaces if he or she had been trapped in a lift.

(7) *Frequency of behaviour* is another specific factor where there are rare or frequent reactions described in the item (scale 9). There is a low association with Factor 2, past (specific) experience, which was unexpected. It seems that subjects can more easily remember the situations they encountered, while the evaluation of their own behaviour seems to be more difficult for them. Attribution theorists would not find this strange because when individuals are doing things, it seems to them as if the environment is always presenting new problems and challenges. Monitoring themselves as well is

difficult. It is the observers — like television-armchair sports 'analysts' — who find it easy to judge others' behaviour passively.

Nowakowska also presents a flowchart illustrating the various pathways and interdependencies of the factors which would be useful if a computer programme were developed. Whether this network is used or not should not devalue the research: what makes a person tick begins a very long time before they begin to tick responses to questionnaire items.

Conclusions

When psychology first became a scientific discipline, its founding fathers believed in a mixture of studies both in the laboratory and out in the field. They were aware of the limitations of working in the laboratory. The development of scientific psychology after the First World War, however, pushed psychology into the laboratory. It would be there that it would prove itself as a science. Every few years the *Journal of Personality* analyses whether most of the research published in its field stems from laboratory work or work in the field. The surveys regularly show that 90 per cent or over of studies published are laboratory studies. The field of real life is not often tackled.

It is because of the importance of grasping how influential this desire to be scientific is, that we return to Scott's and Fuller's work. We think it useful near the start of the book to make its implications as clear as possible because they are good signposts for the rest of the book.

We deliberately chose Scott's and Fuller's research with dogs for our opening test because it was a well-designed, well-controlled, laboratory-type experiment, which are the very reasons why a 'psychological test' failed to produce the expected results. First, we will consider what they actually set out to do, and why their methodology was apparently beyond criticism. Then we will deduce some of the unintentional consequences of what they did. Our simplified paraphrasing tries to reduce the complexity of their research aims.

Hypothesis. Basenji dogs have natural jumping ability whereas cocker spaniel dogs do not.

Reasons for Hypothesis. Geneticists and breeders confirm that the basenji dog is especially noted for jumping ability while the cocker spaniel dog is not. Naturalistic observations in Africa and the United States confirm this hypothesis.

Subjects. An *experimental group* of basenji dogs and a *control group* of cocker spaniel dogs.

Method

(i) *objective psychological test* (that is, the dog's jumping ability will be objectively measured according to *psychometric* criteria; not by intuition or guessing from other measures);

(ii) *criterion-referenced test*: the dog's performance will be judged according to whether it can perform a particular task or not;

(iii) *independent variable*: all of the tests will be carried out in a uniform environment so that the influence of anything extraneous to 'natural jumping ability' will not affect jumping performance;

(iv) as all *variables* except 'natural jumping ability' have been held constant, then the dependent variable (behaviour) will be as near as possible a *'true score'* of natural jumping ability;

(v) the test will have *concurrent validity* because we know from breeders, geneticists, and observation what to expect; that is, the *criterion* is already to hand;

(vi) the *predictive validity* of the test is obvious because there is a straightforward prediction about the jumping ability of different breeds of dogs in accordance with the hypothesis;

(vii) there is no doubt about the *content validity* of the test because the focus is on jumping ability and dogs will be required to perform a particular jumping task;

(viii) *construct validity* is no problem: the theory associates a behavioural trait (jumping ability) with certain dog breeds but not others;

(ix) there should be *external* (ecological) *validity* because the real environment is simulated by piling boxes on top of each other, and dogs will be motivated to jump because of the food placed on top of the boxes;

(x) the usual *null hypothesis* is that there will be no difference between the breeds, for example, basenjis will display very good natural jumping ability while cocker spaniels will also do so.

As every effort was made — according to traditionally-established, laboratory-based criteria — to demonstrate the validity of the test, what went wrong? We will argue that two fundamental errors have been made with respect to psychological testing: first, the experimental criteria of research in the laboratory have been transferred to testing, and as a result, assumptions have tried to make people fit the tests rather than tests fit the people. Some of these assumptions emerge from Scott's and Fuller's research.

(1) It is assumed that it is possible to isolate and measure 'pure' ability or one aspect of an individual independently of others. 'Suspicious' basenjis and 'adventurous' cocker spaniels, as well as common sense, suggest this may not be so.

(2) It is assumed that as everything in the laboratory is *arranged* (no phone calls, no noisy children, no other dogs) the effects of the environment as dismissed as part of the 'error score'. Even Scott's and Fuller's simulated environment was not real enough to put basenjis at their ease.

(3) It is assumed that the sole independent variable controlled and manipulated is the psychological test. Therefore, the dependent variable (test performance) is largely made up of the true score (reflecting real ability) and the much smaller error score. But just as basenjis were poorly motivated and cocker spaniels eager for the food, human beings bring much more to the testing situation than most psychometricians will allow.

(4) It is assumed that, as experiments must be replicable, tests need to be reliable. We do not question the need for reliability as a criterion for tests, but we want to draw attention to the usual emphasis. Usually, the questions are not about people — are they consistent or changing? — but about the test; is the *test* consistent and stable?

(5) It is assumed that representative sampling applies only to how we select our subjects. Scott and Fuller had a good selection of dog breeds. What they did not have was a representative sample of the problems different dogs were likely to solve. In the context of their research, the sheep dogs looked daft and the beagles clever. Yet one command from a shepherd and the sheep dog would round up the sheep. What would the beagle do?

In the course of this book we shall highlight many other assumptions that psychologists are apt to make when dealing with tests. Does everything have to be done against the clock? Are people as passive as most tests assume? Our aim is to evaluate tests according to classical criteria and a bit of common sense, and to show the way tests have been used highlight major issues in psychology today. Scott's and Fuller's work and the implications of Nowakowska offer a good starting point for constructive scepticism.

2 ARE PEOPLE CONSISTENT OR INCONSISTENT?

In the way that we usually describe people, we attribute to them fairly consistent personality traits. We say that 'flapping about in a panic' is 'just like Margaret', who has always reacted to crisis by becoming overanxious. Geraldine, on the other hand, is a rock of calm. If someone changes the way they behave, close friends often notice. The recent spate of publicity about heroin addiction in Britain has made some experts warn parents to watch for abrupt changes in the behaviour and attitudes of children. Though the emphasis in the 1970s on therapy, encounter and 'growth' has led many psychologists to argue that change is positive, most psychological tests still aim to measure the underlying stable traits in a human being. If a test fails to demonstrate consistency – i.e. if someone scores 100 in one year, 80 the next year and 130 the year after — the assumption generally is that it is the test that is wrong, not the person that is changing.

A theory which suffered just such a crisis of credibility was achievement motivation. In the 1950s McClelland, Atkinson, Clark and Lowell (1953) developed a thesis that eras of economic expansion were preceded by periods where people became more motivated to achieve. The time before the growth of trade in the late sixteenth century was such an era; so were the years before the Industrial Revolution. McClelland could not give psychological tests to the deceased, but he could analyse the writings of the time. Shakespeare, Cervantes, Molière and many other lesser authors became his subjects. He suggested that one can use content analysis, a technique which counts the frequency of certain words and themes in texts, to understand the need to achieve in any particular society. When achievement motivation was rising, certain themes would recur more often, such as pleasure in individual effort while there would be less of stress on fate. Literature aimed at children was especially revealing because it reflected the values parents wanted to drill into their young. McClelland linked his literary data with data from tests, especially from the Thematic Apperception Test (TAT). In the TAT subjects are given a set of drawings and asked to make up stories about them. A typical picture is of a boy playing the violin. A high-achievement story would run something like this. The boy is practising the violin every evening because he wants to become a professional musician. There is a concert next week and the prize is a scholarship to the music school. A story low on achievement motivation might be that the boy enjoys playing the fiddle because it gives him something to do while his mother cooks the dinner.

McClelland devised ways of scoring the TAT stories so that he could extract, he claimed, reliable measures of the need to achieve. Individuals tested at intervals would score relatively similar scores whether the interval was a week, a month or a year, because it was fundamental to McClelland's theory that individuals lived with a similar amount of achievement motivation. The theory lost much credibility when it turned out that people were rather inconsistent. It could be argued that this would have fatally damaged the theory but for the fact that it also had very elaborate historical underpinnings. McClelland and Winter (1969) were also able to demonstrate different levels of achievement imagery between the literature of countries with a high rate of economic growth and those with a low rate of growth. So, achievement motivation survived. One of McClelland's co-workers, John Atkinson, has used it to develop a theory of the dynamics of action.

While both everyday life and psychological theories assume that people have consistent traits, language is rather more ambiguous. Consider the sentence: 'Margaret is an anxious person'. Apparently the words describe Margaret, but it is not clear if it means that:

(i) Margaret is anxious all the time. Does she never stop being anxious?
(ii) Margaret is more anxious than most people but there are, of course, plenty of times when she is not anxious.
(iii) If there is something to be anxious about, like meeting the mortgage payments when her husband is out of work, then she will be more likely to be anxious than Judith, who may be very worried about her latest relationship but will never deign to be anxious about money.
(iv) Does it mean that Margaret can never change and that she is doomed to perpetual anxiety?

Our language may not be precise, but the assumptions of psychology are. People are stable and do not change unless it is proved otherwise. However, people do change. St Paul is a prime example but hardly the only virtuous conversion. In Britain today two hardened criminals have abandoned their former lives and become social experts. John McVicar was Public Enemy No. 1 after his escape from prison in 1972. Ten years later McVicar has two degrees and is a free man, not because he had been found innocent but because he has become a sociologist. He studied in jail and renounced his former life of crime and violence. Even more spectacular is Jimmy Boyle, once labelled the most violent man in Scotland. Today he is free, a published author and committed to helping youngsters keep out of trouble. Another convert from crime was Mark Benney, who was a cockney crook. After a youthful career of crime, which he described in his autobiography *Low Company*, Benney took to writing, became a friend of Orwell and H. G. Wells, and ended up as one of the first sociologists to study voting behaviour. He was a reader at the London School of Economics, and his book *How People Vote* is still a classic of political behaviour. Benney left crime so far behind that he did not even make academic capital of his early misdemeanours forever. These three individuals may have been spectacularly inconsistent, but plenty of people appear to change, albeit on a more modest scale. Voting and consumer behaviour has certainly become far more volatile, and a problem for psychological theory.

Classical test theories admit, of course, that no one is perfectly consistent. Most psychometric tests fail to correlate perfectly with themselves because subjects are variable — even over the time of taking the test. Most writers refer to this as random error (which seems to be a better term than error variance) because 'random' implies something that was not forecast or controlled for. If this random error, due to the variability of subjects, can be identified, then tests should become more accurate at predicting behaviour because it would be possible to calculate for it.

Atkinson, in developing the idea of dynamics of action, has made assumptions very different from those of most other tests about the consistency of behaviour. Traditional achievement motivation, like most other approaches, expects constant behaviour given a stable personality and an environment that does not change radically. Dynamics of action expects people to vary. Atkinson sees people as never inactive, or at rest, but constantly choosing how to spend their time. The question of why Fred spends more hours shopping than day-dreaming is an interesting one that ought to provide insight into his motivations. Atkinson uses the concept of *ipsative behavioural variability*. Let us dissect the jargon. Ipsative from the Latin, *ipse*, meaning 'the same', refers to comparisons within the self. You monitor how I change by comparing my behaviour on four separate Sundays. What other people do on Sunday is irrelevant. *Behavioural variability* means, more simply, the extent to which behaviour varies. Atkinson seems to posit as an ideal, looking at the stream of behaviour in real time. If only psychologists could see how long people devoted to answering lonely hearts ads, playing cricket, being at the pub, doing their statistics, we would understand them more. As a result of its theoretical background, dynamics-of-action research has been rather wedded to conventional tests. This is a pity because a new form of testing offers a promising way of establishing basic data on human consistency. And those who go through the apparent ordeal of Experiential Self Monitoring (ESM) are often surprised by the outcome.

Case Study

Test tested:	Experiential Self Monitoring (ESM)
Example of questions:	What was I doing at . . . various points in time
Form of answer:	Diary notes
Our focus:	Establishing a basic record of ordinary activities

Dynamics-of-action theory suggests psychologists study the activities people choose to engage in and what they avoid. A traditional testing approach might ask subjects to rate on paper how much of their day was spent on different tasks. Psychologists whose work stems from the TAT have managed to pose this question of choice in far more recondite ways, by examining how subjects reacted to different sets of instructions for making up TAT stories. But there is a simpler way of studying action. You get people to log their life as it happens. The advent of the electronic bleeper has made this feasible. Subjects are given a bleep which can go off at regular or irregular intervals. Subjects jot in a diary what they are doing, thinking or feeling according to a variety of criteria determined by the testers. ESM is so basic it does not look like a psychological test; but it is — only it happens just to ask elementary, but fundamental, questions. How do we choose to spend our time?

It is not wholly clear who was the innovator of this method. *Psychology News* first encountered it in the work of E. J. Dearnley. On 384 occasions during 1979, Dearnley was jolted by an electronic alarm, and at once grabbed paper and pencil to note the state of his consciousness, what physical position he was in, what he was doing — or not doing — and how he felt. Six times, Dearnley confessed, he failed to be roused to psychological duty — all six being round 2.00 a.m.

At the 1980 British Psychological Society Conference, Dearnley read out some of his notes. Observation 87 seemed to him not untypical. It was a Saturday. At 12.41 Dearnley was sitting in The Railway Inn drinking beer with his friends. The next time the alarm rang was at 14.25 when Dearnley was still drinking beer; but he was no longer in The Railway Inn but in the Conservative Club. He described his mood still as one of contentment. The alarm of 19.35 found the self-scrutinising psychologist checking the length and cut of a new pair of trousers. No description of mood followed. At 23.00 Dearnley was back at the bar discussing the events and introspections of the day with his wife. He noted he was even more contented than at 14.25. On other days, Dearnley lamented, he sampled fewer bars though much time was devoted to studying racing form and watching Mike Yarwood, the comedian.

Dearnley did not restrict himself to amiable impressionistic evidence. He found he spent 41 per cent of his time in work activities and 31 per cent in pleasure. A total of 45 per cent was spent in general bodily maintenance, which included sleeping, eating, ablutions and also, in his analysis, prayer! Only 4 per cent of time was spent in distasteful activities. Rather humbly, Dearnley confessed to having learned a good deal about himself during this experiment even though he always assumed he knew how he spent his time.

One of the attractions of ESM is that though it is very simple, it offers basic answers to basic questions. Psychology has often been criticised for not studying people in real-life situations. Dynamics-of-action theory agonises about what slice of time to study the individual through, and how many choices to present him with. The bleeper test is given to a subject who faces the natural glut of life-choices. Instead of being in The Railway Inn, Dearnley could have been in the library, watching his favourite football team, or teaching a student. The diary yields information and insight, even though it is hard to see how to apply to it traditional criteria for judging tests.

What do you judge its reliability against? A subject may do X on Wednesday and Y on Saturday. When re-tested, the fact that he is not doing X on Wednesday is more likely to represent his choice than failure of the test. Equally, what do you judge its validity against? A further problem is, of course, that subjects may lie. When the psychologist studies himself one is apt to suppose that he will faithfully record what he is up to. Dearnley appeared to honestly record his activities and what he chose to do, so his diary would provide sound data as to his motivations. The need for different criteria to judge the usefulness of such testing devices is a topic we shall return to in Chapter 10.

But ESM need not just involve psychologists testing themselves. Two useful developments of the technique have been by Czikszentmihalyi (1982) and Franzoi and Brewer (1984). In both cases they gave subjects bleepers and asked them to record what they were doing and/or thinking whenever the bleeper went off.

In his study, Czikszentmihalyi was interested also in the quality of the experience, how self-aware people were and whether they felt they were doing X, Y or Z of their own free will. 107 subjects were given a bleep which bleeped approximately seven times every 24 hours. They had to drop whatever they were doing, record what it was and what they felt about it, why, and to leave out no incriminating circumstances. 82 per cent completed the course, which shows how willing subjects are to comply with the requirements of psychologists.

The results showed that people were happiest when thinking about food, and, second, when thinking about other people. They preferred to muse about doing housework, laundry and even death to thinking about themselves. Subjects were asked to note how active or passive they felt when recording their thoughts. When they thought about themselves they said they felt very inactive. The only kinds of thought that were less active were thoughts about radio or TV.

It was at the University of Chicago that John B. Watson began to formulate the behaviourist creed, so it was brave of the psychologists there to ask anything about free will. Czikszentmihalyi detected a curious relationship between how free people felt to do what they were doing and the quality of their emotions. If they felt constrained, as for example at work, they quite enjoyed thinking about themselves. It freed them. But if they found themselves wracked by self-aware thoughts during free time, they disliked the experience. In their own time they preferred to think about food, other people or some pet plan which had no hint of introspection.

A further study using bleepers was that of Franzoi and Brewer, who studied 23 undergraduates over two days. Each had a bleep which went off at 90-minute intervals. Subjects had to fill in a diary, say what they had been doing, and estimate how much of the last ten minutes they spent thinking about themselves, about other people or about something quite different. Roughly, subjects spent twice as much time thinking of others or of 'things' than they did about themselves. Subjects who scored highly on a self-consciousness scale did not appear to indulge in more self-aware thoughts.

ESM is a useful technique in helping to establish how consistent, or inconsistent, behaviour is. Franzoi and Brewer found that their subjects did not feel it was intrusive in the natural setting. In terms of questions of change, the 'bleeper' studies are very promising. They can allow people to see how they spend their time and how much they devote to different activities. According both to dynamics of action theory and to simple common sense, such basic, but elusive information ought to throw some light on their motivation. Subjects could be tested for fairly lengthy periods of time (say a week) at different points in their lives. If the pattern of their behaviour changed, one could ask why. Self-monitoring demands persistence, but it is that alluring technique — a nearly 'pure' test of behaviour.

This simple approach is in stark contrast to the elaborate work that dynamics of action theory has led to so far. Reuman (1982), for example, tried to judge how consistent people were by examining how they responded to a different TAT pictures under different conditions. Reiman challenged the tenets of classical reliability theory by focusing on change. First, he gave subjects three arithmetic problems and then two sets of TAT pictures. The first set of pictures were strongly cued for achievement; the second weakly cued for achievement. On the basis of their responses to the first pictures, he divided his subjects into 41 with low *ipsative variability* — and 20 with high *ipsative variability*, i.e. behavioural change. Since all the first set of TAT pictures ought to evoke the same amount of achievement motivation, those whose replies differed were high in ipsative variability. Subjects were given the second 'weakly cued' set of TAT pictures with different instructions. One group was encouraged to be as imaginative as possible; a second group to impose a common thread on all their stories. Reuman found that subjects with high ipsative variability did indeed vary their stories more when asked to make them different. Subjects with low ipsative variability found this much harder to do and their score correlated best with their performance on the arithmetic problems. Reuman's ideas do raise important issues concerning change, but his study has many limitations.

First, Reuman restricted his actual research to using TAT pictures and made some assumptions about them. He assumed that similar TAT pictures given in sequence made up a constant environment. Secondly, he assumed that the measured quantity of a given type of thought corresponded to time spent in thought. Thirdly, he assumed that whenever there was a change of TAT picture, it was possible to interpret this as a change from one thought to another. These assumptions made it possible to obtain several measurements of an individual's changing behaviour in a constant TAT environment. In contrast to such sophisticated techniques, ESM stands out as a more realistic form of assessment. If people are measured across a longish period of time, say a month, they will often find themselves in the same environment, with the same people. One can then plot how they change, if they do, and perhaps why; self-monitoring also allows subjects to examine whether they want to change — an issue to which we return in our third case study.

Case Study Two: Healthy Changes

Test tested: General Health Questionnaire
Example of questions: Do you feel that you can't cope with problems?
Form of answer: 4-point scale
Our focus: Changes

The desire for consistency affects psychiatry as well as psychology. The history of modern psychiatry could be written as the history of perfecting diagnoses. Since Kraeplin, a good practitioner has been one who can spot whether his patient is a florid schizophrenic, a catatonic schizophrenic, a manic depressive or the victim of a reactive or endogenous depression. Today, psychiatrists accept Freud's view that there is no sharp border between normal and abnormal behaviour, but that took a long time. Barham (1985) has pointed out that most psychiatrists assume that many illnesses are irreversible. Once a schizophrenic, always a schizophrenic. This emphasis on the diagnosis which will pin the patients down once and for all is evident in the work of Wing (1977), for example. Wing helped organise a worldwide effort to improve the diagnosis of schizophrenia using tests like The Present State Examination and the computer based CATEGO.

Not all psychiatrists agree with this emphasis on consistency. Some believe that psychiatry badly needs sophisticated instruments to map changes. Clare (1976) maintains that doctors are not that skilled either at initial diagnoses of psychiatric illness or at monitoring changes. The usual environment in a mental hospital may well hinder the perception of changes. When the doctor briefly sees the patient once a week or so, the patient may be out to impress with his best, sanest or most conformist behaviour. On the other hand, the patient may be 'playing' mad.

The General Health Questionnaire (GHQ) was developed against this background by Goldberg in 1972. He wanted to see how easy it was to measure feelings of well-being. Such measures would allow him to compare the well-being of populations that were 'sane' and 'insane', but excluding psychotics. How different would they be? Secondly, such a test could log the sense of well-being that a person experienced from year to year. Implicit in that was that people did change or, if we wish to rehash the jargon, that one could test for the 'ipsative variability' of their well-being.

Goldberg began by arguing that there was not a sharp dichotomy between 'cases' and normals. 'Psychiatric disturbance may be thought of as being evenly distributed throughout the population in varying degrees of severity.' Goldberg quoted Essen Moller (1956) who arranged individuals on a continuum from frank mental illness through abnormalities of personalities through sheer weirdness to the completely normal. Essen Moller found that 'a large proportion of the population were thought to be personality variants and only 39.6 per cent of men and 32.8 per cent of women were thought to be normal'. Nice to be among the normal minority!

The GHQ begins with questions about physical health and ends with more overtly psychiatric ones. It moves from asking, 'Been feeling perfectly well and in good health?' to 'found the idea of taking your own life coming into your head?'. The questions that Goldberg used in his pilot study yielded five main factors: severity of illness; psychic depression versus somatic depression; agitation versus apathy; personal neglect versus irritability; anxiety at night versus anxiety during daytime. Every one of the initial 93 items had a high positive load on severity of illness, which accounted for 45 per cent of the variance. But this factor included a lot of questions which, on the face of it, covered the same ground such as: 'Dreading things you have to do?' 'Felt unable to face problems?' 'Feeling life a struggle?' 'Felt everything gets on top of you?' After much pilot testing, Goldberg reduced his questions from 93 to 60, which retained maximum validity while not being so long it detracted from the well-being of subjects.

Unlike many tests, the GHQ stresses the 'here and now' situation and how the individual's present state differs from his usual state. Instead of being asked to reply *yes*, *no* or *often* to questions, subjects were usually given the following response options:

Not at all
No more than usual
Rather more than usual
Much more than usual

Where Eysenck stresses stable personality traits in his measures of neuroticism, Goldberg stresses change. He also claims such responses make the GHQ less subject to 'overall agreement set' since subjects cannot parrot *yes*, or, *I agree*, or, *true* and think they're helping the experimenter.

Goldberg's method of scoring the GHQ is also unusual. It tries to overcome problems with yea-sayers, middle users and end users ingeniously. Middle users are people who when confronted with a *yes/no* or *maybe* choice plump for the safe, middling *maybe*: end users are extremists. If faced only with *yes/no* or *maybe*, they will always assert a firm *yes* or *no*. If faced with a 5-point or 7-point scale, they will always tick the extreme graduations. Right-wing and left-wing militants are classic end users. With his 4-point scale, Goldberg forces liberal middle users to the left or right. He lumps 'not at all' in with 'no more than usual', and puts 'rather more than usual' in with 'much more than usual'. Equally, this shifts end users towards the middle. The GHQ can, of course, be used using different scoring methods, but then Goldberg's validation studies don't necessarily apply. He admits that his scoring loses information, but argues it is not important when it comes to identifying cases.

The GHQ was calibrated on normals, the mildly ill and the severely ill, excluding psychotics, however. The normals had to meet stringent criteria. Those who had lost more than two weeks' work in the past three months were rejected, for example. Goldberg found that while traditional psychiatry measures severity of illness in terms of severity of symptoms, many of the GHQ items that best defined illness were those that reflected the extent to which the patient thought he or she could cope, like: 'Felt that you couldn't overcome your difficulties'.

One group revealed an unlikely profile. Phobic patients scored very low. They had had phobic symptoms for a number of years, were used to them and, in many cases, not particularly incapacitated. They recorded 'No worse than usual' to many items because they had not experienced any change, including change for the better. In his early analyses Goldberg did not make as clear as he might have done that these patients were comparing their situation and status with their own previous feelings — not with other people's. He confused ipsative and normative frames of reference and so could mislead other researchers. A crude reading of his data could make one believe that hardy perennial psychiatric patients are the same as the normal minority because neither group feel *worse than usual*.

Goldberg is aware of the possibility of faking the GHQ. He quoted the case of a social worker whose husband had left her and who had attempted suicide. This lady wanted to stay out of the local mental hospital and was strongly motivated to answer the GHQ so as to seem well. Goldberg also believes that some young people with personality disorders and alcoholics in search of asylum may have overstated their traumas.

Given his commitment to testing for change, Goldberg had to test his questionnaire both to see if it identified cases, and also if it charted improvement or deterioration. He argued in 1972 that it accurately monitored both when patients got better and when they got worse. A study reported at the 1981 British Psychological Society Conference accepted the usefulness of the GHQ, but warned that it did misclassify many patients, at least when pitted against the opinion of a psychiatrist.

The 1981 study centred on Broadgate Hospital in north Humberside. The team selected 278 patients at different GPs' surgeries. Doctors deleted 20 of them on the ground they were in no state to be pestered by researchers; 32 refused to co-operate; 10 were never at home. The final sample of 214 people in the community was matched for age, sex and class with 174 psychiatric in-patients. There were women and social class 1 persons among the patients.

All subjects filled in the GHQ, a Mental Health Scale (MHS) and were given a semi-structured interview.

Of the community's 214 subjects, 164 were neither suffering from symptoms nor any ongoing life crisis. 9.8 per cent were bereaved, divorcing or unemployed, which was making them feel worse than usual. But this group did not rate as ill on the MHS. Fourteen in the community scored high on the MHS, but low on the GHQ, which was interpreted as meaning they were chronic patients. Like Goldberg's original phobics, they were used to their symptoms. 15 people in the community managed high scores both on the MHS and the GHQ, suggesting they had recently started a psychiatric episode. In all, the figures suggested that 24 per cent of the community group had some emotional problem or psychiatric illness. In addition, 15 of the 20 patients the GPs refused to let the researchers see were either in crisis or chronically ill.

The Broadgate study highlights two problems with the GHQ. It can classify as ill people who are going through a crisis like a divorce. Also, as Goldberg found, it can classify as being well patients who have become used to their symptoms. Our next case study looks at a test of obsessional illness which has two novel features Goldberg could have usefully incorporated — a *resistance* score (measuring how hard the patient tried to stop giving in to obsessions), and an *interference* score (measuring how much the obsession interfered with their normal life). His phobics would, we presume, have filed a low interference score.

There was one interesting incidental finding. When doing further testing in America, Goldberg found that the mean score for blacks was slightly higher than for whites, but the groups were not matched for social class. When allowance was made for class, a small difference remained between the races ($p > 0.05$). Paul Jackson (1981) used the GHQ and discovered a clear link between being middle class and feeling well, and being employed and feeling well. The correlation between unemployment and poor general health was so great that 'there aren't any statistical tables. There were so many noughts after the p. that the computer couldn't cope'. If any philanthropic wizard would care to do research on the general health of unemployed blacks, perhaps, he could offer them temporary employment writing the noughts after the p! Meanwhile, non-workers of the world unite. You have nothing to lose but your pains! The GHQ meanwhile, for all its problems, has established its usefulness through the 1970s. Goodchild and Duncan-Jones (1985) propose a revision of the scoring technique where 'no more than usual' in response to an item relating to pathology should not be treated as an indicator of good health: rather, it should be seen as a sign of chronicity because to be 'no more than usual'[ly] depressed if you're usually depressed does not mean you are well.

Case Study Three: Washing Your Hands of Obsessions

Test tested: Leyton Obsessional Inventory
Example of questions: 1. Do you often feel that you have to finish a piece of housework?
2. CARD asking subjects to chose from statements that an activity was:
    (i) a sensible thing to do, through to
    (v) try very hard to stop.
Form of answer: 1. *Yes* or *No*
2. One of the five statements chosen
Our focus: Obsessional behaviour and changing it

In Chapter 1 we argued that many psychological tests assume the subject is naïve. Our third test case study focuses on a test which is riddled with technical flaws, but has the merit of asking people about attitude to changes in themselves they want to achieve. The Leyton Obsessional Inventory (LOI) also deals with one of the key problems of psychology — when does a normal personality trait become an abnormal symptom?

The LOI was developed for studying normal families rather than hospital use. The main study concerned the activities of young children at home after health visitors noticed that some mothers were unusually houseproud and just as perfectionist when it came to child rearing. None of these mothers were psychiatric patients. Cooper (1970) aimed at differentiating three groups — normals, houseproud/childproud mothers, obsessional patients.

Cooper constructed two different kind of questions. Items 1–46 were symptom questions; items 47–69 were trait questions. All items refer to common obsessional conditions, but the symptom questions are so worded that replying *yes* implies they are a nuisance and cause distress. The trait questions did not carry that implication and were framed round traits thought to be characteristic of obsessional patients.

The test requires subjects to sort cards and asks a series of questions to which a *yes* or *no* answer is required. Other items test for the degree of resistance the subject offers and the extent to which he or she thinks an obsession interferes with normal life. The Resistance Score asks subjects to choose between one of five options ranging from *Sensible — this is quite a sensible and reasonable thing for me to do* to *Try very hard to stop — this upsets me a great deal and I try very hard to stop it*. The interference items are similar. When reflecting about an item, subjects are shown four cards which go from *No interference — this does not interfere with other activities* to *Interferes a great deal — this stops me doing a lot of things and wastes a lot of time*. Both these innovations are useful.

Symptom questions stressed the domestic such as tidiness and household cleanliness. Unfortunately, they were phrased so that a *yes* always meant subjects were tidy, clean and virtuous. Cooper never seems to have heard of the dangers of yea-saying. The trait questions focused on meanness, irritability, stubbornness, pedantry, conscientiousness and hoarding. Cooper admits that this part of the inventory may be the least satisfactory since it invites subjects to criticise themselves.

It is not clear whether Cooper covers the same topics twice deliberately or not. And, occasionally, different shades of emotion are attributed to the same act. One symptom question runs: 'Do you ask yourself questions or have doubts about a lot of the things you do?' This phrasing is either neutral or a shade negative since doubts are not usually considered positive. A trait question is: 'Do you *pride* yourself on thinking things over very carefully before making a decision?' No doubt Descartes prided himself on his doubts, but the agoraphobic who doubts he can make it to the supermarket rarely does so. Cooper may be wanting to explore the positive or negative aspects of doubts, or his phrasing may be muddled. It's impossible to know.

Cooper also administered the Cornell Health Questionnaire so that subjects did not know just what was being examined. He obtained five scores — a symptom score, a trait score, the Cornell, and a weighted score of interference and resistance. The latter two were meant to reflect the intensity of distress obsessions caused. Cooper argued that interference and resistance ought to differentiate high-scoring non-patients and low-scoring patients. The patients would be expected to suffer more distress given similar symptom scores. That proved to be the case. The sum of the resistance and interference scores was the best differentiator. The range of the two non-patient groups (tidy housewives and normals) did not overlap at all with the range of the patients. The symptom score worked better than the trait score in separating obsessionals from others because, on the trait score, there was not much difference between normals and the houseproud housewives.

In many ways, the LOI incorporates useful features. The idea of testing the extent to which subjects dislike doing something they can't help doing and their estimate of how badly it affects the rest of their lives is original. Cooper might well have followed up to see whether those patients with his high resistance and interference scores got better quicker than others. The only behavioural validation he did attempt was not successful. Houseproud housewives and controls were interviewed about their domestic activities for the previous 24 hours. No difference emerged between the groups, and there was no correlation between the inventory scores and the amount of time mothers said they spent washing, cleaning and polishing. Since no one was going to confess to being a slut, and a clean house is very socially desirable, it was a bit naïve of Cooper perhaps to expect much else. Its poor questionnaire design (with so many *yesses* being obsessional) was not confined to ignoring the dangers of yea-saying. Often people were given only a *yes/no* choice, even when Cooper asked several questions such as: 'Do you feel that even a slight bodily contact with bodily secretions (such as sweat, saliva, urine, etc.) is unpleasant or dangerous or liable to contaminate your clothes or belongings?' There may be people who think than an infant dribbling over them is not dangerous or unpleasant while an old lag peeing over them is both; Cooper gives that discerning individual no accurate answer. Despite its limitations, the LOI does have merits — especially in highlighting the issue of whether those who are the victims of symptoms want to resist them. It is a pity the test has not led, apparently, to research linking resistance and interference with later change.

Conclusions

Romantic literature made women fickle and inconstant, leaving us to presume that the male of the species was a model of consistency. Perhaps because most psychologists who created tests were men, they devised a paradigm in which human subjects were supposed to produce the same score on the same test, time after time. William James claimed that, after 30, human beings became set in their ways, slaves to routine. He only half-regretted this. But what was true in the 1890s may not be true now. In this chapter we have tried to use three case studies to highlight some issues about the consistency of human behaviour. First, there are now better techniques than paper-and-pencil tests for measuring how people actually spend their time, and establishing how consistent we are in real life. This may seem a prosaic problem, but it is actually a rich source of data. Dearnley (1980) was surprised by what he learned from continuous self-monitoring; neither the results of Czikszentmihalyi (1982) nor Franzoi and Brewer (1984) were predictable. Secondly, some recent tests at least tackle the issue of changing human behaviour. Both the GHQ and the LOI may have problems, but they do see human beings as capable of changing. This must count as an advance – especially if it leads psychologists to speculate on whether in an apparently fast-changing world, people are more volatile and changeable than ever before.

3 PSYCHOMETRIC TESTS, PROJECTIVE OR A NEW PATTERN?

The history of testing is riddled with its own internal controversies. Usually, the public takes psychological testing to be IQ tests or personality questionnaires. In fact, a far 'deeper' tradition of tests dates back to attempts to provide scientific evidence for some of the claims of psychoanalysis. In Chapter 2 we looked briefly at the nature of the Thematic Apperception Test (TAT), which was first used about 1942. It was predated by the Rorschach Test, which asked subjects to invent stories and associations to ink blots. The rationale was seductive. If I see a shape which appears to be meaningless, the meanings I impose on it will say something about me. Consider this object:

If I say that it reminds me of a cucumber, I may well be obsessed with food; if I say it reminds me of a penis, I may well be obsessed with sex; if I say it reminds me of a cricket bat, I am probably obsessed with physical prowess; and if I say that it reminds me of a gondola, I am probably being difficult. One can see the apparent sense of it.

The Rorschach test, like the TAT, has been controversial. Eysenck, in one of his subversive moods, sent ink blots to some expert Rorschach scorers and found they could not even agree whether the same reactions to some ink blots came from normals or lunatics. Proof, he claimed, that the Rorschach was useless. Others have defended the Rorschach and maintained that Eysenck's approach was far too crude.

Not all projective tests are as unfocused as the magnificent ink blots. Take the method of incomplete sentences. Interesting differences can emerge from the ways that children finish sentences like:

'Some children work hard at school because . . .'

The sentence does hint at a link between hard work and doing well later on — given current unemployment that link may seem foolish to children, a myth adults want to foist on them — but it is still possible to get interesting data out from the method of completing sentences.

In this chapter we look at four tests which reflect these issues. Our first two tests study very different approaches to pain. The McGill Pain Questionnaire is a carefully devised, conventional test of how people feel pain. It takes many pains, as it were, to handle the tricky questions of the language involved. It is quite different from Petrovich's projective test of pain. That owes something to the techniques of the TAT but is far more focused. We shall argue that these tests are complementary rather than antagonistic. Usually, psychometric and projective test are presented as being radical opposites, but these two pain tests suggest that such hostile attitudes can be unnecessary.

Psychometric tests usually try to affix a number to a subject. Thus, if a test has a task of sorting objects that go together and a number task, the convention is to add their scores together. A score of 15/20 on object sorting and 3/20 on numbers would make for a global score of 18. Subjects could also score 18 in lots of different ways. Traditional psychometric techniques often fail to spot what kinds of errors subjects make, an issue highlighted in our third test, the Kendrick Test. The test that we examine here, The Kendrick Battery for the Detection of Dementia in the Elderly, suffers from four additional faults:

(i)   the old people may not be interested enough to do it properly;
(ii) it may identify errors that are not very relevant to how old people can function;
(iii) it may ignore aspects of their environment which do matter and place them at a considerable handicap;
(iv) all right answers are given equal weight and added to give a total score. Rabbitt (1982) has argued that we should look at memory as a process and analyse the kinds of errors people make — not lump everything together and tot it up!

Our fourth case study is of the Clifton Assessment Procedures, which employs the testimony of witnesses.

Points of Pain

Is it possible to measure objectively such a subjective sensation as pain? The usual laboratory methods for producing and measuring pain are very limited. Ethical considerations prohibit replication of the persistent and intolerable pain that many people suffer. As we can never feel, but only infer, another's pain, we must rely upon the correlation between felt sensation and language.

Case Study One: Objective Pain

Test tested: McGill Pain Questionnaire
Example of questions: Rate your pain along several dimensions
Form of answer: A rating scale
Our focus: Objective versus subjective measures

If pain can be measured accurately it could improve diagnosis, treatment, and doctor/patient communication, saving both time and money.

For too long pain has been thought of as a single sensation that varies only in intensity. But any poor creature who staggers out of bed in the morning with a splitting headache after a night's excesses, will know that one of the best 'cures' for a headache is to bash one's big toe against the bedhead: he soon forgets his head and concentrates on his toe. Pain can be both qualitatively and quantitatively different. Melzack and Torgerson (1971) began to analyse the problem by asking subjects to classify 102 words, gleaned from the clinical literature, into 3 major classes and 16 subclasses. In Melzack's description, the classes are: (1) words that describe 'sensory qualities' of the experience in terms of temporal (e.g. flickering), spatial (e.g. jumping), pressure (e.g. stabbing), thermal (e.g. burning), and other properties; (2) words that describe 'affective qualities' in terms of tension (e.g. exhausting), fear (e.g. frightful), and autonomic (e.g. suffocating) properties that are part of the pain experience; and (3) 'evaluative' words that describe the subjective, overall intensity of the total pain experience (1, mild; 2, discomforting; 3, distressing; 4, horrible; 5, excruciating).

A group of doctors, patients and students were asked to assign an intensity value to each word, using a numerical scale ranging from least (mild) to worst (excruciating) pain. Several words within each subclass had the same relative intensity relationship in all three sets. For example, in the spatial subclass, 'shooting' was found to represent more pain than 'flashing', which in turn implied more pain than 'jumping'. Although the precise intensity scale values differed for the three groups, all three agreed on the positions of the words relative to each other so at least an ordinal scale of measurement was established. This result was especially welcome as the subjects had different cultural, socio-economic and educational backgrounds.

Subjects were shown drawings of the human body so they could point to the sources of the pain. Questions asked about how long pain lasted and the overall, present pain intensity. Melzack tried to tease out individual tendencies to rate pain at the low or high of the scale. Some subjects added words of their own to the 16 subclasses so the questionnaire ended with 20, rather than 16 subclasses. It was given to 297 patients who suffered a variety of ills from cancer to migraine.

The test yielded four kinds of data:

(1) Pain Rating Index based on the patient's mean scale values. This was the sum total of all the scale values of the words in any category.
(2) Pain Rating Index based on the rank values of all the words. Here, the word in each of the 20 subclasses implying the least amount of pain is given a value of 1, the next word a value of 2, and so on. The values of words chosen by each patient are then added up to obtain a score for each category and, also, a total score.
(3) The number of words chosen to describe pain. This is not a good measure as patients may choose words of very different intensity but if they pick the same number they get an identical score.
(4) The present pain intensity.

Melzack warned that the patients might mess up the scoring system by choosing more than one item from a subclass, or might feel compelled to choose a word from every subclass even when it was not appropriate. They might also describe the pain they felt in the morning, or when it was worst, rather than present pain. He recommended reading instructions to patients to make sure they did understand them.

Consistent Pain

To assess consistency of choice, ten patients answered three questionnaires at intervals ranging from 3 to 7 days and reported the same present pain intensity (that is, their pain was unaffected by any attempted manipulation). The consistency of choice of subclasses among the three questionnaires ranged from 50 per cent to 100 per cent, with a mean consistency of 70.3 per cent. Melzack said this high agreement could not be due to patients remembering what they had said because

> most patients are highly selective in their choices, ponder each subclass list carefully, and the choice of a word is usually accompanied by behavioural signs (such as an exclamation of strong agreement) that the words genuinely reflect the properties of their pains.

If Melzack is putting 'consistency of choice' as evidence for the reliability of his questionnaire, then this is not good enough. Three to seven days is a ridiculously short time to test consistency, and using 'weighing and pondering every word' as evidence for patients not recalling the words they chose during an earlier presentation, is strange. They are much more likely to remember if they mull over every word. This is not to say that the questionnaire is necessarily unreliable, merely that Melzack's logic is odd.

The correlation coefficients based on data obtained with specific illnesses were generally higher than those obtained with pooled illnesses. Although it is clear that the pain in some complaints is worse than in others, they were all remarkably close together. One reason is that many of the patients received drugs before the questionnaire since it was unethical to withhold them for research. Scores on the scales might well have shown a much wider spread if patients had been deprived of drugs. Still, some of these results relating to specific illnesses were surprising. Pain due to cancer lesions had a high value on the sensory dimension; the sensory input is prepotent; yet the effect (which should be high because of the serious implications of the disease) is not higher than that for menstrual pain, which has virtually no implications for survival.

More Pain

Taped recordings were made of the patient's comments before and after each session, and these comments regarding pain level, drug intake and activity levels were compared with the four types of data obtained from the test. It was clear that the Pain Index Rating based on the rank values of the words (least amount of pain 1, next amount of pain 2, etc.) was a more valid index of change than the more general assessment of present pain intensity. Therefore, some patients reported that their pain was still at the same (present pain intensity) level, but had changed in a way that was difficult to describe — it was somehow less sharp, less gnawing, not as exhausting and miserable as before.

Although the author admits that the McGill Pain Questionnaire is still a rough instrument, it is a start toward the measurement of clinical pain and permits research in a clinical rather than laboratory conditions. This is a very important step forward.

Melzack's test is a very traditional psychometric one. In 1958, well before Melzack produced it, Petrovich (1958a) produced a very different test, the PAT or Pain Apperception Test. Petrovich argued that normal testing approaches were not useful in judging people's responses to pain. He argued that while pain is vague and individual, it has usually been measured with psychophysical techniques which compare conscious and/or autonomic response with the intensity, duration, or both, of a number of physical stimuli. Hardy, Wolff and Goodell (1952) noted that in analysing the pain experience 'it has been useful to separate the perception of pain from the reactions to pain'. Nemoff (1954) observed that 'changes in experimental procedures often elicited greater psychogalvanic reactions than did responses made to pain'. He suggested that 'the anticipatory element may be the important factor involved in the emotional reaction to pain'. Individual differences can be quite large: what is trivial for one person is catastrophic for another. And some individuals relish pain. Some martyrs seem to have seen it as a spiritual path, while readers of the *Sado-Masochists' Gazette* just like it. Petrovich did painstaking pilot research. 50 male and 50 female students were asked to list ten situations associated with pain, to say whether they had experience any of them, and to rank them from most painful (1) to least painful (10).

To analyse the answers, Petrovich used pain categories based on (i) where the pain was (i.e. headache); (ii) the kind of physical injury (i.e. broken bone); (iii) the situation that led to it (i.e. motor car accident). Four clinical psychologists were independently asked to classify each of the categories so as to judge whether particular pains were physical, psychological or a blend of both.

Instead of devising a conventional psychometric test, Petrovich argued that his survey provided data with which to construct a focused projective test. The TAT was very wide ranging since it dealt with achievement. Pain was a more specific topic. In the Pain Apperception Test (PAT), testers and subjects would have to restrain their imaginations and stick to the point. Everything in the

PAT is about pain, attitudes to pain, reactions to pain and causes of pain. This narrowing has benefits.

Case Study Two: Pictures of Pain

Test tested: Projective Pain Apperception Test
Example of questions: Respond to 25 pictures of painful situations
Form of answer: Explaining what is going on in the pictures
Our focus: Subjective impressions of pain

The PAT contains 25 pictures, which fall into three major divisions. The first contains pictures 1–9 and depicts different situations where actual pain is felt (e.g. cut forearm). The second division includes eight pictures (four pairs) and is concerned with Nemoff's (1954) point about anticipation of pain versus actually experiencing pain. One member of each pair depicts imminent infliction of a specific pain while the other member depicts the same person and situation except that the anticipated painful situation has happened. One example is a hypodermic syringe nearing a man's arm while in its pair it has actually punctured the skin. The eight pictures (again four pairs) are concerned with the origin of the pain sensation (self-inflicted versus other-inflicted). One member of each pair shows a man who has inflicted pain upon himself, such as getting a fishing hook caught in his neck, while its counterpart is identical except that the pain has been inflicted by someone else. A rival angler cast the offending fish hook.

All of the pictures show a man in his middle thirties, and each has differing facial and bodily characteristics 'to facilitate projection into the various pain situations'. Petrovich adds

> Thus, the pictured person's dress, build, posture and facial expression were drawn to be commensurate with the activity and painfulness denoted in each instance. In those pictures that need the presence of others, only a portion of their bodies or background figures were utilised.

Petrovich (1958b) justifies the rationale of the projective technique: 'By the process of identification and projection, the subject may vicariously experience the pain which has befallen the pictured individual and interpret the pictures in accordance with his own predispositions'. Yet, in the test's instructions, it says: 'This is a Test of the imagination. . . . Imagine the feelings of *the man* in the picture and choose the best possible answer for each question'. (Emphasis added). This is a common Freudian muddle that confuses sympathy with empathy when the difference is absolutely crucial. A good psychiatrist or psychologist must have empathy whether he is dealing with rapists or child murderers. But he would not be able to draw upon personal experience of these crimes to understand the individual's feelings, motivations and predispositions, so external cues (e.g. signs of remorse, bodily agitation or composure) are essential if any insight is to be gained. So, if a subject is asked to imagine how that man feels (empathy) it is a totally different question from 'If it were you, instead of that man, in that situation, how would you feel?' (sympathy model where this is a common shared experience). If Petrovich wants to know how his subjects would feel in the variety of painful situations then he should ask them. If he wants to know how well his artist portrayed the situation, then he should ask his subjects to imagine how the man in the picture feels. What Petrovich shouldn't do is to confuse both.

A welcome feature of the PAT is that it is structured so that the responses and interpretation centre on pain. The clinician does not have *carte blanche* to interpret at will. The pain qualities of intensity and duration are assessed for each picture by two questions with a 7-point scale: (i) How does the man feel? (from 'no pain' to 'can't stand the pain'); (ii) How long will it hurt him? (from 'not at all' to 'months').

Petrovich (1959) did carry out three interesting studies using the PAT. In the first, 50 male and 50 female professional and clerical personnel of Jefferson Barracks Veterans Administration Hospital were used (aged about 39–40) to test for sex differences. Females were generally predisposed to see more pain — both intensity and duration — in the PAT pictures than were the males. Petrovich admits that the depiction of males in all the PAT pictures was a possible complicating factor.

The next study was of 100 white, male patients at the same hospital drawn from the medical and surgical wards (aged about 37), but excluding neurological and amputee patients. Petrovich found significant positive correlations between the PAT and anxiety (Taylor Manifest Anxiety Scale) and between the PAT and neuroticism (Medical Questionnaire). Five factors were important:

(i) the degree of physical painfulness commonly associated with the impending injury; (ii) the proximity or imminence of the pain; (iii) the degree to which the intended recipient could control the receiving pain (for example, one picture shows a very large ice cube in the process of dropping on a man's foot, and it was felt that he could have moved his foot out of the way); (iv) the intention or effect (beneficial or harmful, so an injection or tooth drilling is seen as 'beneficial') of the impending pain; (v) the degree of neuroticism and/or anxiety possessed.

The last study was on 100 diagnosed chronic schizophrenics who were compared with the 100 patients non-psychiatric group. The schizophrenic group tended to react less than the normal group where the pain was self-inflicted or sustained. However, two individual pictures did elicit a higher 'normal' response (cut forearm and an electric shock from a plug socket). As the majority of schizophrenics had previously received electro-convulsive therapy (ECT), Petrovich says 'It seems reasonable to assume that picture 6 re-arouses affect previously associated with the unpleasant ECT experience'. For the other picture, 'Suggested clinical explanation for the schizophrenics' heightened reaction to picture 2 involves the castration anxiety symbolized by the cutting or partial severance of a physical projection (forearm) of the body'. This stands out as the only picture that shows blood, so Petrovich's interpretation about 'bodily projections' and 'castration anxiety' could be wrong: simply the sight of blood. In absolute terms, the chronic schizophrenic perceives greater than normal painfulness when another person is about to inflict, or is inflicting, the pain, and less than normal painfulness when the pain will be, or is, unintentionally self-induced. Petrovich notes:

> it is possible that normals can more realistically appreciate and tolerate the infliction of beneficial pain than can the schizophrenic who is often ultra-sensitive to the possibility of bodily harm from other people, even where genuine altruism exists. It is also possible that unconscious homosexual fears of bodily penetration are heightened by the relatively innocuous hypodermic needle and dental drill. (1960)

Perhaps if more normals had the benefits of ECT, they too might become 'ultra-sensitive'. As for unconscious homosexual fears, whether or not schizophrenics saw the hypodermic needle as a phallus, they certainly saw the tooth-drilling as being more painful: they might have even noticed that the pictured dental patient was gripping the arms of the dental chair!

The results with the 100 schizophrenic patients were the most fascinating because although they feared most harm from others, they could still differentiate between 'self-inflicted' and 'other-inflicted' pain. The fact that all the pictures are of males could be a confounding variable in further research, as well as a slight cultural bias (rifle-wounds in the shoulder are not that common an injury outside of the US). Bearing these points in mind, and if Petrovich could possibly make up his mind whether he wants a sympathetic or empathetic response from his subjects, this is one of the better projective tests around.

The areas of concern about pain which these two tests focus on are rather different. Melzack (1975) wants his subjects to provide a precise description of where they are feeling the pain and how intense it happens to be. Though much of the test is concerned with feelings of pain, none of the questions set by Melzack highlight emotional reactions to pain. Here, the Petrovich tests succeeds much better. Responses to the PAT will not tell the doctor just where the patient is in pain, or even how intense that pain is, but they may well be useful in revealing the feelings they have about the pain. Given recent discoveries about the importance of psychological factors in controlling pain, one can see that the two tests provide valuable data within certain limits. Certainly, they need not exclude one another. This may seem to be a rather banal plea for tolerance, but many advocates of testing are really only advocates for one kind of testing. To the IQ fetishist, the Rorschach is a blot on the history of psychology; to the Rorschach lover, the IQ test is a fascist perversion. These two pain tests offer useful comparison because both can be sensibly used; though, curiously, Melzack (1977) in his recent pain book does not seem ever to mention Petrovich.

Those in pain are probably well motivated to answer doctors' questions. Old people may be less kindly disposed to experts, especially if those experts pester them with questions that seem fit only for children. Tests for detecting loss of function in old people are likely to become increasingly popular. Again, it may be useful to compare two tests that hone in on the same problem. Interesting differences emerge between them, and one problem with both tests parallels the differences between Melzack's test and the PAT.

Case Study Three: Old Mistakes

Test tested: Kendrick Battery for Detection of Dementia in the Elderly
Example of questions: Remember pictures on a card; copy digits
Form of answer: The correct one
Our focus: What mistakes are most valuable

The Battery consists of two main tasks which are designed to assess those cognitive abilities most likely to deteriorate with age. The Object Learning Test consists of four large cards with pen and ink drawings of common objects (cat, watch, banana, newspaper). The first card has 10 objects which are repeated on the second card, which has 15; the third has 20, the fourth 25. The subject is shown the card — longer exposures are used for cards with more objects — and is then asked to recall the objects in any order. Scoring is flexible so a donkey is acceptable if the right answer is a horse.

The Digit Copying Tests consists of a 10×10 matrix of the digits 0–9, each occurring randomly ten times within the matrix. Subjects are not told, but the test is interested in speed, not accuracy. To score it, one is instructed 'simply add the number of digits (whether right or wrong)'.

Kendrick says that the Battery should not be used with those under 55 or patients who have become institutionalised. He recommends it is not used after someone has been in hospital for three weeks. Certain anti-depressant and anti-psychotic drugs may depress performance, Kendrick warns. Finally, the Battery should not be used with people whose verbal IQ is below 70. Care has to be taken to ensure that subjects can see the cards, hear the instructions, and are not handicapped by conditions such as arthritic hands.

These warnings suggest that Kendrick is sensitive to some of the problems of elderly subjects, but his Battery suffers from some assumptions. Most seriously, it presupposes that failures due to dementia ought to be assessed quantitatively. As we shall see, Rabbitt (1982) suggested that one way of using tests was to analyse errors qualitatively. Just as Petrovich would claim that people had very different feelings about pain and these might influence the treatment they ought to get, Rabbitt maintains errors have much diagnostic value. *How* one fails can reveal what is wrong.

One of Kendrick's co-authors, Andrew Gibson, found that old people do not recall the objects on the cards in a normal manner. He followed up the work of Miller (1971), who had subjects listen to lists of 12 common words. Usually, subjects recall the first and last items best, consigning middle items to oblivion. Miller (1975) saw that his presenile patients remembered much less, and tended to forget words both at the beginning and the middle of list. Only the most recent words were remembered. Gibson (1981) found much the same with the visual stimuli used in the Battery. He used seven cards of ten pictures each. Each card was shown for 1.5 seconds; after it was shown subjects had to remember what they had seen, in any order.

For both the visual and verbal tasks the depressed group did significantly worse than the normal group (0.001 both comparisons), and the demented group did worse still (0.001 both tasks). The comparisons between the normal and demented groups was obviously highly significant, too. Gibson found no significant interaction between groups and tasks and concluded that the degree of impairment in the groups showing memory loss is not related to modality.

The most interesting finding in respect to the Kendrick Battery was that both normal and depressed samples produced the typical U-shaped serial position curves where first and last items are best remembered, with ones in the middle being most forgotten. But in the demented group there was little sign that the first items were recalled better, and only the last two of the ten items have much chance of being remembered: short-term memory is very much short term in their case. The standard deviations on the visual task for normals and depressives were 7.71 and 7.68; it was only 3.74 for the demented group, indicating greater homogeneity.

Kendrick has promised that a future revision of the Kendrick Battery will consider the merits or demerits of serial presentation of the Object Learning Task. It might be useful to compare the current test, where the items are presented simultaneously, with a serial method to see if performance is independent of mode of presentation as well as of modality.

The Battery raises familiar issues. First, there is the general problem with all testing that psychometricians either are unwilling to, or don't know how to, come to terms with the fact that if a person sees the content of a test as irrelevant to him or her, there are motivational and attentional difficulties. Secondly, if old people are asked to do tasks they associate with young children only, it damages their self-esteem. They may feel that the psychologist is trying to belittle them. Kendrick claimed the Battery could be useful in four areas of research: early recognition of Alzheimer's disease; side-effects of anti-cholinergenic drugs in the elderly; significance of the late onset of depression in the elderly; relation between physical activity, ageing and mental activity.

Alzheimer's disease involves memory loss. Before obvious memory disturbance appears, lack of initiative, difficulty in making decisions and distractability are symptoms which the family dismiss as ageing processes. Once the deterioration becomes so bad that the family seek help for the old person, it is too late to reverse the process but not always to ameliorate it. Both biochemical and neuropathological findings in post-mortem studies suggest that a deficit in the cholinergic system is evident in Alzheimer's disease.

The last two problems have activity — or the lack of it — in common. The onset of depression after the age of 60 is known to have a worse prognosis than before this age. Active lifestyles that stress fitness are a prime factor in reducing the ageing process as measured by simple reaction times, choice reaction times and movement-time tasks. But these may be uncontrolled, independent variables in previous studies. Researchers are often tempted to take samples from Senior Citizens' Clubs, whose members may be more active. A homebound, static sample may give different results.

An Everyday Story of Ageing Folk

To answer all these problems, Kendrick wanted to develop techniques which can assess accurately aspects of everyday behaviour. He added that the use of Wechsler Scales as diagnostic instruments, as well as being measures of intellectual capacity, probably need to be abandoned because these types of tests are both unfamiliar and irrelevant to the life activities of the elderly. Yet tests were vital as they could detect changes, if repeated measurements are taken, before they become obvious and so bad 'patients' could be helped.

It is easy to understand the need for such research, but Kendrick's test seems to suffer from a variety of problems. In the preamble to his paper (1982a), Kendrick argued strongly for realistic tests and castigated other ones for insulting the elderly. Some subjects, he reported, complained of IQ tests being infantile. One woman said she hadn't been expected to fiddle with blocks since she was a child. Kendrick scorns such insensitive tests, but it is not easy to see just how his own is different. How do old people usually react when asked to remember if they just saw a picture of a donkey or a banana? Is this the kind of mistake they might make in a supermarket? Kendrick does not really show that old people were duly motivated to take his tests. Moreover, he seems to suggest that the errors in reaction times and object identification means functional errors in situations familiar to old people. One of the most striking stories that social workers tell is of old people who manage as long as they are living in familiar environments. Kendrick needs to show far more clearly that the kinds of errors old people make on his tasks have implications for their performance in the lives they are used to.

In a critique of Kendrick, the experimental psychologist Pat Rabbitt (1982) noted that testing old people also required more sophisticated models of memory. It was not possible to predict the kinds of errors people made in mental arithmetic, and it was a mistake to lump all errors together on one scale. Rabbitt argues that it is not enough to simply add up the tally of errors in sorting out objects or of slowness in reaction to various objects. To be useful, the analysis of the data has to be much finer; the kinds of errors produced may fall into a particular kind of pattern. The gross IQ score a person produces is, for example, a very inexact guide to how well someone might do on a spatial task. Only detailed examination will show up the differences between spatial intelligence and verbal intelligence. A person with high spatial IQ but no gift for words might score an average IQ. That average performance would mask both where he excelled and where he failed. In all, it would be actively misleading. Rabbitt's claim is that Kendrick's test is open to just such distortions.

Case Study Four: The Usefulness of Witnesses

Test tested: Clifton Assessment Procedures
Example of questions: Reading test, general questions about contemporary society such as who is prime minister and witnesses, accounts of elderly relatives
Form of answer: Correct answers to some questions. Rating by witnesses
Our focus: The use of witnesses

The Clifton Assessment Procedures (CAPE) are similar to the

Psychometric Tests, Projective or a New Pattern? 61

Kendrick Battery in many ways, but with the interesting addition of involving witnesses. Witnesses can make all sorts of mistakes. They may be hostile and make the old person seem worse because they want them institutionalised: they may be sentimental and still think Uncle Fred is only a bit deaf when Uncle Fred couldn't hear an explosion. Despite the need for caution, a test which calls in witnesses who usually observe the performance of elderly people day in, day out, is a welcome development.

The aim of the test is to provide a brief method of assessing the mental and behavioural abilities of the old. It is intended for use by psychologists, social workers, health visitors, general practitioners and occupational therapists. There are two scales: Cognitive Assessment Scale (CAS), and Behaviour Rating Scale (BRS), which can be used either together or separately.

The CAS, it is stressed, is not an IQ test; it is meant to judge the existence and degree of breakdown in mental functioning, and not to establish a hierarchy amongst the able. There are three sections. The first is a self-report called Information/Orientation Test, which consists of twelve questions about who and where the individual is, as well as three oddly chosen 'general knowledge' questions: 'Name the British prime minister'; 'Name the US president' and 'What is the colour of the British flag'. 'What is the name/address/telephone number of your doctor?'; 'What is the address of your local social security/welfare office?'; 'Where do you collect, and how much is, your pension?' would, it seems, be more relevant to non-hospitalised people than knowing the colour of the British flag.

The next part of the CAS, The Mental Ability Test, consists of four measures relating to well-established skills involving counting, saying the alphabet, reading and writing. They examine attention and concentration. The reading test provides evidence for both visual defects and a general indication of pre-morbid intellectual level. The authors add: 'The words selected for the reading list, therefore, are scaled in terms of their difficulty, and correct pronunciation of all of the words can usually be taken to indicate an at least average pre-morbid ability'. The words range from 'free' (simple) to 'precocious' (difficult). When I'm old and doddery, I will choke before I read that word 'precocious'!

The last component of the CAS is The Psychomotor Test (Gibson Spiral Maze) and tests whether the eye can still guide the hand. Scores are based on two criteria: time and errors, but error is the chief criterion because in a community sample (so called because they lived in the community and needed minimum support) 96 per cent were able to complete the maze in a mean time of 106 seconds with a mean error score of 22. However, a psychogeriatric sample (i.e. they needed a lot of support) took, on average, only slightly longer to complete the test but more than doubled the error score. Environmentally based tests of eye-hand co-ordination could be added, such as using the telephone, adjusting the television set, putting plugs into electrical sockets.

The BRS provides four principal measures of behavioural disability: 'physical disability' (Pd), 'apathy' (Ap), 'communication difficulties' (Cd), and 'social disturbance' (Sd). These questions are to be completed by a person familiar with the subject and scored according to what the elderly person does rather than what he/she may be able to do, or at one time was able to do. The authors, quite rightly, focus on inter-rater reliability because other reliability tests would be misleading in that changes would be expected as a result of therapy/treatment. Overall, the inter-rater reliabilities on the four subscales of the BRS are quite high, but tend to be slightly low on 'communication difficulties'. There are two possible reasons for this. First, as only two questions out of eighteen are used to assess this subscale, reliability might be improved by increasing the scope and precision of the questions. Secondly, no details of the status of the raters are given, but 'relatives, caring staff in institutions, health visitors, community and hospital nurses etc.' are recommended, so it might be presumed that the raters had different amounts of contact with the subjects.

Continuum of Care

CAPE can be used in three main areas: individual clinical assessment, population surveys and screening, and identifying patients for rehabilitation and monitoring treatment effectiveness. CAPE has enormous potential value with regard to selection and placement. As people are continuing to live longer, there is an ever increasing strain on hospital and social services. The scales should prove to be invaluable in helping to assess priorities. Pattie and Gilleard (1979) give normative data for different sub-populations ('social services', psychiatric patients — 'acute functional', 'chronic functional', 'acute organic', 'chronic organic'). Although the numbers are small by test standards (two groups of 50 and three groups of 100), it does help in evaluating the level of care required. It would be a great pity if full use was not made of this very valuable test.

Psychometric Tests, Projective or a New Pattern? 63

Neither of these two tests reflect a very interesting recent phenomenon — the development of memory clinics. Psychologist caring for the elderly have found that they enjoy, and benefit from, being encouraged to remember their past. An old person who does not know the name of the current prime minister may well recall what it was like being a young boy in Bow or what Lloyd George did to Asquith. Conventional tests only note that the old man did not know whether President Reagan was President of America. (Testing President Reagan's intellectual capacity became an issue in the 1984 election but, of course, psychologists would have been unable to agree on what would be a proper test for an ageing president if they had been asked to administer it!) Yet, for an old person, the memories of the past may have more emotional and practical value than new items of short-term memory. Subtleties such as these are not usually accommodated in tests.

There is extensive literature on the reliability of both projective tests, psychometric tests and others. The usual assumption has been that such tests are in competition. You believe and use one kind or the other. Throughout this book we argue that no test is perfect and no test is total. Some projective tests, including the perennial Rorschach, may be more dubious than others, but then so are some psychometric tests. The value of projective tests is that they allow more complex and individualistic responses. When, like the PAT, they are well validated, they can reach the parts, or particles, others do not reach. Focused objective tests may be very useful but the lesson of tests of the elderly is that it is not enough to count the number of errors or the scale of delay in answering questions. A quantitative analysis is useful, but it needs to be backed up by a qualitative analysis of the nature of the errors. Piaget offers a good comparison. When he was asked to help standardise the Binet tests, his only means of testing out why small children made mistakes was to talk to them. As he had just studied with Bleuler and Jung in Zurich, Piaget called this 'the clinical method', a nicely scientific-sounding label for probing conversation. His conversations with children exposed gaps in their logic and knowledge, and Piaget wove intricate theories out of the nature of these gaps. Tests that simply log the number of right answers and wrong answers offer a score of performance, but it is a score that may not be very revealing. In some cases, as with a person who is good on verbal tests but bad on mathematical ones, the crude IQ score may be utterly wrong for it could suggest that he or she is average on both. With old people, studying the nature of their errors may be clinically important.

Controversies about testing pit different tests against each other. This combative attitude is fine but it misses two fundamental points. First, very different tests may provide complementary information. Secondly, the way that most tests are scored tells us rather little about the kinds of mistakes people make. Yet the mistakes they make are often crucial both in telling us about them and telling us, as experts, what they may need by way of help.

4 HOW MUCH INDIVIDUALITY CAN WE KNOW?

In 1937 the personality psychologist Gordon Allport blamed the discipline for being pseudo-scientific. It was seeking the general laws of human behaviour, and in doing so it ignored the 'outstanding characteristic of man', which, said Allport, 'is his individuality'. Allport was immediately rebuffed by another psychologist, Henry Murray (1938), who said that any human being is:

(i) in some respects like all other human beings;
(ii) in some respects like some other human beings;
(iii) in some respects like no other human being.

Individuality did not have to be inflated.

The debate between Allport and Murray led to a more general debate about whether personality theory should be nomothetic, i.e. seeking general laws, or idiographic, i.e. seek to understand the unique person in his glowing individuality. Though the debate was largely confined to the study of personality, it has implications for the whole of psychology, especially as many researchers are obsessed with quantification and comparison. Experiments nearly always pit one group of people with another. The experimental group have been given magic drug A, or undergone training procedure B, or been duped by trick C. How do they then compare with a 'normal' group? Other designs compare groups with different histories or experiences. Do prisoners do better than psychiatric patients on tests of this skill? Do they score differently on various personality traits? There is nothing wrong with comparisons or with counting, but often fairly small statistical differences are taken to be facts. All that has occurred is that they have reached levels of 'significance' which psychologists have chosen to make cut-off points. If results go above these arbitrary cut-off points, we have reached significance. In this sense, 'significance' is merely a statistical convention, but psychology plays, of course, on the natural meaning of the word. If there is a 'statistically significant' difference, then it must be really significant. Or else we would not say it was significant.

The slippage between the two senses of 'significance' may well dupe some psychologists.

And even if many of the findings in the journals might be statistically significant, they are not very revealing. They tell me little I want to know about my life or yours. I do not find out why I am obsessed with buxom Mary, gorge on sausage rolls, and love Humphrey Bogart movies. Runyan (1984), in his book on psychobiographies, emphasises the need for more idiographic tests, and provides an up-to-date account of the latest developments in the field. He spots, but curiously does not make much of, a paradox. One might imagine that it would be simpler to study one person in depth than to compare hundreds. In fact, idiographic methods are very complicated. In one case, it took 66 interviews and many tests over 85 days to establish that one girl's asthma attacks were associated with the presence of her mother. Runyan wondered whether, in that case, the findings merited the complex methodology. Perhaps the most extreme instance of effort required is De Waele's and Harré's method of assisted autobiography. Here, a person tells his or her life story to a duly qualified team. The team take it down, note contradictions, ask questions. Questionnaires and psychometric tests flesh out the narrative. For all this expert attention, De Waele and Harré (1979) recognise that they can only arrive at one truth through this method, not the truth. They define this one truth as the best account that a person can give at that time with professional help. Philosophically, assisted autobiography is interesting. It recognises both human self-consciousness and limits of psychological knowledge. But it is a long procedure. It is far less used than many other idiographic methods.

After Allport's polemic there was a spate of idiographic activity. New techniques for studying the 'whole human' careered out of the psychological imagination. Three major idiographic tests were pioneered: Stephenson's Q Sort, the Baldwin (1942) personal structure analysis and Kelly's Repertory Grid Technique (1955). We examine the latter because it has established itself probably as the most used idiographic test.

Case Study One: How Do You Construe the World?

Test tested: Kelly's Repertory Grid Test
Example of questions: See grid

Form of answer: Ticking two people on the grid who are alike and one who is opposite
Our focus: Individual testing

Kelly began life as an engineer. He argued that all human beings are psychologists and that we all construe the world in different ways. He also believed that our way of construing the world changed, often quite rapidly. He devised his Repertory Grid Technique as a technique which would be controlled — to some extent at least — by the subject. The subject could not alter the shape of the grid or the rules for filling it in, but he could make some crucial decisions. Usually, he could decide what were the significant people or elements he wanted to compare, and he could nearly always decide what constructs he wanted to use.

Grid A is an example of a grid. On the top line the person fills in a number of roles or elements. Often they include 'Me', 'Ideal Me', 'Me As Others See Me', 'Father', 'Mother', 'Lover', 'Boss', 'Teacher'. The roles can be adapted for use in a particular environment. Psychiatric patients who do the grids often find that some of the roles they are asked to use include nurse, psychiatrist, occupational therapist, etc. On the right hand of the grid is space for adjectives. On each line a person has to tick two people who are similar in some way and one who is dissimilar. I may rate 'Ideal Me' and 'Mother' as beautiful and 'Me' as plain. Beautiful/plain would then be one of my constructs.

Me	Ideal Me	Me as Others See Me	Mother	Father	Boss	Girlfriend	
			−	×	×		Bullying/Non-bully
	×			×	−		Clever/Dull
−	−			×			Mean/Kind
×				−	−		Likes Pop Music/Hates It
	×		×		−		Beautiful/Plain
	×	−				×	Sexy/Not Sexy

A person uses his or her own adjectives, or constructs, to describe different people in his or her life. The grid can then be analysed in a number of ways. Someone may use many different adjectives but appear to be getting at the same thing. One could fill in the Grid A above in a variety of ways. The grid we depict has someone who sees his mother and his ideal self as clever, beautiful and not bullying, while a third figure (his father basically) is not clever, hates pop music and is bullying. In 1955 Kelly produced a sample grid in which someone rated 19 elements along 22 constructs. Grids do not have to have either that number of elements or of constructs, however; one of the beauties of the technique is its flexibility.

Kelly created the test as a means of studying his theory of personal constructs. He argued that human beings essentially try to make sense of the world using constructs they develop through their own experiences. Individuals with very *tight* constructs found it hard to change the way they saw the world; more flexible people had *looser* constructs. To have nothing but loose constructs, however, is not too healthy because that suggests a person is changing so fast that he or she never gets any fixed view of his or her world. Bannister (1975) found that schizophrenics had a very loose set of constructs. The pattern of constructs a person relied on was, Kelly argued, the result of his or her experiences, though people could consciously decide to construe the world in a different way. Bannister suggested, for example, that there was an early period in doing research where it paid scientists to adopt a loose construct frame of mind so that they could play, quite deliberately, with all kinds of possibilities.

Kelly's Repertory Grid has been the object of many validation studies. It has given rise to a large literature on its uses both in personality research, clinical work and other areas (for a review, see Adams-Webber (1979)).

In examining its idographic uses, we concentrate on two studies. Ryle (1969) used the Repertory Test to examine his own performance as a psychotherapist; Bannister, Adams-Webber, Penn and Radley (1975) used it to study schizophrenic thought patterns and to monitor attempts to improve them. Both these studies reveal that the Repertory Test is valuable, but point to certain limitations it has as an idographic measure.

Ryle (1969) investigated how he saw 28 patients he was treating. He had seen some patients for 3/4 sessions, some for over 100. As Dearnley (1980) broke new ground studying his daily life, so Ryle broke new ground monitoring his own psychotherapy practice. Ryle found that his grids allowed him to divide his patients into four different groups. Each group was defined by a series of constructs. One group struck Ryle as being amusing, expressive, open, original; a second group 'makes me bored' and was assessed by him as having used drugs; a third group he saw as 'can work with me', 'evokes sympathy' and 'I feel involved with'; a fourth group was seen as 'has neurotic work block' and 'makes me angry'. Using the grid allowed Ryle to categorise his patients in sophisticated ways both emotionally and intellectually. He was able to define the patients according to his own reactions. He could eschew the normal, imposed psychiatric diagnoses which would have obliged him to divide them into schizophrenics, depressives and so on. Conventional diagnoses were not that crucial.

Four years later, each patient was rated on what Ryle admitted was a crude 4-point scale which went from definite improvement to nil improvement. Ryle found that his open, expressive and amusing patients had done best. The group that had a neurotic work block and who 'make me angry' had done least well.

Research on the outcome of psychotherapy has long suggested that certain therapists will do better with certain kinds of patients. They can be well matched or mismatched (Truax, Carkhuff and Kudman (1965)). Comparing a patient's grid with a therapist's grid can be a good clue to whether they will work well together or not. Ryle noted: 'These findings clearly had implications for my selection of cases for treatment'. Ryle reckoned too that he was not the ideal therapist for passive aggressives who had work blocks and made him angry.

Bannister explained in an interview to one of the present authors that he had become attracted to Kelly because 'I could make a certain amount of sense of what was happening to me in terms of Personal Construct Theory. I had never seen myself mirrored in Freudian theory or learning theory'. He hypothesised that schizophrenics might have very loose constructs because 'the person had gone too far out on a loose limb and could not tighten and test his new view of the world'. Thought-disordered schizophrenics not only produced loose grids but changed them constantly. Bannister gave them grids at 30-minute intervals. 'The next pattern was as loose as the one before but different'. The ability to think about other people and about human relationships was especially fluid. Kelly argued that human beings constantly make predictions. We believe that the parent who coos 'I love you' will not leave home, and that the stranger who smiles at a cocktail party will not thump people. The schizophrenic has no such confidence. Bannister's findings were replicated. It is interesting that the entire design of his study assumed that the grids were not unreliable because they were producing such erratic results. It was his patients who were so variable. Usually, if a test throws up such results, it is criticised, but Bannister was focused on the people. Did schizophrenics have such loose constructs because they had suffered from 'serial invalidation'? Bannister wondered if the trouble was that the prediction they made always turned out to be wrong. The patient 'is like a scientist whose theories are constantly bashed by the facts. He has no luck. He is always wrong. In the end, he goes in for theories that are so vague they cannot be proved wrong'. The schizophrenic ceases to commit himself to any view.

First, Bannister got normal subjects to judge personality from photographs. They had to fill in 20 grids about the photographs over 20 days. They were asked to say if a person was mean, selfish or intelligent. They were then given feedback from fake biographies. Subjects who were right tightened their constructs. Their correlations got higher, and they 'judged in a very simple way because they were being told they were right'. Those who got negative feedback kept on altering their constructs. At the start, the correlation between judging a person to be *sympathetic* and *honest* was high, 0.7, but by the end it was negative at -0.8. 'People began to despair. They did not give up on all their constructs at one go. Little nodules of constructs stayed quite strong'. But slowly, their constructs, and their confidence, collapsed. It was much the pattern that schizophrenics revealed.

To extend the work, Bannister and colleagues commandeered a ward of 23 schizophrenics. For 26 months patients lived on a ward where everything was altered so that one group had their constructs about people re-affirmed time and time again. One patient had a residual construct system that went:

Bullying	Non-bullying
Loud Voiced	Soft Voiced
Mean	Generous
Flirts	Does Not Flirt
Sides with Mother	Sides with Me
Dislikes Pop Music	Likes Pop Music

This patient has retained the view that the world was divided into bullies who were loud, mean, flirted, sided with her mother and disliked pop music, and utterly different non-bullies. Bannister then tried to get nurses and doctors to be one or the other, to fit in with the patient's constructs. Bannister himself acted the part of the bully each time he saw her, refusing cigarettes, talking loudly and siding with her mother. 'The idea was that she would experience an interpersonal world that would strengthen the theory she had'. Other patients were given similar construct-building experiences.

The evidence of the project 'leans', Bannister chose the word with care, 'towards the thesis'. Not all the experimental group got better, but 5 out of 12 were discharged after two years. Of the 11 in the control group, only 2 were discharged. A battery of other tests including TAT tests, Hospital Adjustment Scales and Word Speech samples all pointed in the same direction, with the experimental group getting better on ten measures. The control group improved on only two measures. Bannister has never claimed the project is conclusive proof that tightening constructs helped cure thought-disordered schizophrenics, but suggested that it was still impressive evidence.

Both Ryle's study and Bannister's project reveal the value of the grid. There are still, however, problems. Often the grids use a set number of elements or roles. The subject does not have to choose these. Secondly, Kelly's whole method assumes that we think in a 'bipolar' way, judging people to be either mean or generous; either clever or dull; either lovers or haters of pop music. Subjects can choose what constructs to use, but they cannot chose not to rate people in this *either-or* way. It could be argued that normally many people do not think like this at all. I may like Fred because he is generous and likes pop music, but I may not think very much about people who do not like pop music. There may be a wide range of people in my world who are neutral about pop music, neither liking it, nor hating it. It does not matter much to them. George may strike me as intelligent, and, therefore, I remark on that. But there may be people I mix with who neither strike me as clever nor as dull. Kelly presumes that we divide the world in this kind of way..In doing that, unwittingly perhaps, Kelly echoes the ideas of philosophers of science who believe that a proposition must be either *true* or *false*. We perhaps inhabit less of an either-or world.

We raise these points about Kelly because it shows the poverty of idiographic techniques that his test should shine as such a star in the firmament. There are many idiographic aspects to his test. Bannister constructed very different grids for different patients. For each one, the roles or elements selected were based on extensive interviews in which the psychologist tried to see what people had been (or still were) important for them. Having done all that, subjects were still obliged to squeeze their perceptions into a bipolar pattern. On the traditional psychometric criteria, Kelly's test works well. Normal individuals do produce fairly stable grids at different times. The clinical research done suggests that the test is a useful tool for sorting out people who think alike, and therapists and clients whose view of the world is sufficiently similar for them to be able to work together. Yet, from an idiographic point of view, the test leaves a good deal to be desired. People are constrained into expressing their thoughts in a perhaps distorted either-or way which may negate the idiographic effort to know the whole person.

Kelly required his subjects to make *either-or* descriptions, but gave them considerable freedom, nonetheless, to set the agenda of their test. Some tests appear to tackle idiographic concerns, but because their methods are so steeped in psychometric conventions they undermine the whole enterprise. An interesting example of this is the widely used Edwards Personal Preference Schedule (Edwards, 1959a, 1959b).

Case Study Two: Personal Choices or Forced Ones

Test tested: Edwards Personal Preference Schedule
Example of questions: Would you criticise someone in authority or say nothing?
Form of answer: Yes or no choice
Our focus: Forcing subjects to choose

Personal preferences are, on the face of it, very individual. The subject matter of the Edwards Personal Preference Schedule (EPPS) ought to allow subjects to express all kinds of idiosyncrasies. In fact, the form of the test makes this impossible. The test is a self-report inventory that has been widely used in selection, counselling, and even marriage guidance. It has been employed by the Peace Corps to judge how effective their volunteers would be, and on engaged couples to see if they are likely to enjoy the company of similar friends. The EPPS uses the personality variables that Henry Murray devised when he was claiming that all human beings were, in some respects, unique. Its pedigree is idiographic; its execution is not. Murray (1938) claimed we all had fifteen needs — achievement, deference, order, exhibition (showing off), autonomy, affiliation (loyalty to friends), intraception (insight), succorance (kindness to others), dominance, abasement, nurturance, change, endurance, heterosexuality and aggression. One way to examine these might be through interviews. Instead the Schedule consists of 210 pairs of items and the forced-choice technique makes respondents choose either statement A or statement B rather than endorse 'Yes-No' to a single statement. This method is claimed to reduce faking in order to make a good impression.

Fifteen items are repeated to judge consistency. The pairing of variables against one another is intended to give an assessment of the relative strength of competing needs within the person not between persons, so the resulting scores is ipsative. Gustad (in Buros, 1978) states that no reasons are given in Edwards's manual to show that the EPPS does measure the manifest needs proposed by Murray. Even face validity is suspect! Four items presume heterosexuality. What about those for whom boots evoke sexual arousal! Edwards purports to measure normal personality variables, but this is no excuse for presuming normality of responses or equating sexuality with heterosexuality. Aggression, too, is mainly refined, bitchy and verbal, not overtly physical.

Edwards admits that his fifteen variables are not wholly independent and there is a similarity between some of the questions professing to measure different needs: autonomy (to say what one thinks about things, to criticise those in positions of authority); aggression (to tell others what one thinks of them, to attack contrary points of view, to criticise others publicly).

The Norms of the EPPS were established on 749 college women and 760 college men aged 15–59, but 82 per cent of the sample were aged 15–24. Kirchner, Dunnette and Mousky (1960) found that scores on the EPPS for 362 male applicants for sales positions differed significantly from those of the college males on nearly all of the fifteen scales. Probably, the sales applicants were different from the student population, but Anastasi (1976) has questioned the practice of mixing ipsative and normative frames of reference. Ipsative scores permit comparisons of the relative strength of characteristics within the individual, while normative scores permit comparisons with others.

Rubenowitz (1963) found the 'Correlations between EPPS variables and total suitability for promotion, assessed in a comprehensive selection procedure' for five selection studies. He concluded that achievement, dominance and change make subjects good bets for promotion, whereas deference, succorance and abasement suggest they should stay where they are. On Edwards's normative sample, men have signficantly higher means than women on achievement, autonomy, dominance, heterosexuality and aggression, but women have significantly higher means than men on deference, affiliation, intraception, succorance, abasement, nurturance and change. Given how bad the norms are, this makes a prima facie case for better research into sex discrimination and employment.

Great caution should be exercised in interpreting any of the EPPS profiles. Dicken (1959) found that scores on three of four scales of the EPPS differed significantly when a group of college students took the inventory under standard instructions, and when they took it with instructions to make the best impression on a specific trait described to them: it can be faked! Each of the four subgroups was instructed to consider a different trait on the second administration.

What does a need-score mean? One very shy boy scored very highly on exhibition but showed himself to be quite diffident in an interview. Further probing revealed that he did always take a back seat, but more than anything else would like to be the centre of attention. In another case, a middle-aged, married man received a high score on heterosexuality (older and married men are supposed to have less of a need than the college stud). He turned out to be in the midst of an extra-marital affair — his first really satisfying relationship with a woman. The shy boy had an unfulfilled need while the older man had found someone to satisfy his heterosexual need. It is obvious, then, that the EPPS, in and of itself, says nothing about an individual's past, present or future behaviour.

Without interviews to reinforce the findings or to allow some rather basic points to be raised, the EPPS seem rather little use. Its widespread employment suggests that psychologists want a test that looks personal but are easily seduced into using an easy and conventional one. Lamiell (1981) made some attempt to make the idiographic approach more scientific.

Case Study Three: Idiothetic Testing

Almost all tests attempt to compare the performance of different individuals along one or more attributes. My IQ score of 117 only establishes my IQ in comparison with an average drawn from others tested. When psychologists correlate scores on a personality test with success in a job, they are not studying an individual so much as a linear trend using data from a group of subjects. It is easy to think of the correlations as relating to one person, though. The history of psychological testing owed much to work on individual differences, and one irony of studying individual differences is that they tend not to focus on individuality. Our third case study in this chapter examines a proposal by Lamiell (1981) to devise *idiothetic* testing.

Lamiell begins by pointing out that there used to be a distinction between the study of personality psychology and differential psychology. Differential psychology was quite correctly concerned with important questions of whether I am more extravert than Fred and what implications that has; personality psychology had a less specific aim: to describe personality. Traditional tests, Lamiell argued, 'generated data that reflected differences between individuals along the same common attribute'. Within this tradition there was little use of ipsative measurement. The data thus generated provided 'aggregate indices' that made Lamiell wonder; for 'data computed on this the basis of data *summed* [his italics] across individuals . . . virtually precludes their appropriateness as grounds on which to infer anything about the consistency or inconsistency of one individual'.

Lamiell suggests that any correlations that are obtained — say, between assertiveness and the number of speeches made in a group setting — are proof of inconsistency unless they reach the perfect 1 yet psychologists often gasp with pride when their data turns up a correlation of, for example, 0.7. (The square of the correlation 0.49 defines how much of the variance of scores is due to that factor). But, in fact, that number means that the correlation is far from perfect. For 50 per cent of the variance, being mathematically crude, there is no link between assertiveness and speech making.

There is also a more philosophical objection. Tests are used in personality research in an attempt to discover what the individual is like and how he or she got there. 'How can empirical research that does not even describe the personality of individuals possibly illuminate the process of personality development?' For Lamiell, it's a rhetorical question.

In place of the correlation paradigm, Lamiell proposed a paradigm which has similarities with some of the ideas discussed in

Chapter 2 under dynamics of action. He noted:

> The framework for personality research to be proposed here is grounded in the basic notion that an individual's personality is best described in terms of information about what that person tends to do — not in direct contrast with what others tend to do but in direct contrast with what that person tends *not* to do but could do.

By way of illustration, Lamiell suggests that the best way of defining Mary on a continuum of rebellious to compliant is to get her to describe eleven potential behaviours that she might engage in in a week. Table 4.1 illustrates these.

From this table it would be possible to work out the maximum or minimum values that could be obtained on some underlying attribute. The figures for 'conceptualisation' come from asking Mary to imagine how likely she is to engage in a particular kind of behaviour. She might have been as 'compliant' as 1.20 or as 'rebellious' as −1.78. In the week in question she notched up a score that indicated 0.61 of compliance.

There are some obvious points to be made. First, Mary's

Table 4.1: Illustrative Application of Proposed Measurement Rationale

Perceived behavioural alternatives	Conceptualisation of perceived behavioural alternatives	Recorded behaviour over a given week
1. Drinking beer/liquor	−0.24	No (0)
2. Engaging in premarital sex	−0.20	No (0)
3. Studying/reading	0.18	Yes (1)
4. Participating in extracurricular activities	0.32	Yes (1)
5. Engaging in acts of vandalism	−0.26	No (0)
6. Doing nothing in particular	−0.23	Yes (1)
7. Smoking marijuana	−0.28	No (0)
8. Participating in church-related activities	0.36	No (0)
9. Skipping school	−0.28	No (0)
10. Shoplifting	−0.29	No (0)
11. Participating in volunteer work in the community	0.34	Yes (1)

Note: Assuming an additive integration function, the application of Equation 1 to these data yields an S_{pa} value of 0.61.

behaviour is being compared against — and only against — Mary's previous behaviour. Lamiell does not make it clear whether Mary chose the eleven 'perceived behavioural alternatives' or whether these were imposed by the psychologist. Certainly, Mary or any subject could be asked to choose a number of things she might do if rebellious, and a number if conformist. Lamiell argues that by getting such data across time, psychologists would be better able to monitor changes in patterns of behaviour, personality and motivation.

Developing these ideas, Lamiell also reported an attempt to study 19 undergraduates using self-report scales. Every two days the subjects had to fill in various items and log on a 10-point scale the extent to which they had indulged in them. The items were meant to highlight four different personality attributes. In classical personality theory one would compare the scores of different kinds of individuals — say, students in class B, and students in class C, when class C had had a special training programme. Instead, Lamiell compared each subject with himself on all the four attributes. These ipsative comparisons (Figure 4.1) allowed Lamiell to note that respondent 1 was fairly consistent on attribute II but inconsistent on the others; respondent 10 was relatively consistent over time with respect to attributes I and IV and inconsistent over II and III. Respondent 17 was most consistent about attribute I and most inconsistent over the rest. Lamiell stressed that in every case the definition of an attribute would be individual, and derived from asking each subject (like Mary was asked) what he/she might do and might not do. The attributes were, in effect, individually tailored.

Lamiell argued that such an approach would have much to commend it. It would be firmly rooted in individual lives. Subjects would help construct the scales which were used to test them; a rich picture of a particular life could emerge; people could be studied not at isolated moments or 'slices in time' but through meaningful periods of time. At the same time the techniques would have more to offer than simple descriptions or assisted autobiographies. The use of a formal measure of what people might do (and not do) and whether they did it (or not) would reassure 'hard' psychologists that this was still the realm of science. Moreover, Lamiell claimed that using such a strategy could help develop 'hypotheses pertinent to questions of personality development'. Gathering such data on large numbers of individuals, 'one could very well accumulate empirical support for general principles of personality, the (in)

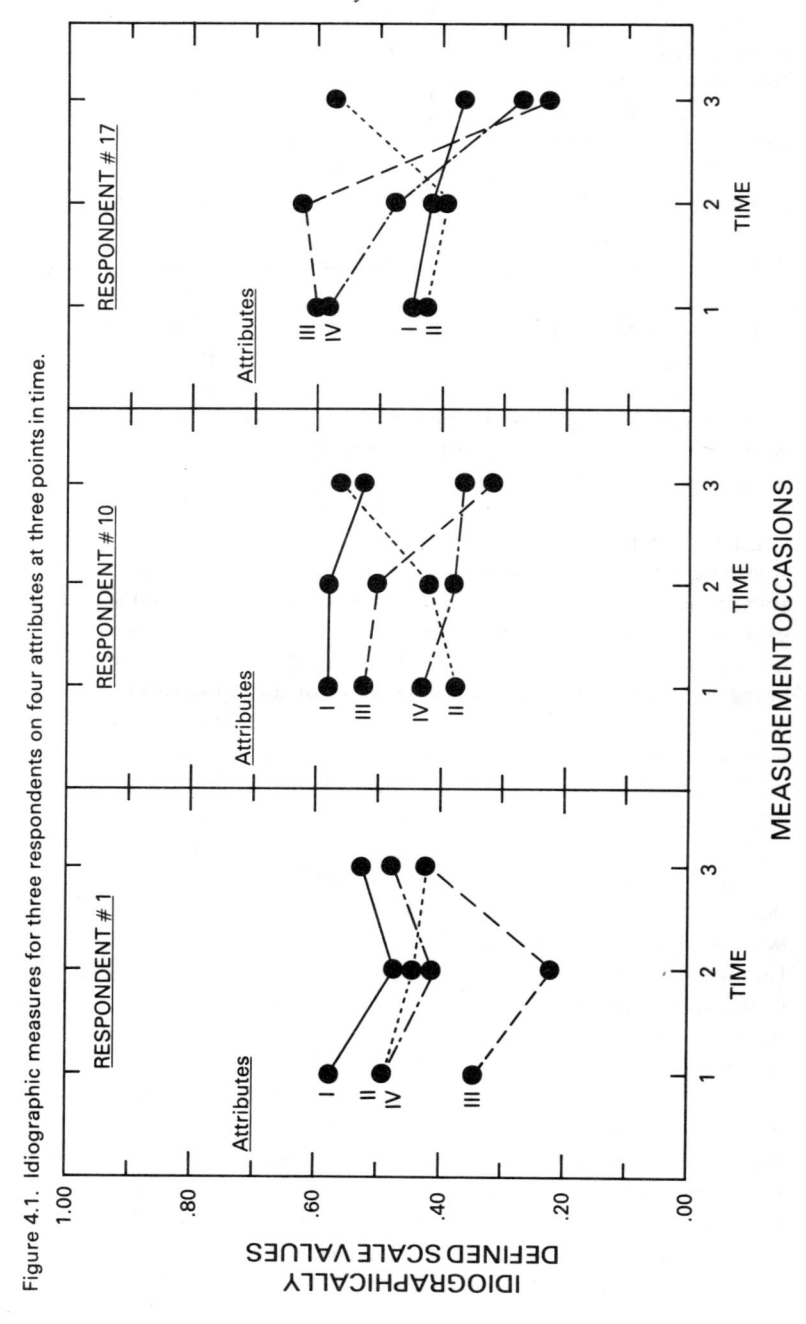

78 *How Much Individuality Can We Know?*

Figure 4.1. Idiographic measures for three respondents on four attributes at three points in time.

compatability of individuals notwithstanding'. Essentially, Lamiell believes that such research paradigms would mean enough information would be collected to allow some very sophisticated comparisons as opposed to the rather crude ones we are currently saddled with. In a nice attempt at synthesis, Lamiell (1981) proposed:

> Programmatic research of the type just described would be idiographic in the sense that it would be predicated on idiographic measurement rationale and would literally involve the study of single individuals across time. It would also be nomothetic, however, in that it would seek to confirm, across individuals, the applicability of certain basic principles to an understanding of the theoretically relevant principles. In a word, the research would be *idiothetic*. (p. 286)

Lamiell's idea is attractive in its marriage of in-depth understanding and sound measurement principles. There are, however, some basic problems. First, the alternative behaviours that a person lists initially may be designed to impress the questioner. Mary never listed, for example, the most obvious rebellious act for a teenager — being rude to her parents, defying them or anything direct of that nature. Was that because she did not want such 'bad manners' monitored? By excluding certain kinds of behaviour in the desire to be idiographic, would Lamiell let subjects write the agenda too much? Secondly, there remains the practical problem that very little such research is actually carried out. Attractive as Lamiell's paradigm is, it has not led to an outpouring of research. There have been some amusing self-studies, like Dearnley's report on his own behaviour. But the kinds of serious longitudinal research that Lamiell proposes is costly, time-consuming and rare. As Runyan (1984) points out in his book on the study of lives, there is always more interest in idiographic research than actual idiographic research completed.

In this chapter we have argued that the majority of tests can hope to provide only very partial information. Much of that information will be comparative and relatively meaningless to the individual. According to Lynn, the average IQ scores of Japanese executives is higher than that of their western counterparts by up to 7 points! It is nice to imagine that means that the boardrooms of Nippon outsmart those of Wall Street by a 7-point margin, but, of course, averages don't produce such neat effects in real life. The main case for idiographic research is that psychology is about people, and non-ideographic techniques provide only very partial data about individuals. The tests and the issue relating to testing that we have covered in this chapter show that for a long time many critical psychologists have pined for a less narrow psychology. For all their pining, we still do not have well-established techniques that allow us to 'psychologise' a person in depth. Lamiell's idiothetic programme is idiosyncratic, and in terms of conventional practice rather eccentric.

The debate about idiographic testing has been a long one. Undergraduates are often asked to comment on it. What is striking, perhaps, is how the terms of the debate have been fixed for so long. The question is how to get the psychologist to understand the subject better. Not even relatively radical thinkers like Kelly embrace the idea of the psychologist collaborating with the subject more. We would agree with Runyan (1984), that attention needs to be paid to devising more sophisticated idiographic techniques. We would also suggest that the notion of idiographic testing would become more interesting if psychologists could loosen their control a bit and see it as an enterprise in which their subject comes to find out more about himself or herself. Later on we return to this idea. At present, despite much effort and good intention, psychological tests remain poor instruments for getting to understand individuals as individuals. Whatever it is that makes us, as Murray would have it, 'unique' escapes nearly all tests.

5 TYPES OF VALIDITY

Anyone can devise a test or a quiz. All it takes is the imagination to think up a few questions. Popular newspapers since the 1920s have often carried tests to tell readers whether they will succeed in life, how romantic they are, what will impress their bosses, and how shy they are. Such tests have not been scientifically vetted. That does not matter to readers who may be gullible about the niceties of verifications. Even the most gullible reader though expects the questions to look relevant. Consider this batch of questions:

1. When you meet a new date, do you often feel nervous?
2. Are you sometimes unable to tell your partner how you feel?
3. Is it you who usually ends your romantic relationships?
4. When you first started to go out with members of the opposite sex, were you (i) under 15, (ii) under 18, (iii) under 20, (iv) over 21?
5. Which of the following statements reflects your views most accurately:

    (i) I want to remain a virgin until I am married.
    (ii) People who do not have experience of sex by the age of 18 are weird.
    (iii) I believe pre-marital sex is moral as long as you expect your partner to become your spouse.

Questions 1 to 5 would seem very odd if they were part of a test of business acumen or of parental skills. Not one appears to be connected to work attitudes or experience. Questions 1 to 5 would carry some conviction though in a test of petting even if they might need more vetting. The issues raised need to look relevant to have face validity.

In selling psychological tests, face validity is important. Customers become convinced that an instrument which raises these kinds of questions has some relevance. There may well be cases of a valid test that does not have apparent face validity. The TAT (see Chapter 2) is just such a test. On the 'face of it', why should making up stories about boys playing violins or families at dinner reveal one's need to achieve. The TAT has a rationale that makes unexpected questions relevant. Most tests are more direct and need, 'on the face of it', to be valid by tackling the issues at hand.

Psychometricians agree that there are basically four different kinds of validity — content validity, concurrent validity, predictive validity and construct validity. As the issues involved are complex, we shall offer a brief definition of each of these terms, which have often been confused.

Content validity requires that the contents of a test should adequately reflect the problems involved. Take again questions 1 to 5. While they are certainly about sexual behaviour, they make unwarranted assumptions. For the homosexual, some questions are irrelevant since the phrasing assumes that the only object of desire is someone of the opposite sex. The foot fetishist would also not find much to arouse him. Most of the questions also seem to hinge around dating or the first period of marriage. Unless other questions were very different, the test would not be very appropriate for discovering the secret (or not so secret) lusts of 35-year-old marrieds. The questions suggest a test which is neither very comprehensive nor very apt; it is short on content validity.

Concurrent validity is an attempt to assess a test's validity by comparing how subjects do it as against their performance on other tests. In Chapter 2 we saw researchers had contrasted how subjects scored on the General Health Questionnaire with how they scored on the Mental Health Scale. Tests of a particular aptitude or attitude ought to have concurrent validity. It is worrying if Test A shows prisoners to be more neurotic than average while Test B shows them to be less neurotic than average. The problem with concurrent validity, however, is that some psychologists feel it is enough to test tests for that. Two tests can have impressive concurrent validity, going hand in hand, correlation matching correlation, but bear no relationship to how subjects behave in the outside world. The Vendors of Ices Test (VIT) may correlate nicely with the Selling Aptitude Scale (SAS), but their concurrent validity is rather irrelevant if those who do well on the VIT do not sell ice-creams better than average, or those who do well on the SAS don't excel at selling. Our last case study in this chapter warns against the dangers of relying too much on *concurrent validity*.

Construct validity is assessed by seeing whether scores on a given trait are linked with behavioural differences which a theory assumes are associated with the trait. One would expect extraverts as defined by the Eysenck Personality Inventory to go to parties more, and to be more likely to become actors than introverts. In some ways, construct validity is predictive since one would predict actors would be more extravert.

Predictive validity is perhaps at the heart of the matter. Competing visions of psychology disagree about the importance of prediction but, traditionally, it has been a key aim of the science. In his behaviourist manifesto John B. Watson (1913) declaimed that psychology had to be about the control and prediction of behaviour. Ever since then, psychologists have tried to devise tests which would usefully predict how individuals would behave and perform in the outside world. The problem, as we shall see, is that it is hard for tests to live up to these hopes of predictive validity.

In this chapter we look at a number of tests that illustrate some of these issues. Our first test (the Rathus Assertiveness Scale) reveals some fairly gross flaws. There is rather little evidence that it is valid, largely because the test authors did not carry out sufficient studies. The second test (the Columbia Driver Judgement Test) highlights problems of *content validity* and *predictive validity*. It seems to assume that one can study a complex cognitive, perceptual and motor skill like driving through getting subjects to solve pencil-and-paper problems. It does not then go on to show those who do well in the test have fewer accidents or reveal any other superior form of car-behaviour. One of the authors of this book who failed his driving test on every item apart from parroting the Highway Code did reasonably well on the Columbia Driver Judgement Test.

The third test we test, Department of Employment Vocational Assessment Test (DEVAT), faces up squarely to the problems of using tests to predict success in jobs. Extensive work on the DEVAT ironically, shows that it is less good at doing this than predicting success at O-level and at completing job training schemes. Much effort has been used to validate DEVAT, and much has been claimed for it.

The fourth and fifth tests we examine deal with sex roles and androgyny. Bem's Sex-role Inventory was used to suggest that we would all be better off if we become less rigid in our sex roles. Men should become more feminine; women should become more masculine. Bem's work arrived at a time when feminism was on the crest of a wave and, therefore, it won quick acceptance. It led to much fruitful research, but it seems one of her central claims was totally wrong, according to a re-analysis of validation studies. The inventory may be quite wrong in the prediction that feminine men and masculine women were in better psychological health.

The final test (a series of EEG batteries) illustrates the problem of concurrent validity. It is validated against performance on other tests. We want to argue that tests ought to predict behaviour in real life not just on other tests. We map an insidious process by which psychologists argue for the validity of a test on the grounds that it correlates with scores on other tests.

Case Study One

Test tested: Rathus Assertiveness Scale
Example of questions: 1. 'Most people seem to be more aggressive and assertive than I am'
2. Say how well certain adjectives describe you
Form of answer: 1. Yes or No.
2. On a 6-point scale
Our focus: Assertiveness

Most tests show some attempt to validate them properly. This cannot be claimed for the Rathus Assertiveness Scale. Assertiveness training has become nearly as fashionable as behaviour therapy techniques, according to Rathus (1973). His Rathus Assertiveness Schedule (RAS), can be used both to evaluate research into how effective assertiveness training is, and to check how much clients/patients have benefited. Assertively, we assert that Rathus asserts a deal too much.

The first question on the RAS is disastrous: 'Most people seem to be more aggressive and assertive than I am'. It is ambiguous in that a person may think that he is very assertive but not aggressive, and vice-versa. A person may quietly and firmly maintain a position but threaten none; another may rant, rave and bully, but be ignored. Secondly, the question implies that assertiveness and aggressiveness are synonymous so there could be an agenda-setting effect; if you are aggressive then you are also assertive, or if you are assertive then you are also aggressive.

Question 11: 'I often don't know what to say to attractive persons of the opposite sex' is pretty dreadful, too. Does this imply that we have a lot to say to ugly, repulsive people of the opposite sex, or that we are so totally mesmerised by heterosexual beauty that we are incapable of conjuring superlative-enough adjectives to describe the physical wonder before us? I don't know if I should say 'Gee you look great' or 'How gorgeous you are'. This question seems to have been framed for the all-American-boy-film-hero who is the successful college stud.

Question 15 shows even more bias and parochialism: 'If a close and respected relative were annoying me, I would smother my feelings rather than express my annoyance'. First, why 'relative' rather than 'friend' or even 'person'? A mystery unless we look to the good old days of the West when boys and girls always showed 'Ma' and 'Pa' respect and did as they were told. Presumably this question was framed for young people living with, or having a lot of contact with, older generations of family. If a young person doesn't show unwavering deference to 'Ma and Pa, Grandma and Grandpa, President and Country, home-made apple-pie', then they are assertive.

Question 18 is the most myopic and parochial of all: 'If a famed and respected lecturer makes a statement which I think is incorrect, I will have the audience hear my point of view as well'. It may be a surprise to some academics, but the vast majority of the population — be they American or British — do not spend their time sitting in an audience listening to 'famed and respected lecturer(s)'. Even in the academic context, the use of the question is questionable. Arthur Jensen and Leon Kamin are both famous and infamous, respected and despised, depending upon one's biological, ideological, psychological and sociological viewpoint.

Some of the other questions were not beyond question either, so where did they come from? Some were deduced from the literature and others were 'suggested by diaries the author requested be kept by two classes of college juniors and seniors. In them were recorded behaviours the student would have liked to exhibit but refrained from exhibiting because of fear of aversive social consequences'.

To establish how reliable the RAS was, it was given to 68 undergraduates (aged 17 to 27). Eight weeks later they were re-tested. Then, to check on validity, 18 college students gave the RAS to 67 subjects they knew well, aged 15 to 70. The 18 subjects also rated them on 17 items such as bold/timid, quiet/outspoken, poor/prosperous. The rating was done on a 6-point scale. This whole procedure is a doubtful means of establishing validity. First, you fill in my test of assertiveness. Then, I fill in another test to see how well my first test agrees with my second test. Matching two doubtful scales makes for doubtful testing.

Rathus factor-analysed his 17-item schedule. Four main factors emerged — assertiveness, contentment, intelligence and prosperity. Scores on the RAS correlated positively with boldness, confidence, outspokenness, assertiveness and aggressiveness as rated by the 18 college students. There was also a negative correlation with awful/nice. The author uses this one negative correlation to claim there is nothing to suggest that their test is affected by respondents' desire to give socially acceptable answers. That seems rather skimpy proof.

Three questions did not correlate with any of the personality traits tested. Ambiguous Question 1 where individuals have to assess both their assertiveness and their aggressiveness, was one. The second was the 'famed and respected lecturer' question, so perhaps there is a need for more famed and respected lecturers to go round giving public talks and exhorting the timid toadies to state their point of view as well. The other question was 'I am open and frank about my feelings'. This could have been confused with 'emotionality' rather than assertiveness: people who make uncontrolled outbursts tend to lose their authoritativeness and hence their assertiveness.

Of the 30 RAS items, 28 correlated negatively with 'niceness', and six of these did so significantly. One of these six questions (which is scored in reverse direction to indicate assertiveness) is: 'I have hesitated to make or accept dates because of "shyness"'. Perhaps the more conservative elements in society may think it is 'not nice' for 70-year-olds never to hesitate to make or accept dates, but the question is muddled. Surely assertive persons will have no hesitation in trying to make a date with a person they desire, but have no hesitation in refusing a date with some they don't.

Because of this strong association between being assertive and not being nice, Rathus (1973) notes 'Therapists should consider that a global stimulation of clients to behave more assertively . . . may result in strong aversive social feedback which the client receiving assertion training is likely to be particularly ill-equipped to handle'. This is true, but the therapist may be very unassertive so, despite what the patient is exhorted to do or told to do, he or she may use the therapist as the model rather than the training itself. Secondly, the purpose of a clinical test can differ radically from other purposes. It is not every therapist's aim to train patients to be super-normally assertive but normally assertive, whereas an employer may want the super-normal assertive type. Remember that Rathus's middle-class, confident, highly educated college student was asked to record in a diary 'behaviours the student would have liked to exhibit but refrained from exhibiting because of fear of aversive social consequences'. If the most privileged young American citizens fail to show these behaviours, what chance has the underprivileged, downtrodden patient in a psychiatric clinic got? The RAS is not even appropriate for a normal sample of the population, let alone as a clinical tool for assessing behavioural change in patients.

In summary, the face validity of many questions is poor where two — sometimes contradictory — questions are asked instead of one. There is little conceptual clarity, and there is no discussion of similarity or differences between assertiveness and aggression: they are treated as synonymous. To standardise a test on a college sample and their friends and relatives, take typical student behaviours as typical of the population as a whole, and then recommend it for 'obtaining pre- and post-measures of patients' assertiveness in clinical practice' is foolish, especially when students themselves are not assertive enough to display such behaviours. It is methodologically appalling. The RAS should not be used outside of 17 to 27-year-old American college students — and then only after all the ambiguities have been weeded from the questions. Better still, 'dump it down the memory hole'.

It is not only badly designed tests which may be useless for predicting behaviour. Some tests may be well designed internally and have apparent validity, but they incorporate very evident flaws. Among the improbable tests we have found, few compete with the Columbia Driver Judgement Test, which claims that performance with the pen predicts performance on the road.

Case Study Two

Test tested:	Columbia Driver Judgement Test
Example of questions:	Judge how safe it is to turn in the given picture
Form of answer:	Which of a number of options is the correct answer
Our focus:	Is driving a skill you can test on paper?

According to the Freudian Highway Code, 'man' behind the wheel becomes a macho member. He drives to assert his masculinity. His car becomes an expression of masculinity. Woman, too, is capable of anonymous, but equal aggression with men, once behind the wheel. Can any pencil-and-paper test be a valid assessment of safe-driver behaviour when this very important psychological symbol — the motor car — is absent? More importantly, does knowledge of theory facilitate, or increase the desired safe-driver behaviour? Will a safe-driver test, irrespective of its content or mode of assessment, reduce collisions? If not, the test fails the test.

The Columbia Driver Judgement Test (CDJT) claims to be 'an objective measurement of a person's ability to formulate correct decisions within the context of specific traffic situations'. But it does not measure 'a person's ability to act on his decisions'. There are two equivalent forms of the test comprising 40 multiple-choice items each, and time for completion is unlimited. Incidents descriptive of 'good' and 'bad' driver behaviour were collected from 1,057 professionals concerned with traffic safety. In all, 2,111 incidents were received, from which 3,809 critical driver behaviours were abstracted. These included speed adjustments, lateral positioning, headway, passing, turning, intersecting and merging traffic, communication between drivers, emergency or hazardous conditions, courtesy and vehicle maintenance and preparation.

While the test was being developed, each driver was given the Gallup-Thorndike Vocabulary Test, and questions were rejected which related significantly to intelligence as measured by the vocabulary score. However, later the Manual admits that some studies suggest that a high level of education will raise scores on the CDJT. It was a good idea to try to control for intelligence, but 'vocabulary test score' was probably the weakest and most inappropriate intelligence measure that could have been used in relation to this test. The questions require a high degree of logical reasoning from the information given (necessary in 'solving' an Agatha Christie novel but not for one of D. H. Lawrence's) and good spatial ability to follow the diagrammatic representations of hypothetical traffic situations. It is not the actual words of the questions that would cause too much difficulty — unless the individual was totally illiterate — but relating these to 'As' and 'Bs', moving and stationary vehicles, directional arrows, and various positions at crossroads, not to mention working out where you were and want to be. We would guess that the test is far too abstract for many commercial (i.e. lorry and truck) drivers, and might be improved (made more concrete) by using model cars and model roads. This seems yet another test designed by, and by implication for, middle-class people. The further a test divorces itself from reality, the more likely it is that the working classes will perform badly on the test, but possibly perform more accurately than a test score would indicate.

The aim of any safe-driver test should be either to reduce the number of collisions, or to predict 'good' and 'bad' drivers (preferably both). Unfortunately, the CDJT gives no evidence that it does either of these things. At first, the evidence for validity looks convincing because criterion groups are used. In one study, the mean score for 94 behaviourally classified 'good' drivers is 31.95, while the mean score for 182 'bad' drivers is 28.12 ($p > 0.001$). This still leaves the age-old question of whether psychological tests sort out the 'good' and the 'bad', the 'sane' and the 'deranged' when Joe Bloggs can do the same with no psychological tests and no psychological training. The crucial thing is whether this test can differentiate between a group of apparently 'normal' drivers and predict who will be 'good' and who will be 'bad' drivers, or to show that drivers who have been trained with the CDJT will have fewer collisions than a very comparable group of drivers who have not been trained with CDJT. This test has established its claim to be used as a research instrument, but it is a long haul before it could be recommended for commercial use.

Even though no grand claims are made concerning 'vehicle maintenance and preparation', it is mentioned, and there is a sad lack of any such items. In view of the overall theoretical and abstract nature of the test, this omission is very grave. All the questions seem to treat the mechanical reliability of the car as a constant, while it is only the driver behaviour and weather conditions that vary. One of the questions does raise the possibility in a very oblique way:

23. A red flag displayed on the back of a pick-up truck usually indicates:
    a.   an over-hanging load
    b.   a load containing explosives
    c.   that the truck is not in perfect condition
    d.   that the load is not tightly tied down

As far as this test is concerned, it is not 'in perfect condition' and needs to be 'tightly tied down' with evidence that it can differentiate 'normal' drivers and that it can predict or reduce collisions. If the test fails to develop these qualities it is something of a one-way street to obscurity, reflecting many traditional problems of validation.

Case Study Three: Job Testing

Test tested: DEVAT (Department of Employment Vocational Assessment Tests)
Example of questions: If $2x = 50$, does $x = 100, 48, 25, 20$ or 5?
Form of answer: Correct answer
Our focus: Predicting job ability

Tests of assertiveness and driving skills are, in some ways, esoteric. The bulk of psychological tests are in employment. Ever since the American Psychological Corporation started in 1919 the production of tests which claim to be able to predict how well people will do in jobs has been big business. Despite over half a century of scientific testing, many companies still create their own tests and use them without the slightest hesitation. The Commission for Racial Equality in one report in the 1970s complained that one road haulage firm gave prospective lorry drivers essays to write: that ensured all Asian applicants failed this even odder test of driving than the Columbia one. No one asked what connection there was between writing a nice essay on flowers, or even on, 'why I want to drive a lorry . . .' and getting the goods to Dover on time.

Even scientific tests with long pedigrees are not easy to validate. One of the best established tests in vocational training is DEVAT, the Department of Employment Vocational Assessment Tests. It incorporates six tests — arithmetic, shapes, same words, reasoning, mechanical reasoning and mathematics. Its roots lay in the Alpha Test used by the army in the First World War to sort out recruits into poor bloody infantry, officer potential and those too disastrous even to put into uniform.

John Toplis (1981), Director of the Occupational Psychology Unit at Barking College of Technology, was optimistic when he began research intended to update information in the two DEVAT manuals. He contacted 181 companies which had hired recruits who had completed the DEVAT — usually while they were still at school.

The way Toplis's sample of 181 companies fell apart is an object lesson in the problems that face the tester of tests. Only 33 of the 181 companies replied positively. Toplis was given 644 names, but only 437 of these young people had actually done the DEVAT. School records were not available for most of them so he ended up with 198 subjects whose DEVAT scores were available. To add to his sample, Toplis tested three groups of subjects of college courses.

Employers rated the job abilities of Toplis's subjects on a 25-point scale. That gave, in the end, distinctions between well above average, above average, average, below average, well below average. Toplis gave the test to twelve different occupational groups. There were thus six different tests given to twelve different groups, yet a range of eight to nine stanines were covered on 30 per cent of occasions. Only six per cent were below job ability — according to DEVAT.

If that was the good news, the correlations between test scores and ratings of job ability by employers were poor. They ranged between −0.57 and 0.77. But while 88 correlations were positive, 56 were negative. In other words, in over 40 per cent of cases the DEVAT score predicted abilities *opposite* to those employers found.

There were two other major findings. First, despite the dismal prediction score, DEVAT did differentiate between those who passed and those who failed an electrical technician's training course. Secondly, the higher the DEVAT score, the more likely the young person was to achieve one or more O-level passes. DEVAT seemed to be predicting ability to succeed on other tests better than ability to succeed at work. The short-term needs of teachers and the long-term needs of employers may be different. Success on a course requires, perhaps, being quick on the uptake, but in traditional manufacturing industries what counts is performance over 20, 30 or 40 years. Less bright individuals can be trained, but it will take longer. Motivation will play a crucial role. The sharp, but slapdash, may do worse in the end than the plodding but persistent. Tests rarely note this distinction. Arthur Jensen (1983) drew attention to the different ways people perform when they start a job and when they have settled into it. If a test predicts how well people will be trained but not how well they will do, it has some kind of validity — but of a rather impractical kind.

Writing in *Psychology News* (1981), Toplis noted that correlations of 0.30 and above were meant to indicate a test was valid for training criteria. This magic correlation of 0.30 was, he added, mainly derived from Ghiselli's (1966) *The Validity of Occupational*

Testing. Toplis censured Ghiselli who 'continues to quote progressively higher correlations, ending thus, "Therefore a final statement of the maximal predictive power of tests, based upon experience with them, is a validity coefficient of 0.75 for trainability and 0.65 for job proficiency"'. These sound impressive, but Toplis added that Ghiselli also said that tests with far lower correlations had 'substantial power to predict occupational success'.

In a subsequent contribution to *Psychology News* (*17*), Toplis agreed that all too often little was said about negative correlations. He had been surprised that nearly 40 per cent of correlations were negative. Like one of the present authors in his original comment on the DEVAT research, Toplis was interested to note how rarely negative correlations were referred to. Toplis quoted the manual for *Differential Aptitude Tests* which included correlations between numerical ability and science skills. 30 correlations ranged from 0.70 to 0.19 and *below* (our italics). The use of the category *below 0.19* would include negative correlations, but by using that category the appearance of negative signs has been avoided.

The saga of the DEVAT tests highlights three major problems for predictive validity. First, how it is extremely difficult to conduct large-scale occupational research following up how well tests do predict industrial performance. Secondly, one of the best-established occupational tests in the UK is better at predicting performance on other tests than in predicting job performance. Many correlations between success on the test and in industry were, actually, negative. Thirdly, there is a tendency for research into the validity of tests to focus only on positive correlations and to ignore negative correlations. Toplis and his colleague Tol Bedford (1980) had the courage to highlight negative correlations, too. Summing up the experience, Toplis said: 'Tol and I wanted to draw the attention of professional colleagues to the range of data available about the validity of tests (rather than the average correlations) and caution that it might be appropriate to exercise professional caution when using some tests'.

DEVAT was designed out of Alpha at a time when it was vital to assess people correctly for jobs. Controversies about the use of tests for selection have receded slightly with the recession. We raise this nebulous notion of the prevailing political and economic climate because the next test we consider hit the market just at the right time. It fed a cultural fashion, and perhaps as a result, some issues about its validity were not considered too rigorously.

Case Study Four: A Question of Androgyny

Test tested: Bem's Sex-role Inventory
Example of questions: Given a set of 60 adjectives such as 'dominant', 'gullible', etc. rate how you see yourself
Form of answer: Ratings on a 7-point scale
Our focus: Testing the influence of sex roles

In 1974 Sandra Bem published her Sex-role Inventory. She asked students to rate how desirable 400 traits were in order to find 20 adjectives that were characteristically feminine, and 20 that were characteristically masculine. Twenty socially desirable and undesirable adjectives were also included in her final list to help detect students who tended to exaggerate. These adjectives included:

Feminine	Masculine	Socially desirable and undesirable
Affectionate	Acts as leader	Adaptable
Cheerful	Aggressive	Conceited
Childlike	Ambitious	Conscientious
Compassionate	Analytical	Conventional
Does not use harsh language	Assertive	Friendly
Eager to soothe hurt feelings	Athletic	Happy
Feminine	Competitive	Helpful
Flatterable	Defends own beliefs	Inefficient
Gentle	Dominant	Jealous
Gullible	Forceful	Likeable
Loves children	Leadership abilities	Moody
Loyal	Independent	Reliable
Sensitive to others' needs	Individualistic	Secretive
Shy	Makes decisions easily	Sincere
Soft spoken	Masculine	Solemn

Sympathetic	Self-reliant	Tactful
Tender	Self-sufficient	Theatrical
Understanding	Strong personality	Truthful
Warm	Willing to take a stand	Unpredictable
Yielding	Willing to take risks	Unsystematic

Many adjectives in this list are virtual synonyms. Aggressive, forceful, dominant, acts as leader, leadership abilities and assertive would all seem to be very close.

Bem was frank about her motives. In an interview with *Psychology News* (no. 29), she said she started 'when there really were no data in the field'. But she had a definite feminist aim. She wrote (1979) illustrating how psychologists sometimes exercise control:

> I consider myself an empirical scientist and yet my interest in sex roles is and has always been frankly political. My hypotheses have derived from no formal theory but rather from a set of strong intuitions about the debilitating effects of sex role stereotyping and my major purpose has always been a feminist one; to help free the human personality from the restricting prison of sex role stereotyping and to develop a conception of mental health which is free from culturally-imposed definitions of masculinity and femininity.

The process of collecting these adjectives was typical of most testing. Bem's subjects were American college students. As they were so young, their vision of what is typically male and typically female might be actually unrepresentative of all age groups. Bem did not even consider this issue in her first paper in 1974. Three years later *Psychology Today*, inspired by the success of androgyny, surveyed its readers. Twenty-eight thousand replied; of this admittedly self-selected group only 30 per cent of men said that their ideal man was aggressive while 64 per cent said the ideal man was gentle. Eighty-two per cent of men in the *Psychology Today* survey suggested the ideal woman 'stood up for her beliefs', an assertive stance which you would not expect of the soft-spoken, gullible, eyelash fluttering floozie Bem's sample thought of as characteristically feminine. Most of the *Psychology Today* sample (over 80 per cent) had had some college education, but over 50 per cent were aged 25 plus. Bem's sample were all much younger. They may well have been reflecting both their lack of experience and also a certain ambiguity in Bem's instructions. She asked subjects to say what adjectives were 'characteristic' of women. Were they being asked to say what was characteristic of those women they knew personally, or what was characteristic 'in general'? The second would make it possible that subjects felt they had to regurgitate social stereotypes. Bem never clarified this confusion. It is also possible that Bem's research shifted attitudes, making *Psychology Today* readers far less likely to endorse the John Wayne school of maleness.

Having established her 60 adjectives, Bem got subjects to rate themselves on a 7-point scale saying how affectionate, gullible, aggressive, leadership-minded, etc. they were. From her scale she could derive a score both for femininity (F) and masculinity (M). The difference between the M scores and F scores were, for her, crucial. Joseph, for example, might give himself a score of 3 on aggressiveness, 3 on analytic, 3 on assertive, 3 on self-reliant and 3 on masculine. That would make 15 M points. He would also score 2 on loyal, 4 on warm, 3 on gentle giving him 9 F points. His 'balance' would be 6. Bem would rate as identical a man who ticked no feminine qualities at all, but gave himself a 1 on each of Joseph's first four adjectives and 2 on masculine. Those who scored low on masculinity and low on femininity often showed up as equal to those who scored high on both. Spence, Heimreich and Stapp (1975) criticised this scoring technique, and argued that only those who scored high on both masculine and feminine items should be rated as androgynous. Low scores had no hope. Eventually, Bem adopted this position.

As Bem's research arrived at a time when there was much questioning of traditional sex roles, some assumptions about its validity were not raised by many commentators, including *Psychology News*. It may have flattered intellectuals to show that those who were androgynous did better. The *Psychology Today* survey in 1977 took Bem's study for granted as a classic. In its preamble, the survey quoted the reply of a young minister from Georgia who trumpeted

> I feel I must say very loudly that I'm tired of American male stereotypes. I have a beard, two biceps, a penis and I'm capable of

showing warmth, sharing housework and shedding a tear. Why are so many men threatened by a combination of characteristics.

'Worried but enthusiastic' of Georgia seemed not to know that women also have biceps.

But Bem's inventory has many problems. First, she asked people to describe their personality using the adjectives. You could feel ambitious but never do anything about it. The traits might never be reflected in behaviour. Secondly, since Bem accepted that only those with high scores on both masculine and feminine items bloomed with androgyny, it is worth re-examining the original adjectives. Many of the 20 feminine and masculine adjectives on Bem's list veer towards extreme behaviour. The characteristic male is reckoned aggressive, dominant, forceful, willing to take a stand, willing to take risks; the characteristic female is gullible, childlike, flatterable, yielding. A person with a high score on both these sets of attributes might well be, in P. G. Wodehouse's graphic phrase, 'a suitable candidate for Colney Hatch'. He, or she, would be aggressive and gullible, dominant and flatterable, childlike and dominant. We may have just described an idiotic bully of psychopathic tendencies who would emerge from the test as a paragon of androgyny and a model of psychological health. Again, the comparison with the *Psychology Today* survey is interesting. That found that the following percentages of subjects rated the ideal man as:

Trait	Males	Females	Highly characteristic of 'me'
competitive	38	27	26
aggressive	35	28	16
takes risks	34	35	21
able to cry	40	51	—
able to love	88	96	54

The picture of men to emerge from this survey is much softer than Bem would allow. Less than 50 per cent see it as ideal to compete, aggress or take risks: 40 per cent want to be able to cry, 88 per cent to love. John Wayne must have been shooting himself in his grave. The important point though is that an older, educationally none-too-different sample yielded a quite different version of what was 'ideal' masculine behaviour. How valid did that leave Bem?

Bem's political purpose was honestly admitted, and we might as well say that we would applaud it. Androgyny should be good for you. Masculine men ought to work on their feminine sides; feminine women ought to work on their masculine sides. Yin and yang, animus and anima should all vibrate together. Bem inspired enthusiasm for honourable reasons. By the mid-70s poor Dr Spock had become something of a baddie. Feminists pointed out that he advised little boys to play with guns and little girls with dolls. Each ought to learn their sex roles and not be confused or else they might become well . . . not androgynous but worse. Bem showed this wisdom to be reactionary. The androgynous were more likely to be healthy and well adjusted. The prevailing liberal mood allowed harsh questions not to be posed. First, did it make sense to go from self-ratings on a list of adjectives to a grand theory about how people behaved in very intimate situations? Feminists have often complained about men who pay lip-service to the creed but never change dirty nappies or do the ironing. Such men would no doubt rate themselves as sensitive, caring, androgynous etc. Secondly, when an individual scored high on both masculine and feminine traits, were they equally important in making him or her well adjusted? It is easy to see how one might avoid asking this question because it might subvert the whole trend of Bem's work. What if it was the masculinity that mattered in terms of adjustment or success?

Taylor and Hall (1982) re-examined some hundred studies which had used Bem's inventory. Many of these studies had looked at how well masculine, feminine and androgynous subjects did on various other scales and a few real-life situations. First Taylor and Hall criticised Bem for accepting that only those who scored high on both dimensions were androgynous. Using a two-way analysis of variance (ANOVA), Taylor and Hall claimed that what was important among the androgynous was the high masculine score. This led them to succeed and be well adjusted. Most of the variance could be accounted by their scores on masculine items. In American society the crunch is to be macho. It did not please Taylor and Hall to come to this conclusion for they both claimed to out-feminist Bem. They noted 'that it is primarily masculinity — not androgyny that yields positive outcomes for individuals in American society'. They attacked Bem for emphasising personal psychology as opposed to general social solutions, and pointed out that she had to adjust one scale of socially desirable items because too few feminine items were desirable enough. Instead of openly saying that reflected the nature of sex bias in society, Bem fudged to make the statistics smooth. Taylor and Hall added:

the misconception that androgyny brings the good things in life carries multiple liabilities . . . possibly encouraging educational and therapeutic practices that are dysfunctional, in fact but even more important, fostering a kind of false consciousness that problems entailed in current sex role definitions have psychological rather than social structural solutions.

Far from revealing the value of androgyny, Bem's work actually showed the power of masculine values.

Ironically, the success of Bem's work led to the interest in developing scales for children to see if they could be cajoled/educated out of traditional sex roles. Judith Hall herself worked on one such scale.

Case Study Five: Androgynous Children

Test tested: Children's Personal Attributes Questionnaire
Example of questions: Rate where on adjectives like being 'gentle', 'considerate', 'aggressive', 'tactful'
Form of answer: Rating scale
Our focus: Sex roles in children

The authors of the Children's Personal Attributes Questionnaire (CPAQ), Hall and Halberstadt (1980), based it upon the adult version, PAQ (Spence and Helmreich 1978) so that researchers can investigate 'developmental aspects of gender-role-related personality attributes'. The first two scales, labelled *masculinity* and *femininity* contain attributes that are socially desirable for both the ideal man and ideal women *according to college judges*; a third scale, *masculinity — femininity*, contains attributes that were judged to be *differentially* socially desirable for the two sexes. These ideological stereotypes have other labels, too: *masculinity* or *instrumentality* and *femininity* or *socio-emotional orientation*. The authors follow this trend 'because research has shown that males and females are typically described as differing in the degree to which the two clusters of attributes characterize them'.

The 'ideal' man resembles Bem's version with differences — adventurous, outgoing, ambitious, intellectual, superior, active, good at sports, independent, competitive, stands up under pressure, never gives up, always acts as leader, bold, self-confident, not excitable in minor crises, always takes a stand, not easily influenced, outspoken. The 'ideal' woman is predictably, the ego-reflecting chattel of the male: warm in relations to others, helpful to others, aware of the feelings of others, emotional, considerate, kind, able to devote self completely to others, gentle, does not hide emotions, expresses tender feelings, enjoys art and music, understanding of others, grateful, tactful, likes children, is neat in habits. In his original assessment of the test, Shelley (1982) (*Psychology News*, no. 24) went on:

> The ideological male embodies all the values of capitalist ideology, entrepreneur, private enterprise, individual initiative, dog-eat-dog, as well as being a big-mouthed bigot: what an ideal person to have in your family! The ideological female incorporates all the undesirable qualities of socialism: caring for and helping others, being gentle and considerate, as well as indulging in typically 'useless' pursuits like art and music; wasting time by doing things for reasons other than commercial profit. These images say far more about the college students, the media to which they are exposed, the economic, political and social system under which they live than any psychological aspects of 'gender-role related personality attributes'.

Two preliminary studies examined the equivalence of both the children's and adults' versions of the inventory, which corresponded item by item except for three items judged to be inappropriate for children ('skill in business', 'knowledge of the way of the world', 'interest in sex' — William Blake would blush at such a picture of prime innocence!). Needless to say, this 'equivalence' was done by college students. Until now, we thought the idea that children were merely miniature versions of adults — both physically and intellectually — had died out *c.* eighteenth century, or at least post-Piaget.

Another validity study asked each class teacher to rate his or her children on three 9-point rating scales on popularity, leadership, and social maturity so these could be compared to the children's responses on the CPAQ. This further confuses the 'equivalence of adults and children' question. Are the terms of reference the teacher's or the child's? One child may be an attentive, apple-polishing creep and be judged as 'popular' and 'socially mature' by nobody except the teacher, while another child may be the undisputed leader of a violent, disruptive, anti-school subculture and popular with almost everybody except the teacher.

The authors found that teachers had the highest opinion of conventionally gender-typed boys and girls, which is not surprising considering the methodology. As the initial categories were assigned by a college sample — presumably going through the same type of educational process as their own teachers and as those in the validity study — then, this may simply be a perpetuation of the college students' notions of the 'ideal' man and woman but have little in common with common ideals of the same. The authors explain that 'masculinity is defined more in terms of overt behaviour whereas femininity is defined more in terms of inner states or interpersonal motivations that are less easily observed'.

Having asked a college sample to define what they took to be masculine and feminine, they ought not really to have been surprised by that. Nor should the authors have been surprised by the fact that there was 'only one instance of androgynous children looking "more healthy" or "adjusted" than other children'. Hall and Halberstadt concluded that androgyny might not be as useful a concept as had been originally hoped.

It seems likely that it was such conclusions that led Hall to re-examine Bem's original work. Her latest analyses suggest a progressive disenchantment with androgyny. Karl Marx said long ago that the point of philosophy ought not to be to understand the world but to change it. It seems possible to argue that because Bem wanted to change the world she failed to understand it as thoroughly as she might. Seduced by the ideal of androgynous Americans who could excel at both sensitivity and the Stock Market, Bem did not think of checking whether it was the masculine part of the androgynous personality that was responsible for all the success. Sympathetic as one might be to Bem's political aims, her work made a personality trait out of an ideal. The Inventory seems to lack validity and in a somewhat ironic way.

A final area of confusion about validity is that of comparing scores on different tests.

Case Study Six: Brainwaves

Test tested: Brainwaves and Academic Promise Test

Example of questions: Perceptual Task
 Wechsler Similarities Subtest
Form of answer: Correct responses
Our focus: What do you judge a test against?

Concurrent validity means assessing the present validity of a test by comparison with another, currently available criterion. Too often, though, this 'criterion' is just another test, so, for example, a score on an intelligence test is compared with a score on a school examination. If the correlation between the two is too high, then this would tend to make the second test redundant because they are apparently measuring the same thing; but if the correlation is too low then they may be measuring completely different things and the two tests bear no relationship to each other. Psychologists are never satisfied! It is rare, but Apter (1982) correlated the Telic Dominance Scale with Eysenck's Personality Inventory to demonstrate that despite some superficial similarities, they were *not* measuring the same thing. It is not very satisfactory to compare one pencil-and-paper test with another because there may be just a few variational frills around the same theme. Another approach to establishing the validity of a test is to use a qualitatively different measure such as a physiological one. The trouble is, if both tests are meant to be predictors and the criterion is rather vague and imprecise, we are in a similar situation to trying to measure an unknown quantity of water using a leaky bucket on the one hand and a sieve on the other. We do not know the volume of water in the first place, and neither do we know if we are going to lose more out of the leaky bucket than the sieve, or vice versa.

Electroencephalograms (EEGs or measurement of brainwaves) have shown differences between learning disabled and normal children on some cognitive tasks. Previous tests used to identify children with learning difficulties have used a 'clinic' sample and a 'normal' sample for comparison. The futility of some of these comparisons is that it has been like comparing the physical performance of an athlete with someone who has a broken leg: tests can identify the differences, but so can any damn fool without any fancy test apparatus. It is borderline cases where clinical judgement fails, and, unfortunately, so do the tests.

Before considering in detail the research of Grunau, Purves, McBurney and Low (1978), we should explain a little more about EEG recordings. Physiological measures are attractive because they seem to be monitoring the real functioning rather than any learned, social veneer that is literally skin deep. But consider the analogy between electrical activity in the brain (as measured by EEG recordings) and electrical 'activity' in a house as measured by an electricity meter. Solely observing the electricity meter may not be a good guide as to what activity is going on, and what conditions are like, in the house. Bulbs give out a lot of light, not much heat, and use little power. Electric fires give out a lot of heat, not much light, and use a lot of power. If every heating appliance is working to full capacity, the heat or energy may still be dissipated if all the windows and doors were left open in freezing weather. To date, we have both pessimism and optimism about EEG.

In 1982 the Association for the Advancement of Science (AAAS) met in Washington, 3–8 January. Alan Gevins, Director of the EEG Systems Laboratory at the Langley Porter Psychiatric Institute, reported an experiment where volunteers did a spatial and a numerical task wearing a helmet with a dozen leads attached. Subjects either had to move an arrow on a screen or respond to a number somewhere between 0 and 100. Their EEGs were monitored. Traditional models of the left hemisphere (serial) and right hemisphere (spatial) would suggest that the EEG would find the left side *on* and the right side *off* for the numerical task and vice-versa for the spatial one. Gevins found instead, very complex, rapidly changing patterns of electrical activity between many areas in the front and back of both sides of the brain. New computing techniques allowed the research to sort out the muscle and irrelevant signals. The research suggests that even simple judgements require complex barrages of brainwaves. Gevins was hopeful that within a few years such techniques would allow more precise diagnosis of disorders of higher brain functions. We do not believe we have reached anywhere near this advanced stage yet, so with these reservations in mind, on to the research by Grunau and his colleagues.

Grunau *et al.* set out to evaluate the results of a psychological test battery and compare them with EEG measures derived from spectral analysis of EEG measured at rest and during a verbal and a perceptual task, in a group of 12 to 15-year-old children (which included those in the middle range of academic achievement). The subjects were taking part in a longitudinal study of low birth-weight children and their full birth-weight controls. There were 25 boys and 20 girls. Thirteen of the low birth-weight children had earlier been diagnosed as showing minimal cerebral dysfunction at age 6.5 years, while the rest of the children were neurologically normal. All children were given the Wechsler Intelligence Scale for Children (WISC-R) and had a full-scale IQ above 80.

The abstract reasoning (visuospatial) and verbal reasoning subtests of the Academic Promise Test were given. Children who performed below the median (based on norm group scores) comprised the 'low' group, and those at/or above the median comprised the 'high' group. The EEG was recorded from the left and right parietal regions under three conditions: (a) resting with eyes open, (b) during performance of a perceptual task, and (c) during performance of a verbal task (WISC-R Similarities Subtest). The stimuli were presented on a TV screen and the EEG for analysis was recorded from the time the stimulus appeared until the children began to respond verbally. The EEG analysis had to stop here because speech would have introduced all sorts of artifacts which would obscure the EEG waveform.

For visuospatial reasoning aptitude, 67 per cent of the children were correctly classified with the EEG measures alone and the same percentage with the psychological test battery alone. When the EEG and the test battery were combined, the correct identification level rose to 82 per cent. Amongst the 33 children at or above the median ('high') in the visuospatial reasoning, there were 9 cases misclassified by EEG measures and 10 cases misclassified by the psychological battery. However, in only 2 cases were the same children misclassified by each set of data. Nine children who had been classified as minimally cerebrally dysfunctioning were in the 'high' group for visuospatial reasoning. The EEG measures alone correctly classified all of the 9 cases, but 4 were misclassified with the test battery.

For verbal reasoning aptitude, only 60 per cent of the children were correctly classified with EEG measures alone, but 80 per cent were correctly classified using the psychological battery results alone. When the two sets of results were combined, 87 per cent of the children were correctly classified.

There were some differences in the identification rates comparing children 'low' and 'high' in each aptitude. The EEG measures alone correctly identified 73 per cent of the children 'high' in visuospatial reasoning, but only 56 per cent of those 'high' in verbal reasoning. Conversely, the psychological battery alone best identified children 'low' in verbal reasoning (85 per cent) but only 58 per cent of those 'low' in visuospatial reasoning.

What is Classifying What?

The authors first conclude 'Of particular interest was the finding that for visuospatial reasoning, the two data sets were to some extent identifying different children. Thus to achieve greatest overall accuracy for visuospatial reasoning both sets of measures are required'. What claims are the authors really making here? Three measures were used: Academic Promise Test, WISC-R and EEG. The first of these is chosen to be the criterion by which to judge the accuracy of the other measures, but no reasons are given as to why this should be the definitive measure and the others not. This is very similar to abuses in construct validity. A researcher devises a test and uses correlations with similar tests which purport to be measuring the same or a similar thing as evidence for this new test's validity, yet even well-researched tests like DEVAT are poor at predicting performance. When Grunau claims that either EEG measures or the WISC-R misclassified individuals, it is also possible that the Academic Promise Test did the misclassifying in the first place or, most likely, all three tests did their share of misclassification.

Some of the conclusions Grunau and his colleagues come to are interesting. They argue EEG measures offer the best test of visuospatial tests and that the psychological test battery is sharper on verbal attitudes. The socio-economic status of the child (based on the father's education and occupation) was a highly significant predictor for verbal, but not for visuospatial, aptitude.

Despite these intriguing results, Grunau's research never comes to grips with a fundamental dilemma. What is the point of judging how effective one test is by reference just to another test? As the number of tests increase, the temptation to validate tests by reference to each other increases. This is a dangerous trend because the whole rationale of testing was to use a laboratory instrument to illuminate how people would behave out in the world. Despite these faults, Grunau's work left us with one idea. If children have different preferred modes, why not focus the way they are taught on the mode they are best at? Perhaps children should be streamed not according to their global intelligence, but according to whether they are good with words, pictures, or numbers. It would be difficult but in some subjects, in economics, for example, some people understand the words, others the equations, while yet others are happiest with the graphs.

Conclusions

Being human, psychologists fall into different groups. Some have insight, some have the statistics, and some have a profound affinity with rats. It has been suggested that conflicts in psychology may have as much to do with the personality of psychologists as with anything else (McClelland 1961; Cohen 1977; Kendler 1982). Different visions of psychology place a quite different emphasis both on prediction and on testing. There are certainly many clinicians who use psychological testing to describe their clients rather than to predict behaviour. In the main, however, the value of tests has been judged by their power to predict. IQ scales claim to predict who will do well in schools; Eysenck's Personality Inventory would claim to make useful predictions about how extraverts and introverts behave, yielding some surprising results. We would argue that perhaps too much emphasis has been placed on the predictive use of tests. Some psychologists have claimed recently that it is high time psychology stopped trying to ape the hard sciences (Chein 1972; Harre and Secord 1974; Shotter 1984 among many). Moreover, many perfectly respectable sciences like geology and astronomy make relatively little use of prediction. It is time that psychological testing reflected this shift. We shall argue later on against completely abandoning the ideal of using tests to predict behaviour. Nevertheless, we need to recognise that so far tests have not predicted human behaviour too accurately. Better prediction may involve a shift to more sophisticated forms of assessment than paper-and-pencil tests. These would include both how people actually do when being trained and, we shall suggest later, a kind of collaborative testing. In that, it will not be just the psychologists who controls what the important variables are. Imagine what might happen if, using her test, Bem had worked with a group of men who said they wanted to become less masculine and to embrace more androgynous ways!

6 HOW RELIABLE ARE TESTS? HOW VARIABLE ARE PEOPLE?

We have argued that tests often assume people do not change. Tests also seem to assume that subjects will be well motivated and obsessed with a desire to please psychologists. It would be nice to have a Freudian interpret the extensive literature on how subjects tend to produce the results psychologists want. Is this true? Or does it just show how desperate psychologists are to show they are needed? Such slightly bizarre issues affect the question of the reliability of tests.

In our technological world machines are credited with being reliable. The gas meter and the speedometer do not tell lies. Psychometricians often seem to want their instruments to be as reliable even though the nature of what they are measuring is radically different. The CAT scan permits a minute and accurate, second by second, analysis of activity in the brain; this allows it to measure, among other things, the circulation of blood inside the skull. Reiman *et al.* (1984) have shown a link between asymmetrical blood flow in the cerebral hemispheres and panic attacks. In normal people blood travels equally in the left and right half of the brain. Those who suffer panic attacks tend to have an excess of blood flow in 'emotional' areas of the brain like the hippocampus. The excess can be measured reliably, though hardly ever during a panic attack. No one imagines there will be a perfect correlation between the asymmetrical excess of blood and the extent of panic attacks, or that it will be possible to predict the depth of panic from a simple measurement of the blood flow, however reliable. One is a physiological measure; the other is a psychological one. The two may correlate but, at best, imperfectly. What is crucial initially is that the CAT provides a consistent, reliable measure of brain activity. In normal language, 'reliable' has two slightly different meanings. We say a thermometer is reliable if it works and provides, time after time, a correct reading of temperature. We also say a person is reliable if we can depend on him or her to turn up on time to do what they have promised to do. In testing terms, reliability is much closer to the first meaning. If a test is reliable subjects will turn up roughly equivalent scores whenever tested. Traditionally, the reliability of a test depends on two measures, its *internal consistency* and its *test/re-test stability*.

For a test to be internally consistent, the items that cover similar kinds of behaviour or attitudes should get similar answers. Imagine a test which includes questions like 'Do you enjoy going to parties?' and 'Do you dislike social meetings?' People who answer *yes* to the first ought to reply *no* to the second. A test becomes internally inconsistent if the pattern of replies is erratic. The second measure of reliability looks not at the coherence of items within a test, but at how likely people are to give the same kinds of scores at different times. Intelligence tests do throw up generally similar results when people retake them, though there is a tendency for people to do better the more IQ tests they take (Heim 1948) and for IQ to decline in old age, reflecting it has been said, a genuine decline in skill. In general, though, IQ tests reveal good *test/re-test* scores.

It is easy to confuse how reliable a test is with how valid it is. A test could be designed to judge the performance of ice cream vendors. If we use our wit to vet the Vendors of Ices Test (VIT) we might discover the following. Ice cream vendors who take the test at six-months intervals come up with fairly similar scores. The items on the test which are supposed to tap knowledge of ices and skill at communicating with the public are coherent. Each set of items forms a natural cluster so that vendors who say 'yes' to 'Do the public like to have a choice of flavours?' usually say 'no' to 'Do the public only buy chocolate?'. Despite this promising start, the Mega Ice Corporation notes that there is absolutely no relationship between performance on the VIT and how much ice cream each vendor sells. The VIT is reliable but not, alas, valid, and ought, of course, to be put on ice!

The reliability of tests is not just a technical issue. The manner in which subjects react to test items does affect the test/re-test stability of a test. People may get bored with a test or remember the answers from the last time they took the test.

In Chapter 2 we argued that people were less consistent than literature on tests wanted them to be. The first three case studies in this chapter attempt to examine some reasons for inconsistent behaviour on tests. The first looks at the growth of automated testing; the second study looks at changes in IQ, and asks how we can judge whether a change detected by a test is a minor or a major one. I may, after all, change my routine of 20 years tomorrow by buying *The Times* rather than *The Guardian*.

This may be a profound alteration in personality, indicating the mid-life crisis and that I have swung politically to the right on becoming a fat cat. However, it may mean that I have just decided to succumb to Portfolio, *The Times*'s up-market bingo, because I want to win £20,000. How do we interpret the change in my newspaper-buying behaviour? Can tests do that at all?

Case Study One: Automated Testing

Test tested: Digit Span + Perceptual Mays
Example of questions: 1. Remember 371423
2. Plot dots to link points A, B and C
Form of answer: 1. Correct recall
2. Any line
Our focus: Computers in tests

Doctors are feeding computers 'symptoms' and getting out remedial action. Garages use similar tricks to 'diagnose' your car. Psychology is latching on. Most standard psychological tests have only one set of answers. Some have parallel forms of the same test but rarely more than two. If a clinician wants to test a patient often, for example, to see what effects a particular drug treatment is having, the subject may eventually parrot the answers because he has had so much practice. Furthermore, the scoring of most conventional psychological tests is so insensitive to small changes in mental competence that it sometimes seems the only definitive result you get is whether the patient is dead or alive. Here, computer testing does have a role.

Elithern (1981) gave Digit Span, where the subject has to repeat a number of digits read aloud as an example of a test with one correct answer. There are a million ways of arranging six digits and 100,000 ways of arranging five digits. Subjects cannot guess or predict the numbers beforehand. However, 123456 is much easier to remember than 495318. Automated testing is useful in making questions more random and their presentation more reliable. Filters can be built into a computer program to stop easy strings being generated, and the computer can control very precisely the duration of a stimulus and of a response. The time a patient takes to respond may say more about his condition than the actual response. Elithern argued that automated assessment could present questions both more neutrally and more precisely. Assessment would become less subjective. Computer testing allows the testees to complete the tasks in their own time, and this can yield additional information. Elithern warned that some subjects had been reared on an absolutely pernicious ratio of reinforcement so they would never give up unless physically dragged away from the computer. Similar problems exist with some young people and 'Space Invader' machines.

Many of Elithern's ideas stem from work on the Perceptual Mays Test (a series of dots randomly superimposed on a matrix or criss-cross lines, the shape of which is a triangle). The task is to find the pathway to the apex using a minimum number of dots. Very different results are obtained depending on whether the subject is told how many dots to use or to find out how many by himself. The test can be broken down into: solution time (the time taken overall); search time (how long the person takes before responding); track time (the time the person takes before he fills in the pathway); and check time (the time the person takes before he says that he is satisfied with his answer). Two people may take exactly the same time to complete the test, but use it in totally different ways. One person may spend almost all of his time 'looking' and suddenly complete all the dots at once, while another may carefully scrutinise each aspect and fill in the dots one by one. Their cognitive styles differ but conventional tests don't identify such different strategies.

Daily tests can be used in assessing various treatment and non-treatment programmes. One comparison Elithern made was between performance first on amytal and then on amytal plus amphetamine. The latter was more beneficial to the patient so she remained on that combination-drug treatment for a period.

Computer-automated testing may be the testing of the future, but Elithern's enthusiasm needs some balancing. First, he has not used any control groups so it is presumed, and not established, that computer testing doesn't suffer from the same wild fluctuations as other testing methods. Secondly, some clinical psychologists feel that they can put subjects at ease and reduce their anxiety in a way no machine can do. Ansaphones evoke a host of individually varied responses. Some use messages as requested; others immediately ring off since talking to a machine feels awkward; others, perhaps even more oddly, insist on talking *to* the machine as if it could answer like the human being it is substituting for. While computers have much to offer, Elithern is being a bit over-optimistic in some of his claims. Automated testing is a breakthrough both in giving questions to subjects and in the sheer bulk of the numbers of subjects that can be handled but it is not problem-free.

It is not just the form of questions that makes for variable responses. As we argued in Chapter 2, human behaviour is less consistent than test theory would like. That is true even for handicapped children. For example, John Morss (1981) of Ulster Polytechnic took a small group of Down's Syndrome children aged 12 to 22 months. He compared them with normal children using a classic test in developmental psychology. According to Piaget, if an object disappears behind a cushion children younger than 6 to 9 months will make no attempt to retrieve it. Out of sight is out of mind for them. Only after 9 months do they structure their perceptions in such a way as to see that objects continue to exist whether they see them or not. Morss wanted to see how Down's syndrome children performed on such tests.

With normal children, performance is usually fairly stable. They either have, or do not have, object permanence, though there is a transitional period. Down's Syndrome children were slow in their cognitive development. But Morss also found that both their errors and the variability of their behaviour differed from a control group of 26 normal children. The Down's Syndrome children were quite likely to succeed at the task at one time and then fail at it the next. Their behaviour was less stable, and they made quite different errors from those of normal children.

In analysing his results, Morss warned of the dangers of relying on a one-off test to assess the status of handicapped children. It could mean overestimating their ability, or ignoring the kinds of errors that stood in the way of progress.

A related problem is that of being able to interpret change properly. We have studiously avoided getting embroiled in the repetitive debate about the value of IQ tests, but our next case study looks at the stability of IQ scores. If tests scores suggest change, how is one to judge whether the change is a major one or a minor one? It is well established, for example, that IQ declines with age. Some five years before death, there is often an abrupt drop in an individual's IQ. Here, the tests scores would seem to be mapping a major personality change.

Case Study Two: IQ

Test tested: IQ tests in various forms including the Wechsler, Ravens' Progressive Matrices
Example of questions: What is the missing number, 3, 7, 13 ?
Form of answer: Correct solutions
Our focus: Change

There has been more energy devoted to validating the IQ test than to any other. The way the test is used to assess 'intelligence' encourages one to assume that intelligence is constant. After all, it sounds odd to say that Fred was more intelligent than Joan in 1983, but in 1984 Joan fizzed with brainpower. Devotees of IQ tests rarely challenge this assumption of stability but, as we hope to illustrate, IQ tests reveal some curious inconsistencies: first, the Japanese are much brighter; secondly, children fluctuate. Richard Lynn (1982) of the Psychology Department at the New University of Ulster has shown that the IQ of the Japanese is significantly higher. Lynn looked at 27 different studies. He relied heavily on evidence gathered in 1975 when a new version of the standard American Wechsler Intelligence Scale for Children was standardised for Japan. 1,100 children were tested aged from 6 years to 16 years old, with 100 6-year-olds, 100 7-year-olds, 100 8-year-olds and so on. The performance of 1,100 Japanese subjects was compared to that of 2,200 Americans.

The analysis of the tests revealed, first, that in Japan the mean performance IQ is 111, against an American mean of between 100 and 102. The Japanese subjects were particularly good at picture arrangement, mazes, block design, and object assembly parts of the test which examine spatial ability. They were less good at digit span and coding.

Lynn also analysed the trend in IQ scores across the generations. The earliest subjects who were tested were born around 1910. The youngest were the 6-year-olds of 1975. The pattern of IQ scores shows that the Japanese sample born in the early part of the century — from 1910 to 1945 — have a mean IQ of 102–105. This is slightly higher than the current mean IQ for American and Western Europe, but only fractionally so. But the subjects who were born between 1946 and 1969 have a mean IQ in the range of 108–115. The very high mean of 115 applies to those born in 1960 and 1961. The level slipped back then to a consistent 111 or 112. Over a generation then, the mean IQ in Japan has risen by something like an average of 7 points.

Lynn also brings forward some more unnerving evidence. In America and Europe only 2 percent of the population have an IQ of above 130. And while many people (including the editors of *Psychology News*) are apt to poke fun at the pretensions of MENSA, an IQ of above 140 is, at least, statistically rare. But in Japan over 10 per cent of the population have an IQ of 130 or above. Lynn concludes that on average 77 per cent of Japanese have an IQ higher than that of a European. Is that why they don't buy British cars?

Lynn's results show inconsistency (or progress) on a grand scale. But does the shift in Japanese IQ — and the differences between their 'mean' and the Western 'mean' — have important consequences? Crudely, does it account for their economic success? The Japanese certainly tend not to think so. In a recent trip to Japan one of the authors interviewed many Japanese psychologists who attributed the economic miracle to the Japanese capacity for hard work. In an article in the *American Psychological Monitor*, a number of Japanese psychologists tried to explain the reasons for the boom in IQ, but not one of them directly claimed that the higher brain power led to commercial success. Lynn's analysis of the IQ results documents a major shift in IQ, but it is far from clear what its actual implications are.

Lynn's results have been used by writers like Eysenck to counter the accusation that they are racist. How can they be racist when they use IQ scores which show that whites are not the top race but that orientals are? Intriguingly, Lynn does not accept the hereditarian position. He does not think that the kind of increase he found 'could be accounted for by a change in the genetic structure of the population. Instead the explanation probably lies largely in environmental improvements'. Better health care and nutrition have made the miracle. P. G. Wodehouse would not have been stumped for the explanation since the Japanese, like the inimitable Jeeves, live on a diet of raw fish. Fish is the best brainfood, the rawer the better! There is, however, no evidence at all that the Japanese have better health care than Americans. In so far as their diet has changed since 1900 it has become more Western, with less raw fish. The problem with Lynn's results is interesting. No one doubts their *internal reliability* because the Wechsler has been so well validated, but it is hard to know what they mean. Do they explain the economic success of

Japan? Are they due to an educational system which, *inter alia*, trains children to dazzle on the IQ? The fact is, no one knows.

From a practical point of view, it is telling how a well-respected test can accommodate all kinds of fluctuations in its reliability. Soon after the war Heim and Wallace (1948) persuaded undergraduates to take intelligence tests weekly for eight weeks. They got no feedback and no results, but the scores kept on going higher and higher. Mandleburg and Brooks (1976) found a quite different pattern. They gave intelligence tests to patients who had suffered head injuries in road accidents. Thirteen months after the accidents patients finally returned to near normal levels of IQ. On paper they were not lame brains. Mandleburg and Brooks wondered why, then, these patients seemed unable to perform as well as they had done before. They recovered their intelligences, but could not pick up the pieces in their old jobs. This study has implications both for reliability and validity. It is slightly surprising that, despite brain injuries, patients should recover all their IQs. It is even more intriguing why, given recovery, life did not resume as before, as they were not physically disabled. Two studies of English children have also attacked this question of how stable scores of intelligence are over long periods of time. They came to rather different conclusions.

Petty and Field (1980) found children's IQ over four years was rather unstable while Yule, Gold and Busch (1982) found it to be stable. When similar and well-established tests throw up such different results, the reasons are problematic.

Petty and Field tested 355 8-year-olds every year for four years. They gave them a non-verbal test and observed their achievements in English and mathematics. The IQ scores varied considerably over the four years. Yule *et al.* (1982) did an eleven-year longitudinal study of 85 children. These children were given the Wechsler Pre-School and Primary Scale of Intelligence, and eleven years later an adult IQ scale (the WISC-R). It is a pity that there was no intervening testing. The full-scale IQ on these two tests intercorrelated at the very hefty score of 0.86. Correlations with attainment variables were less at around 0.6 — still far from negligible. How does one explain the contradictory nature of these two studies? It is clearly an important issue because, in the maelstroms of testing, intelligence test scores have a reputation for being, at least, reliable.

There appear to have been two essential differences — first, the mode of test being used; secondly, the statistical techniques. At the end of Chapter 5 we commented that Grunau's work led us to wonder why schools did not try streaming children according to their preferred mode. Petty and Field used two tests which place little emphasis on the verbal: Raven's Coloured Progressive Matrices and the Australian 'Junior Non Verbal Test'. This involves problems with time sequences and patterns, and Yule relied on a series of intelligence tests with verbal as well as visual items. Petty and Field argued that their tests had the merit of being relatively culture-free and, therefore, a 'purer' measure of intelligence than culturally loaded verbal tasks.

The statistical techniques differed, too. Petty and Field (1980) used standardised scores; Yule *et al.* (1982) used correlation coefficients. Clarke and Clarke (1975) warned that correlations can provide a misleading impression of consistency for individual scores even when test-retest correlations are as high as 0.9. The pattern of change is obscured by the correlation coefficient. Ironically, teachers need to know about changes, for the good or the bad, in their pupils. So do educational planners. If most pupils are stable in English from year to year but a few fluctuate wildly, the implications are very different from where all pupils fluctuate a bit.

One potential, though far from proven, explanation is recent work which suggests that high verbal ability may go with rapid maturation while good spatial ability may go with later maturation. Petty's and Field's sample were maturing late, and so their non-verbal scores shot up! But this is highly speculative.

Yule argued that his research is 'a sobering finding for those educational advisers who have been abandoning the use of tests of general intelligence over the past few years'. As we shall see in Chapter 10, more testing goes on in British schools than is admitted, but the contradictions between these two studies are worrying. If IQ is not reliable, what is likely to be? Is our adult IQ score made up of the same relative weightings of different abilities as when we are young, or do the combinations that make up the total score change? And do psychologists, consciously or not, choose different shades of intelligence tests to suit their theoretical positions? As one cynical student said of Piaget, for him, intelligence is not 'what the tests test, but what his tests test'. Psychologists, by their choices, affect how reliable test results can appear, which should be no surprise except to those who imagine the reliability of tests to be some abstract entity remote from human behaviour.

We have argued so far that reliability is crucial to tests. If a medical thermometer were not very accurate, it would not be much use as a diagnostic tool. Nevertheless, psychometricians ought perhaps to make more use of inconsistent and unreliable behaviour on tests when it appears, and to examine why subjects — especially on well-proven tests — are producing inconsistent results.

So far we have looked at what might be termed sincere unreliability. People cannot help answering questions differently at different times. Very different dynamics affect the way people behave when they want to please or impress others. A recent study of 12 to 21-day-old babies had to be re-run when the experimenters discovered that some mothers had been trying to teach their babies to stick their tongues out. The mothers had been told the psychologists were studying whether babies could imitate their mothers doing that. One mother explained her reasons for 'training' the newborn. She did not want him to fail the first examination of his life. In the face of such attitudes it is not surprising that psychologists have been at pains to study the ways in which subjects do their best (or worst) to please them. Our next two studies look at how our desire to please and to conform affects responses to tests. The second case study looks at related issues of prestige. All these dog the question of reliability.

Case Study Three: The Truth About Liars

Test tested: Eysenck Personality Inventory
Example of questions: Do you like going to parties?
Form of answer: Yes ? No
Our focus: Lying

One problem in psychological testing is usually guaranteed to make the rest pale into insignificance. Whether it be labelled 'social desirability', 'response set', 'yea-saying', it amounts to the same thing: the subject is telling lies.

Edwards (1957) described the 'social desirability factor' as subjects responding in a manner that would be expected of well-adjusted people so as to present themselves in a socially acceptable light. But what is a good light in one situation is a bad one in another.

Sometimes a test constructor will incorporate a lie scale, and say that beyond a certain point all the answers should be discarded. Other scales (MMPI-K, for example) use correction measures to adjust scores. The most refined statistical techniques will not salvage poor data. Cronbach (1980) also noted: 'If the subject tells lies to the tester there is no way to convert the lies to truth'.

Elliot (1981) and Dunnett, Koun and Barber (1981) have been investigating the apparent lack of truthfulness in some psychological test respondents. Even lie detector scales — no one has introduced the Galvanic Skin Response into tests yet — have failed to detect liars. McKerracher and Watson (1968) found that pathological liars scored lower on Eysenck's Personality Inventory (EPI) Lie Scale than other patients at Rampton Hospital, and concluded the Lie Scale was a lie. This is very worrying, for if we cannot even rely on pathological liars to tell lies on our psychological tests, what hope do we have with the non-pathological liars? The EPI consists of questions like:

Do you enjoy going to parties?
Do you often feel depressed for no apparent reason?

Subjects can answer 'yes', 'no' or tick a '?'. The test has been used to derive various important personality traits including extraversion, introversion and neuroticism.

Gorman (1968) used an EPI on American students to assess the effect of social desirability. He found that the mean desirability rating of extraversion items was significantly higher than the mean rating of all other items, but the mean rating of neuroticism was significantly lower. In a second experiment, Gorman tried to get subjects to answer honestly, fake what they thought to be a good image to be, and, finally, fake what they thought a bad image to be. Some of Gorman's methodological techniques were unsound, so Dunnett decided to replicate them on a British sample, but with a better experimental design. An equal number of subjects were run under four conditions in a completely randomised design: (1) rating EPI items on a 5-point scale from 'desirable' to 'undesirable'; (2) completing the EPI under 'fake a good image' instructions; (3) under 'fake a bad image' instructions and (4) under control instructions emphasising honesty. Eighty men aged 18 to 64 and eighty women aged 19 to 64 were selected. Approximately half the subjects of each sex were professional people and the rest were students, but none had encountered the EPI previously.

Dunnett found that items in the EPI contributing to the extraversion score were considered to be socially desirable. This result agrees with Gorman's findings for middle-class suburban students, but disagrees with Farley's (1966) report of a negative relation between extraversion and a measure of social desirability for a group of British apprentice mechanics. Gorman explained the discrepancy in terms of national differences in cultural values. Dunnett also studied a middle-class British sample, so for him the disparity is probably due to socio-economic class differences. It is a pity that Dunnett and his colleagues do not expand upon this as we do not know whether 'undesirable extraversion' is a social judgement, occupational judgement, or both. For example, if a young mechanic applies for a job that requires working with machines rather than people, should he stress the social aspects of his life? The company might infer that every Monday he would be a total wreck after a riotous weekend at parties. Class differences are reflected throughout the whole of society and especially in the occupational sphere. Are not middle-class people — be they professionals or managers — expected to have a certain gregariousness, while their proletarian brethren are merely expected to get on with their job and not be distracted by gossiping and showing-off to their mates?

Promoting Truths

Dunnett found that extraversion items were thought of as desirable, neuroticism items as undesirable, and lie-scale items as relatively neutral, which is surprising since they are meant to show 'perfection'. Subjects instructed to 'fake good' tended to present themselves as stable extraverts, but when asked to 'fake bad' showed themselves as neurotic introverts. These results, based on a middle-class sample, are intriguing for they may be based on a stereotype. If folklore is right, the stereotype of the typical professor in the lower socio-economic circles is of some bumbling, socially inept individual who is rather clumsy, cannot remember the date or his wife's name, and is fixated on his own absentminded brilliance rather than the 'normal' but uninspired stable extravert. It would be interesting to know whether 'social desirability' is a function of actual, or imagined, ideal people in society.

Elliot's research blamed the majority of previous studies for using students which limited the usefulness of the findings in predicting how people in operational conditions will behave. His main aim was to see whether groups tested in different circumstances displayed any coherent change in the pattern of responses to Cattell's Personality Factor which measures extraversion and Cattell's NPF which measures neuroticism. The tests were designed to be used together, but a lie scale was incorporated into each so that they could be independently administered. The subjects studied were:

(a) 11 male promotion candidates of a paper-manufacturing company on an assessment at Trinity College, Dublin;
(b) 42 male applicants for managerial posts in a food-processing company;
(c) 136 female bank employees tests in a promotion screening programme;
(d) 298 female bank employees applying for in-company training in computer techniques;
(e) 142 male programmers and systems analysts applying for posts in a computing bureau;
(f) 84 male bank employees applying for in-company training in computer techniques;
(g) 70 male graduate students on master's courses in management, most with managerial experience.

Elliot showed that if there is a relationship between lie-scale extraversion (i.e. 'social desirability' according to other middle-class samples) then it is hardly linear. The only group to produce a significant correlation was bank promotion candidates. According to Michaelis and Eysenck (1971), applicants score higher on lie scales than controls because they are motivated to present themselves well. The graduate students in Elliot's study scored significantly lower on both lie scale and stability. When the Bradford School of Industrial Technology incorporated the EPI in its admissions procedure, it obtained the highest mean extraversion scores ever (21) and the lowest mean neuroticism (2). Applicants guessed rightly the school wanted stable extraverts and produced the profile wanted. This would seem to support the idea that distortion of responses is a function of motivation. Elliot adds that it is unlikely that men applying for managerial jobs in a food plant (who scored high on the lie scale) would be significantly more highly motivated than programmers and analysts (who scored low on the same scale) applying for posts where salaries and job interest are reputedly high. And why should female bank officials undergoing screening for promotion be more highly motivated than female bank officials actively seeking computer training?

Elliot treats 'social desirability' as a unitary concept that should manifest itself across all occupational categories. He doesn't consider the more logical term 'occupational desirability', which would be occupation-specific. A degree of extraversion might be desirable in bank promotion candidates but not in computer programmers. The conventional interpretation of a combination of high-lie score and low anxiety is that the candidate should be treated as if he had returned a high anxiety score. Elliot asserts that it would be more appropriate to see him as apprehensive but in control: he is able to present a brave face to the world, which indicates better adjustment than a high anxiety score (whatever the lie score).

Elliot concludes that his results have followed the pattern of previous studies in finding significant correlations between lie scale and neuroticism. This may provide the answer to problems of 'social desirability' replacing it with what is socially or occupationally undesirable. For example, if an employer wants an audio-typist, he may well think it better to have an introverted type who will get on with his or her work, rather than an extraverted type who will spend all his or her day chatting. Extraversion may only be a socially desirable quality when it is seen in the context of certain middle-class ways of life and middle-class occupations. Instead of test constructors looking for people who claim to have the perfect shining halo, perhaps they should look towards lie scales based on social or occupational undesirability to see how many people would admit to being rude, illogical, unreliable, constantly working in chaos, etc. An unsubstantiated, hazardous guess is that a 'social undesirability/unreliability' measure would make the 'social desirability' lie scale redundant.

It may seem odd to include a review of how papers get accepted in scientific journals as part of a study of psychological tests. But what gets published is passing a test and, as it happens, a test with considerable implications for science. What is taken as being scientific knowledge depends almost entirely on what is accepted, as by journals. There is a clear hierarchy of journals, with general ones like *Nature* being at the top of the greasy pole, with lesser organs like *Psychological Reports* well below it. The process of scientific publication seems to be completely as prone to the unreliability, and as unreliable and variable as any other human performances tests of human performance. Only here, the consequences are actually quite serious.

Case Study Four: Peer Review: Who Lords The Journals?

More than 20 years ago when Robert Rosenthal was at the University of Dakota, he was not able to publish between 15 and 20 articles in mainstream psychological journals. After he had been at Harvard a few years most of the same articles were published in mainstream journals. Are these examples of systematic bias based on ascription, or of what the famous sociologist Robert K. Merton (1968) called the 'Matthew Effect', based on the biblical aphorism: 'Unto every one that hath shall be given, and he shall have abundance: but from him that hath not shall be taken away even that which he hath'?

Scott Armstrong (1980), of the University of Pennsylvania, has an alternative explanation. His empirical research on scientific journals revealed an 'author's formula' which is likely to speed acceptance of manuscripts: (i) not pick an important problem; (ii) not challenge existing beliefs; (iii) not obtain surprising results; (iv) not use simple methods; (v) not provide full disclosure; and (vi) not write clearly. Peters, from the University of North Dakota, and Ceci, from Cornell University, presented some research to *Science* which, after a long delay, was rejected with the advice that it would be appropriate for the *American Psychologist*. After another long delay, the paper was rejected by the *American Psychologist*. But submission was encouraged by the editor of *The Behavioral and Brain Sciences* — a journal specialising in peer interaction on controversial papers — and after a final round of major revision, the paper was accepted. Never violate the 'author's formula' would seem to be the conclusion.

Peters and Ceci selected 12 already published research articles by researchers from prestigious and highly productive American psychology departments: one article from each of 12 highly regarded and widely read American psychology journals with high rejection rates (80 per cent) and non-blind refereeing practices. With fictitious names and institutions substituted for the original ones (Tri-Valley Center for Human Potential), the altered manuscripts were formally re-submitted to the journals that had originally refereed and published them 18–32 months earlier. Of the sample of 38 editors and reviewers, only 3 (8 per cent) detected the re-submissions. This result allowed 9 of the 12 articles to continue through the review process to receive an actual evaluation: 8 of the 9 were rejected. Sixteen of the 18 referees (89 per cent) recommended against publication and the editors agreed. The grounds for rejection were in many cases described as 'serious methodological flaws'.

Many of the invited commentators charged Peters and Ceci with unethical research, but Steven Harnad, editor of *The Behavioral and Brain Sciences*, thought that the deception was rather innocuous. Harnad argues that perhaps some editors regard themselves as too important, or their time too valuable, to contribute to empirical efforts to study and improve the peer-review system under natural conditions. However, there were also 'serious methodological flaws' with Peters's and Ceci's research. The sample was very small and the design highly unbalanced.

It is worth noting just how subversive Peters and Ceci's project was. Publication in scientific journals is the method that is accepted for the *creation* of scientific facts. What the journals and the editors accept passes on the record as a duly accredited finding. To show that the standards used to assess papers were so very varied was worrying, and it is, of course, an interesting example of how assessment varies. Not surprisingly, therefore, Harnad found that many of those he invited to comment were acid in their comments. One professor noted that the so-called Tri-Valley Center for Human Potential did not sound like a research institution at all; another noted that the statistics used were poor, and that if the experiment were repeated many times some previously rejected manuscripts would always get accepted. Katherine Nelson of the City of New York Graduate Center, had a wilier explanation of why manuscripts were not recognised a second time around. She said: 'Most manuscripts will soon be forgotten by editors, reviewers and the general reader simply because they are eminently forgettable'. Other criticism said that the final original published versions had often been altered and honed to meet specific criticisms of specific reviewers, so for the articles to be acceptable to different reviewers, different honing would be needed. Some comments picked up the fact that Peters and Ceci had made purely cosmetic changes, replacing titles like *Gone with The Wind* to *Off with The Breeze*. That might have been important.

Harnad did not restrict comment to psychologists. One of the most useful comments came from David Lazarus, editor-in-chief for the American Physical Society, which publishes many prestigious journals. Lazarus said:

Even in my science which is by common consent (however misplaced) regarded as far less subjective than psychology, there is no way that we can run a journal with even far higher acceptance rates (45% for Physical Review Letters) without encountering enormous discrepancies between the opinions of different referees. In only about 10 to 15% of cases do two referees agree on acceptance or rejection the first time around — and this with the authors and institutions known. Perhaps objective science is as hard to come by as objective criteria.

The final comment worth citing is from D. S. Palermo, editor of the *Journal of Experimental Child Psychology*:

I do not wish to play God because I know the system is fallible. The article by Peters and Ceci makes clear the humanness of the enterprise. Let us hope that it results in more human decisions in the future — our science may depend on it.

Conclusions

It may seem odd to include a review of Peters and Ceci's work in a chapter on the all-too-frail reliability of tests. But the case studies all show how hard it is to assess human behaviour and skills by a study taken at one moment in time. In its eagerness to be productive, psychology is apt to elevate very partial results based on such fallible tests into grand laws of human behaviour. It is important to see this not as a necessary truth but as a move in a scientific game. Publishing research articles and books (like this one, too) is also, after all, one kind of move in the 'science game'. Looking at the whole issue of reliability suggests we should be wary of making too grandiose claims. In Chapter 7 we look at an issue which is usually treated early on in most books on testing — sampling. We have deliberately first examined questions of consistency and reliability because the problems these present would exist even if tests tested a perfect sample. As well we shall see, the perfect sample is as rare as the consistent human being.

7 THE PERFECT SAMPLE

We have argued that human beings are less consistent and tests less reliable than enthusiasts would wish. The defects of both human beings and of testing may reveal something of the problems of psychology. It is not the same as a physical science by virtue of the knowingness of its — are they 'subjects', or 'objects'? Subatomic particles may exhibit all kinds of quirks and quarks, but at least they don't know they are doing it. Many of the sampling flaws we point to are curable. Psychologists cannot alter the fact that people are inconsistent, but they certainly could alter the fact that their sampling is often poor.

The literature stresses the importance of sampling. A sample should either be representative of the whole population or, more often, relevant to the problem at issue. No point in checking a test for the senile on 20-year-old athletes. Sixty-year-olds who are still working might be a good control. Throughout the book so far we have made some points about sampling, especially the dangers of relying too much on samples of college undergraduates. In this chapter we examine three cases of where the sampling practices used reflect problems in psychology. Our first study is of a test of menstrual symptoms. The sample was limited to young women studying together. Our second test looks at work on industrial psychology. Warr, Cook and Wall (1979) took a sample of workers from different sized companies and of different socio-economic classes, gathering together a better than usual sample. Our third case study highlights an unusual problem given that we have complained of psychologists controlling testing too much. Haley (1964) let some of his subjects determine the sample with, we believe, odd consequences. There are further pitfalls good sampling has to avoid — racial bias, educational bias and class bias. In Chapter 5 we condemned the Rathus Assertiveness Scale. It used only 68 undergraduates in its original sample; and some of these 68 were also ranked by their friends who were also undergraduates. On the basis of this narrow sample, grand propositions about assertiveness were made. The author of the Rathus neglected the fact that many of his questions were clearly designed for American male undergraduates who were infatuated with baseball, bubblegum and pleasing their teachers.

Our first case study in this chapter looks at an instance of sampling where the faults were less glaring than the Rathus but still fairly important.

Case Study One: Menstrual Symptoms Questionnaire

Test tested: Menstrual Symptoms
Example of questions: 'Do you suffer from dull, aching pains?'
Form of answer: 5-point scale
Our focus: Differentiating symptoms

Before the feminist literature of the 1970s, the literature on premenstrual tension was small. One of the few psychologists to study the phenomenon was Katherine Dalton. In her book *Menstrual Cycle* (1969) she argued there were two very different kinds of menstrual symptoms — spasmodic dysmenorrhoea and congestive dysmenorrhoea. *Spasmodic* involves painful spasms like labour pains which begin on the first day of a period; *congestive* involves dull, aching pains which precede the start of the period. Lethargy and depression accompany the pains. Dalton believed that dysmenorrhoea was related to hormonal imbalance between the levels of ovarian hormones — oestrogen and progesterone. Women whose progesterone levels were much higher than their oestrogen levels were likely to suffer from spasmodic pains because too much progesterone seems related to tightness of the cervix. This tightness produces cramp-like, labour-like pains. High oestrogen levels, on the other hand, lead to *congestive* dysmenorrhoea because a lack of progesterone seems involved with the biochemistry of depression. Dalton's ideas are clearly crucial in determining what treatment to give. In 1975 Chesney and Testo designed the Menstrual Symptom Questionnaire to differentiate the two.

Chesney and Testo amassed 51 items from the descriptions of the symptoms. They tested these on 56 volunteer subjects from the introductory psychology course at Colorado State University. These volunteers said they had menstrual discomfort. They were given the 51-item questionnaire and then retested two weeks later. At the second testing the typical profiles of spasmodic and congestive dysmenorrhoea were read out to them, and they were asked to say which they felt they suffered from.

Before being able to analyse their data properly, Chesney and Testo had to rewrite some items for clarity. A factor analysis of the answers did show up two factors after eliminating items which did not correlate with either kind of dysmenorrhoea. Twelve of the remaining 24 items were characteristic of spasmodic dysmenorrhoea; twelve of congestive. Chesney and Testo used a 5-point scoring scale, but they introduced one variation. The scale was used so that a score of 1 = *never* for items indicative of spasmodic dysmenorrhoea, but for items indicative of congestive dysmenorrhoea it was the opposite. Setting out as a table may make it clearer. Take a congestive question:

'Do you suffer from dull, aching pains?'
It would be scored as follows:

$$1 = \text{always}$$
$$2 = \text{often}$$
$$3 = \text{sometimes}$$
$$4 = \text{rarely}$$
$$5 = \text{never}$$

A question about spasmodic symptoms would be scored the opposite way so that 5 was 'always', 4 'often' and so on. By this technique, subjects with spasmodic symptoms get the highest score, while those with congestive symptoms get the lowest score. It is a nifty piece of statistics which is apt to exaggerate the differences. The highest possible score was 125, and the lowest possible score was 25. When the authors ranked subjects, they found a 14-point gap between the highest low (i.e. congestive) subject (68) and the highest lowest high (i.e. spasmodic) subject (82). The authors conclude that Dalton is right in her assertion that there are two kinds of dysmenorrhoea.

There were, however, some problems with the sampling which suggest their conclusions may have been premature. First, Chesney and Testo never explained how old their subjects were. They may have all been in their late teens or early twenties as undergraduates. If so, their descriptions of symptoms might not fit older women. They do not say if any of their subjects had had children, which often affects menstrual symptoms. Such simple lack of information verges on the perverse.

In their preamble to the test the authors say nothing of the fact that all their subjects lived on the same campus and were doing the same course. Research on mice has shown that if female rats are caged together, this will affect their menstrual cycles. They will tend to synchronise them. Studies of convents and other female institutions have suggested that this sisterly phenomenon is not restricted to the non-human mammals. Women living together often have periods together. Since Chesney and Testo tested one group of students who were sharing a course they ought at least to have been aware of the possibility that this might affect their results. Work has shown that even the smell of someone else's sweat can affect periods. Sweat was taken from the armpits of volunteers who had a very regular 28-day cycle. The sweat was mixed with alcohol and placed on the upper lip of eight volunteers three times a week for four months. The control group were given alcohol but no personalised sweat. The periods of the control group did not alter. But some of the experimental group were, by the end of the research, beginning their periods within one day of the donor's. The sample was small, the study in some ways bizarre, yet it shows how social and chemical factors can affect menstruation.

One reason why it is important to be sceptical of the testing done by Chesney and Testo is that they eliminated no less than 27 items. Laconically, they write: '27 items which did not meet criterion were eliminated'. They give little more information about these dumped items. Yet they begin their paper by explaining that they scoured the literature (mainly, one presumes, Dalton) for symptoms of spasmodic, as opposed to congestive dysmenorrhoea. Over half these symptoms then 'did not meet criterion'. Though they must have been initially chosen by the authors because they thought these items would separate the two kinds of menstrual symptoms, they failed to do so. The questions used in the final analysis, therefore, were very selective. Choosing the symptoms from descriptions of two different illnesses in the literature meant that Chesney and Testo ran the risk of making circular findings. Their sampling compounded that risk.

As a result of the inadequate sampling, no reader of their tests can know if their sample is typical of young women, old women, women living close together, women living apart or any other group. There was no control group. It would have been interesting to see what women who did not complain of menstrual symptoms felt — never any discomfort? — and even better to have a control group from outside the university. Without any of these basics of sampling, who knows what their results mean?

The Menstrual Symptoms Questionnaire may well, given better sampling, prove itself an effective instrument. The authors certainly believe they have bolstered Dalton's ideas. For us, the real lesson to learn is to guard against the seductiveness of such evidence. It is all too circular. The theory of hormonal imbalance is presented with examples of symptoms that are presumed to signify this imbalance. These symptoms are then remoulded into questions. Those that do not fit the factor-analytic model are thrown out. Then, by some deft sleight of argument, the theory that there are two types of dysmenorrhoea is confirmed though there is neither hormone nor a proper sample in sight.

Case Study Two: The Will to Work

Test tested:	Work Attitudes
Example of questions:	'I would be soon bored if I had no work'
Form of answer:	Agreeing on a 7-point scale with statements
Our focus:	Sampling

Samples often have a class bias. This is especially true in occupational tests. One of the merits of a recent study at the University of Sheffield is that it has developed a test of the will to work on a realistic sample. Warr *et al.* have devised 'Scales for the measurement of some work attitudes and aspects of psychological well-being' to examine the precise areas of work satisfaction and dissatisfaction. Our main focus here, though, is on the sampling methods used.

Understandable Questions

Warr *et al.* are aware of the particular problems associated with their samples, and are careful not to patronise. They write;

> questionnaire items are sometimes difficult to comprehend, especially for blue-collar workers. . . . Of particular value would be short scales which are easily completed by unsophisticated respondents, which are known to be psychometrically acceptable, and for which normative data are available.

Very welcome; far too many tests are standardised on psychology undergraduates and then used indiscriminately on the rest of the population.

A Relevant Sample

This was not an 'opportunity' sample of using the local factory next door whose workers were 'available' for research because the occupational psychologist played golf with the manager, but a very carefully prepared sample. Altogether, respondents were 590 blue-collar workers employed in the manufacturing industry within the UK. All were employed full-time and had a mean length of service of 9.02 years. They were aged between 20 and 64. The subjects were drawn from widely dispersed, sampling areas, so the 'two-nation split' (affluent South and poverty-stricken North) was avoided. Half the sample from each area were from firms employing fewer than 300 employees and half from larger companies. Within each half of the sample, 50 per cent were above, and 50 per cent below, 40 years of age. Within each quarter sample, half were skilled, 30 per cent semi-skilled, and 20 per cent unskilled. The skill level was judged by the amount of training an individual required before being considered competent at his job (years or months, several weeks, or a few days for the three levels of skill).

These researchers started out with one of the most obvious questions of all, but one that is so rarely asked, even in some surveys: 'Will our sample understand the questions?' If psychologists and sociologists wrote plain English, Arabic, Chinese, or what have you in research publications, then the pseudo-scientific jargon that is meaningless to the ordinary person might no longer appear as a problem in devising questionnaires that are meaningful. There has been a tendency to ask workers if they have 'An instrumental orientation towards work?' or if they 'Are intrinsically motivated towards their job?' Gobbledegook rules OK if our subjects are fellow gobbledegook merchants, but any data is worthless if subjects do not understand the questions asked.

Warr *et al.*'s sample was *representative*, and psychology students embarking upon research for the first time should appreciate the wealth of data and comparisons this can generate. Admittedly, some of the numbers may have been rather small, but Warr and his colleagues could have compared:

(1) Older workers versus younger workers (are older workers

more fearful, for example, that new technology will make their skill redundant?).
(2) Workers in the North versus workers in the South of England (are workers in the North more anxious about losing their job because unemployment is higher than in the South?).
(3) Larger versus smaller companies (do smaller firms where there is more contact with the boss have better industrial relations than larger firms?).
(4) Skilled workers versus unskilled workers (do skilled workers get more satisfaction — other than money — from doing their job than do unskilled workers?).

The need for a representative sample of people — such as that used by Warr and his co-workers — is well advised, but rarely adhered to. But the proper sampling of questions rarely receives such prominence although the lesson is quite simple: if your sample cannot understand your question, then you will not be able to understand the reply, no matter if the reply was ticked or not.

Using the sample, Warr and his colleagues looked at the relationships between work involvement, job satisfaction, 'higher order need strength' (which means how much individuals want to use complex skills), life satisfaction, happiness and self-rated anxiety. They found that there was a link between self-rated anxiety and poor work involvement, happiness and job satisfaction. There was a correlation (0.20) between higher order need strength and self-rated anxiety, but the self-rated anxiety scale had rather low test-retest reliability. Part of this seemed to be due to changing perceptions of Britain's future economic prospects. In his original assessment of Warr's scale, Shelley argued that both the range of its issues and the excellence of its sampling made it welcome. We have focused here on the merits of its sampling because it does show how thorough and imaginative investigation can produce interesting results and a useful test to develop.

Warr's sampling had the merit of testing actual workers. In Japan (perhaps due to their higher IQs) a more perfect method of sampling has been achieved. At the Japanese Productivity Centre, 130,000 workers are given an annual stress test. Workers do not have much of a choice about whether or not to take the test if their company has agreed. The sampling is very large scale, and allows comparisons to be made between small, large and medium-sized companies and between various jobs. The benefit of such a huge sampling is that it is representative of Japanese industry. We shall return to this study in Chapter 10 because it incorporates many benefits for those who take the test.

One key point is that workers do not get paid for taking tests. One of the problems with many samples is that their subjects are American undergraduates who are either paid for taking part in the test or given some form of course credit. This raises a host of niggling questions. First, are such undergraduates typical either of the rest of America or of humankind in general? We know that the American undergraduate is better educated, better motivated, and richer than most of their contemporaries elsewhere in the world. In America the undergraduate has to pass certain tests (well of course!) to get to college. The college population is disproportionately white, male and middle class. Secondly, even among undergraduates, there may well be differences between volunteers and those who do not volunteer.

Case Study: When Family Conversation is Disturbed

Test tested: Family Interaction Analyser
Examples of questions: Who speaks when?
Form of answer: Patterns of conversation
Our focus: Who chooses the sample?

So far, we have complained often that far too many tests rely on American undergraduates as subjects. Studies of families need wider samples. In creating an instrument to study family dynamics, J. Haley committed a novel sampling error.

Haley argued that the conversations of disturbed and non-disturbed families ought to be different. He assumed that in enlightened America it would be 'normal' for all members of a family to take equal part in a conversation; though he pointed out that in Europe, still riddled with feudalism, children would speak only when spoken to — normally, that is. Haley arranged for families to come into the laboratory to discuss (i) the items on a questionnaire, and (ii) some TAT pictures. He devised a simple form of analysis where father could be followed by child (FC) or by mother (FM). Other variations were CF, CM, MF, MC. He made a special machine, the Family Interaction Analyser (no less, shades of

H. G. Wells!), so that any conversation could be assigned to one of these categories. Haley decided to ignore pauses, so if father spoke, paused, no one dared answer, and then father spoke more, it all counted as one patriarchal speech.

The idea behind Haley's research was intriguing. He devised four main hypotheses:

(1) the order in which family members speak should not be random.
(2) the more pathological families will be more limited and less random in their speech.
(3) If one creates a scale with the zero point being that distribution of the six possible sequences (father-child, mother-child, mother-father, mother-child, child-father, child-mother) which would occur if the speaking order was random, every family will deviate from that random point.
(4) if a family falls on the disturbed range on the scale of deviation (obtained from the scale in (3)) it is then treated successfully by family therapy, the family will move towards the normal range.

Haley selected a group of 80 families, and now his design began to be affected by his bizarre sampling practices. Parents of 40 normal children were asked to come with *one child of their own choosing*. The children ranged in age from 10 to 20. It is hardly likely, given such circumstances, that a normal family would bring its most difficult child. More probably, the parents would succumb to the temptation of bringing the child who they thought would do them most credit. Haley excluded from the normal sample any family who had contacted a psychotherapist or where anyone had been arrested.

The disturbed group were not given the freedom of choice the normals had. Haley deemed as being 'abnormal' families where one member

(a) was suffering from schizophrenia; or
(b) had committed a delinquent act; or
(c) had a school problem which had brought him to the attention of the authorities; or
(d) had sought treatment for some neurotic complaint; or
(e) had parents who had sought marital or family therapy.

By definition, Haley made his disturbed families those where the community had got wind of the problems. They had not been able to deal with their troubles themselves. The children were meant to be aged from 10 to 20, but four children older than 20 were included. In this group, if the child was the identified patient, the families were asked to bring him to the group interview. There was totally skewed sampling, therefore. Normal families could bring their 'best' child; disturbed ones had to bring their 'worst' child.

Microphones were hung round the neck of each family member as they discussed a list of items, talked about the TAT picture. Haley always gave the TAT picture as the last thing to discuss. He found, as expected, a different pattern of conversations between the normal and abnormal families. In abnormal families different members of the family speak far less equally both in dyads and triads. Nevertheless, 10 abnormal families were misclassified as normal in that their conversation fell well into the normal range, while 10 normal families were misclassified as abnormal. Not that that meant his testing was wrong. Haley suggested that, perhaps, the 10 normal families had an as yet undiagnosed family member about to become depressed or delinquent. That, alas, does not explain why his 10 abnormal families were classified as normal!

Making families discuss the TAT picture last also produced problems. There was less difference between the abnormal and normal groups on this part of the test. Was that due to fatigue? Or was it due to the fact that, given the nature of the TAT, conversation was more free-flowing? Haley could only speculate and say that a further project would need to alternate the designs.

Throughout the paper Haley argued for a systems approach to family dynamics rather than an individual approach. Following Laing, he argued that one could not study the 'sick' member of the family in isolation. 'What the individual does is not separable from what the other two individuals are doing,' Haley observed, commenting on his conversing threesomes. If that is true — which we believe — it has the effect, ironically, of damaging the credibility of his own research. If the individual is not to be studied in isolation, is it right to limit the study of family conversations to a group of three, and then conclude this is typical of the family as a whole? The sampling errors Haley made with normal families bringing the child they chose could lead to all sorts of distortions. For example, it might well be that Mother, Father and Fred are the paragons of normality when they are together because they do not have to accommodate disruptive Derek. Derek would never come along to an interview with them, so what we witness is a group within a family. If disturbed families had to bring their disturbed child along, then perhaps they talk quite normally in other situations. The sampling errors here are a great shame because they spoil an ingenious piece of research.

Conclusions: Sample Who Ye May

It is all too easy to be highly critical of sampling, because there is no such thing as the perfect sample. Very few studies have the resources either of Kobuta's massive study of Japanese stress (Cohen 1984) or Alan Smithers's (1984) analysis for the astrological birthdate data of the 1971 census. Most researchers struggle to get a sample together at all. In some fields of study, like criminal behaviour, much credit is given to researchers who actually manage to follow up most of their initial sample after they leave jail or treatment. One of the present authors (Cohen 1981) has published two studies of highly specialised samples — one, 'Famous Psychologists', the second, 'Inmates of Broadmoor'. In both cases there were problems in getting hold of all of them, persuading them to answer questions, continuing to keep in touch. It is not surprising that so many studies pounce on the students at hand because they form an ever available sample.

What is important, however, is not to make outlandish claims on the basis of poor sampling. It may well be that it is better to do an imperfect study than no study at all, but that does not mean one should delude oneself that one can generalise from that sample. What we have tried to show in this chapter is how, in the fine grain of doing experiments, researchers often get carried away and fail to use what seems to be common-sense caution. They claim to reveal a great truth when, because of flaws in sampling, a study can provide only partial insight. Psychology is, obviously enough, about all kinds of people — even those you can't seduce into your sample.

8 ODDER TECHNIQUES

Most of the tests examined so far have been based on classic tests of intelligence, attitude or personality. Either answers to a questionnaire or to a set of problems illuminate the person. Such tests can lead to superficial or misleading results. In this chapter we examine four instances of less conventional testing which have tended to emerge either in response to particular needs or as a result of special situations. As we have seen in previous chapters, industries often test applicants for jobs to predict how well they will do in real life. But often, even with well designed tests like the DEVAT, validity coefficients are low. Good performance on the test does not mean good performance for real. Gordon and Kleiman (1976) compared how well an aptitude test and a sample of behaviour while training predicted future performance. The sample of behaviour was better. Their work suggests perhaps that instead of devising tests to look at how well people will do, tests should aim at seeing how trainable people are.

Case Study One: Trainability Testing

In a trainability test, the applicant is expected to learn how to do the task as an integral part of the test procedure. Robertson and Mindel (1980) wanted to see whether it was feasible to introduce trainability tests in a 26-week bricklaying course at skill centres. Instead of paper-and-pencil tests of how to lay a brick, they wanted to devise a much more practical test. In bricklaying, for example, trainees were shown how to lay bricks and then urged to complete a wall. In the milling test they learned how to operate a steel-milling machine to produce a specific component. Such trainability tests are the very opposite of generalist tests like an omnipresent arts degree. What better qualification is there for working at the Department of Employment than a degree in Classics? Robertson and Mindel take the opposite view.

As the procedure they used is radically different from paper-and-pencil tests, it is worth describing in detail. Specially trained instructors give the test. Each instructor has a set of routine tasks that applicants must complete and a standard checklist for each trade. The trainee has two attempts. All trainees are tested during the first three days, and then continue as usual without their normal instructors being given the results of that initial test. Based on the trainee's performance in all task, instructors are asked to predict, using a 5-point scale, how well they will do. The special training instructor also makes two predictions: a personal estimate and one based simply on the number of errors made on the standard checklist.

The procedure is elaborate, with two subjective predictions (one by the special training instructor, one by the usual instructors) and an objective one based on errors. Robertson and Mindel did not have complete control of the procedure, and they had to compare these predictions with performance at the end of the third week of the course. This is generally a cut-off point. Trainees are either rejected or accepted then for the full 26-week training. The hopeless bricklayer is removed. Intuition might lead one to expect that for all trades practical tests would be equally effective, or ineffective, as predictors. Intuition would be wrong. For the six trades, the correlations between the initial tests scores and performances at the end of the third week ranged from *zero* to a monumental 0.80. In their report, unfortunately, Robertson and Mindel do not specify just how trainees' performances were assessed at the end of the third week. Was it a subjective impression of the instructors? Was there another formal test? Maddeningly, we do not know.

Despite this shortcoming, the idea of trainability testing is extremely interesting because it is much more specific than general-aptitude tests. Trainees could have the chance to do tests for a number of skills or trades. Robertson and Mindel noted that applicants often seemed much more at ease with practical testing than with sitting down to do an examination. Given concern among ethnic groups whose English may be less good, about unfair discrimination, trainability testing seems an idea that is worth developing. It would seem better, though, to add to the number of tasks and to make them increasingly difficult. At the end of week 3, the apprentice bricklayer should be able to lay a wall that does not fall down; by week 20, his wall should not be aesthetically repulsive.

In technical terms, the kinds of tests investigated by Robertson and Mindel have a high face validity. That those who take them seem more comfortable with them also indicates their potential value.

Physiological Testing

The merit of trainability tests is that they are based on something more real than most psychological tests. In their desire to achieve solid results, many psychologists have tried to see how well psychological tests correlate with physiological ones. One reason for this is that physiology seems more real and more basic than psychology. Your pulse-rate is easier to measure than your attitude to — well, anything. Certain psychological theorists have suggested that the main aim of psychology ought to be to catalogue psychological events in such a way that would allow scientists to discover the physiological changes that underlie, and *cause* all mental events. To understand how emotions operate, therefore, one needs very subtle measures not of what a person is feeling, but of what his or her body and brain are doing. A recent controversy that highlights this debate is the one surrounding lie detectors. Those who favour lie detectors believe that when we lie, we experience stress. Stress can be measured physiologically through changes in heart-rate, pulse-rate, sweating, galvanic skin response. Once a base-rate for a particular subject is established, then it is possible to monitor deviations. If a subject deviates wildly when giving a particular answer, he is lying. His physiological fluctuations prove it. Many psychologists deny that lie detectors can be used in this way, but it is a crude example of trying to use physiological measures to validate mental states.

Generally, paper-and-pencil tests do not make much use of physiological measures. An interesting exception is the Telic Dominance Scale. Subjects have a variety of questions and tasks, including supplying biographical data, doing paper-and-pencil questions, and sometimes having their physiological responses monitored. This mixture leads us to put the Telic Dominance Scale among 'Odder Techniques'.

Case Study: The Playful Test

Test tested: Telic Dominance Scale
Example of questions: Choose which of the two you would rather do
Write a short story for fun or compile a short dictionary for financial reward

Form of answer: The choice is yours
Our focus: A rounded test?

Sometimes we do things because we enjoy doing them, while at other times we feel it is essential to do something irrespective of whether we enjoy doing it or not. A pilot for British Airways flies to live; the weekend aviator may slave at the bank all week and live to fly at weekends. Reversal theory — to which the Telic Dominance Scale (TDS) is indissolubly linked — proposes that an individual will interpret means-end relationships in two opposite ways and that there are two stable states. The 'telic' state is where the individual sees himself as pursuing some essential goal, and pleasure is derived from achievement of the goal or anticipation of such an achievement. By contrast, in the 'paratelic' state, the individual does not see himself as pursuing a goal at all, or if a goal is being pursued this is not seen by him as being essential; rather, it is an excuse to perform (most people swim for pleasure, not to train for the Olympic Games). In this state of mind, pleasure derives from the performance of the behaviour itself and from related sensations and feelings. In addition, the telic state is one in which the individual's focus of attention tends to be on the future, whereas in the paratelic state of mind it tends to be focused upon the immediate sensations — on the 'here and now'. The theory has very far-reaching consequences for society. Crime and punishment, pension schemes, long years of education and much else in society assumes that individuals can project themselves into the future and think through the consequences of their current behaviour. Western society tries to make good telic citizens. Is that perverse? From a testing point of view, the TDS is an attempt to devise a very comprehensive test marrying psychology and physiology.

Not An Optimal Theory

According to reversal theory, not only does the individual interpret means-ends relationships in two different ways, but he also interprets the arousal he feels in two opposite ways at different times. Two stable states are postulated. In one of these, the individual attempts to gain as much arousal as possible, high arousal being felt as pleasant ('excitement') and low arousal as unpleasant ('boredom'). In the opposite stable state, the individual attempts to reduce arousal as far as possible: in this case high arousal is felt as unpleasant ('anxiety') and low arousal as pleasant ('relaxation'). It is not the absolute levels of arousal that are seen to be bi-stable, but the way in which arousal is interpreted. The theory of psychological reversals is about 'experience', not behaviour, although there are implications for behaviour, of course. Most previous theories of arousal/motivation assumed on biological, rather than appropriate psychological evidence, a homeostatic model (i.e. there is a single optimal level, not two levels).

For Fun Or Not

The aim of the TDS is to measure the degree of dominance of the telic state over its opposite state, paratelic, for individual respondents. There are three subscales of 14 items each:

Serious-mindedness — the degree to which an individual is oriented towards goals seen as essential or important to himself or herself (or others identified with), physically or psychologically, rather than goals seen as being trivial, arbitrary or inessential.
Planning Orientation — the degree to which an individual plans ahead and organises in pursuit of goals (future orientation), rather than taking things as they come (present orientation). Pleasure is gained from achievement of goals, anticipating goal achievement rather than from immediate behaviour.
Arousal Avoidance — the degree to which an individual avoids situations which generate high arousal and seeks situations in which arousal levels are low.

Validity, Oh Validity

Each item requires the respondent to make a choice between two alternatives which represent a telic (e.g. compile a short dictionary for financial reward) and paratelic (write a short story for fun) choices respectively; 'not sure' responses are scored as half (i.e. midway choice).

As the respondent is asked to make the choice in terms of which alternative he would usually prefer, it is important to show that subjects are responding in terms of their usual rather than current performances. All of the Test-Retest Reliability Studies — covering 6 hours; 6 weeks; 6 months; and 12 months — had reliability coefficients significant at 0.01 level irrespective of time interval.

The most interesting validity study was done by getting 14 subjects to rate themselves at hourly intervals each afternoon on scales which related to the telic/paratelic dimension to see whether the preferences expressed in the TDS represented real preferences in everyday life. Two problems with this method are: (i) if an individual is truly paratelic and solely concerned with present behaviour, would he or she bother, or remember, to complete the rating scales; and (ii) does an 'afternoon response' take adequate account of an individual's bio-rhythm and changes of state? Nevertheless, every effort to test the validity of psychological tests against everyday experience must be highly commended.

An End In Itself

There were two problems with the normative sample of 945 adults consisting of 368 females and 577 males, aged between 21 and 78 (mean age 32 years). All were Open University students who usually work full-time, study part-time, meet constant deadlines, pay for their own fees as well as choosing courses ten months in advance. Murgatroyd does point out the dangers of extrapolating from this highly telic sample to the population as a whole. Next, the survey method was used to gather data, with a response rate of 75 per cent. Non-responders often have characteristics different from responders/volunteers, but how this would skew the data would only be guesswork (i.e. in the telic direction).

In his original assessment, Shelley welcomed the TDS, but warned it was only 'appropriate for the normative sample in which it was standardised'. Many of the questions were middle-class orientated and required a fair degree of literacy. From our current perspective, what is interesting is the way in which further studies tried to validate the TDS by linking internal states to physiological measures. The sophistication of Svebak's work (1980) makes the lie-detector studies stand out as rather crude.

Svebak built on a study by Murgatroyd (1984), who took details from individuals on what they had done yesterday and meant to do tomorrow. Their patterns fell neatly into telic and paratelic clusters. Svebak gave this same sample a game like Space Invaders, but where the player had to drive a car projected on a TV screen.

Fourteen male students participated in the first experiment. The car on the screen was run at double speed and other cars bobbed up to intercept it. The subject had to avoid collisions by shifting the position of his own car with a joy-stick and using his preferred hand. One group was told the purpose of the game was to avoid collisions; the second that if they did not perform very well, their non-preferred hand would get a shock. Each group then received the other condition so that the experimental procedure was counterbalanced (threat and no threat). The threat of an electric shock ought to induce a telic, serious-minded state in subjects.

At the end of both versions of the task, subjects had to complete a questionnaire which asked how difficult, interesting and well-liked the game was. In addition, they also had to state how serious-minded, planning-oriented, and worked-up (aroused) they were during the actual performance.

Sven Svebak (1980) carried out physiological tests during the game as well. EMG (monitors muscle tension) measured in the *passive* forearm, which was the arm not used in the game. This EMG also measured 'physiological gradients'. Fatigue is a problem in any sort of task. Physiological gradients are a control mechanism which compensate for fatigue in the motor systems by gradually increasing muscle tension in passive muscles to keep subjects concentrating on what they are doing.

The differences between the 'no threat of a shock' and 'threat of a shock' (no shocks were ever given) situations were most striking. The threat condition produced more muscle tension (remember this is in the non-playing arm and *not* the playing arm), higher heart-rate and lower skin temperature. There was also an increase in respiratory frequency and amplitude. Two measures of respiration were taken because it is possible for one person to breathe fast and shallowly while another will breathe deeply but slowly. Not only were all differences due solely to the subjects' self-perception of instructions ('Perform well or you'll get a shock'), they also saw themselves as significantly more serious-minded, planning-orientated and worked-up during the threat than during the no-threat condition. However, there were *no* significant differences in perceived difficulty, liking, and interest in the game.

The next experiment had 10 extremely serious-minded and 10 extremely playful subjects — according to scores on the TDS — given by 180 undergraduates. Both extreme groups performed the car-driving game five times at a moderate speed and then once at very high speed. Muscle tension in the non-involved arm was again measured, but Svebak also measured the force or the thrust of the arm that was manipulating the play-stick (active forearm flexor EMG).

The telic subjects performed better (fewer crashes), but again there were no significant differences in perceived liking, difficulty and interest in the game. One of the most interesting findings was that there was very high muscle tension in task-irrelevant muscles (the non-involved arm) in the serious-minded subjects, while there was high phasic task-relevant muscle tension in the playful subjects. In other words, the playful subjects used much more forceful arm movements to shift the play-stick and tended to over-react.

As mastery of the task improved, the muscle tension in the 'unused' arm also reduced (if you are a driver of a real car, compare the tenseness when you were a learner driver to the comparatively relaxed feeling that comes with experience). However, if mastery of the task does not improve, telic subjects do not reduce muscle tension. Svebak explained this last point. During the slow condition, as subjects got more practice, they improved performance. But in the fast condition, cars were bombarded from all angles and at a frenetic pace, confronting subjects with an impossible task. Whereas telic subjects increased muscle tension in their passive forearm (indicating greater concentration and control) paratelic subjects did not. However, as telic subjects showed a steady decline in the force used by their active arm, it is difficult to say whether they were 'controlling the game better' or at the point of giving up a hopeless task. After all, it's only a game to the paratelic subjects, and only when games are taken seriously do people mind losing and not want to go on if it is obvious that they have already lost. Imagine a game of football where one side is losing hopelessly. One of the losing players rushes in to tackle and kicks the ball wildly, not helping his side in winning the game. Another of the losing players may stand watching the ball intently, waiting to make the 'right' move. Although it may sound much better to stand on the touchline 'reviewing the situation', it will not do any good if the game is over before the player moves at all. This last point is speculation about differences between extreme telic and extreme paratelic people, but it does emphasise that one does not always know much about motivation simply by observing people's behaviour. There has been a stereotype that those suffering from 'nervous tension' are merely lazy malingerers who enjoy lolling around doing nothing. If we replace 'nervous' with 'muscle tension' then Svebak's results does give some of these people credibility. The more hopeless the car-driving game became, the less the telic subjects *appeared* to respond, but the more tense and wound-up they got. The paratelic subjects did not get tense and wound up, although they might have appeared (from their forceful use of the play-stick) to be the dogged, never-say-die perseverers. The theory of psychological reversals is definitely a theory of the future in more ways than one. It is also one linked to a test that is more imaginative in its implications than most.

Case Study: Do-it-yourself Testing

Test tested: Behaviorpak
Example of questions: A variety, including vocational preference questions, attitude scales and personality questions
Form of answer: Various
Our focus: Testing oneself

For all their novelty, both trainability testing and the TDS are conventional. Experts give them to subjects and experts score them. Behaviorpak breaks new ground in that it is designed to be used, and scored, by those who take it. Unlike the pop quizzes in the media, Behaviorpak is very serious. It hails from California, mecca of new therapies. If the 1970s were the 'Me' decade, Los Angeles was Self City. Encounter groups flourished and begat new encounter groups. The growing 'growth' movement helped turn books like *Passages* (Sheehey 1979) into best sellers. Behaviorpak is a product of that environment and a radical enterprise. It proclaims that subjects have nothing to lose but their roles. They no longer need be experimental fodder for the psychologist. They can study themselves, at their own time, at their own pace, using well-researched materials. Do-it-yourself testing has its limits. Potential employers may be sceptical of your claims to have shone on those vocational tests which prove you should take over IBM. They might want more than your word for it.

The Guidepak (which offers the user a guide to the rest of the material) contains the California Psychological Inventory and the Strong Campbell Interest Inventory. Buyers also receive an explanatory manual, answer sheets and return envelopes. The material is scored by computer and returned to the client together with a narrative report, an interest profile and a workbook containing instructions for interpreting the results.

The tests used are, admittedly, conventional. The California Personality Inventory is meant to assess leadership, initiative, self-control, achievement urge and accuracy. The Strong Campbell

Inventory compares the client's interests with those of people in 83 other professions. It should indicate what kind of work an individual ought to be happy pursuing. The Guidepak relies heavily on a category of six 'general occupational themes'. It is against these typical profiles that people have to judge their own likes and dislikes. Most of the labels are self-explanatory.

R-Theme, or Realist People, are rugged, aggressive, physically strong, politically conventional and sometimes find it hard to express themselves verbally. They like jobs such as car mechanic, air traffic controller, surveyor, farmer or electrician.

I-Theme, or Investigative People, are abstract problem-solvers who shy away from people. They tend to choose scientific jobs like geologist, but show few leadership skills. They are typically analytical, critical, curious, introverted, precise, rational or reserved. They are more interested in things than people.

A-Theme, or Artistic People, are emotional, sensitive, individualistic and, as the label suggests, want to work in the arts or media. They are complicated, disorganised, idealistic, impractical and non-conforming. They do not want jobs that require brute strength!

S-Theme people are social. They like being in social situations, caring for others and often seek attention. They don't like working with their hands. They prefer jobs like teaching, being a social worker, a therapist or, even, a priest. They often lack mechanical skills and scientific ability. They are often convincing, friendly, generous, understanding and cheerful. They can be high achievers and lead well.

E-Theme, or Enterprising People, are good with words, have energy, enthusiasm and self-confidence. They are ambitious, impulsive, optimistic, pleasure-seeking and self-confident. They talk well and enjoy power and money, but they avoid precise work. They can do well as leaders, like Social People.

C-Theme or, Conventional People, usually like structure, do well in large organisations and avoid intense relationships. They are not natural leaders; rather, they sound like the proverbial faceless bureaucrat. They are cautious, conscientious, obedient, inhibited, persistent, and have what might be derided as the soul of a bank clerk. They do like being bank clerks or stenographers or tax inspectors. They dislike using physical skills.

An Administrative Index in the Guidepak checks that clients have not skipped too many questions. The Strong Campbell Interest

Inventory has seven parts, and requires subjects to answer either with a simple 'Yes/No' or 'Like-Indifferent-Dislike'. Part 1 asks whether people have a 'preference or not' for 131 occupations; Part 2 examines school subjects they liked; Part 3 asks how they enjoy spending time; Part 4 asks what amusements they go in for, wearing the latest fashions or turning out for the National Guard; Part 5 asks about the kinds of people they like to meet on a day-to-day basis; Part 6 asks subjects to make a choice between two activities such as dealing with things or dealing with people. The last part is self-descriptive, where you endorse or not such things as whether you have, or lack, patience when teaching others.

The 23 Basic Interest Scales are grouped according to the six general themes, and the results indicate the degree to which the 'like' activities are related to the 23 scales ('very high' to 'very low'). There is an imbalance between these 23 scales and the six themes because Realistic incorporates agriculture, nature, adventure, military activities and mechanical activities, while Conventional has only one: office practices. The themes are not mutually exclusive either, because a psychologist is investigative, artistic and social, but a librarian is merely artistic.

Occupational Scales list 166 specific occupations, and the computer scores show how close your interests are to those who actually do these various jobs. The Workbook points out that these scores are different from the scores on the other two scales. With General Occupational Themes and Basic Interest Scales, the comparison is with 'people in general', but on this last scale the comparison is to people with the specific jobs listed. These Occupational Scales also have different norms for males and females.

The Guidepak Workbook gives detailed instructions about how to combine the various scores and develop an individual profile. The last part of the booklet contains a section on preparing a résumé (*curriculum vitae*), and lists the questions that are likely to be asked at a job interview.

Overall, the Guidepak seems good value for money, but as the heading of the press release makes obvious ('A Self-Help Career Counselling Package'), it is aimed mainly at those who wish to enter the professions and would be of little use to the unqualified school leaver or the redundant factory worker. However, if the current Guidepak is successful, perhaps Behaviordyne will be encouraged to concentrate on the bottom end of the employment/unemployment market taking into account Kasl (1980);

Overall, it would appear that lower skilled industrial workers have a rather tenuous attachment to the work-role. They would continue working in the absence of financial needs, not because of any intrinsic satisfaction in work, but because society has not provided any meaningful alternatives.

There is evidence that some tests are less reliable when self-administered, but the Behaviorpak appears to be the first concerted attempt to develop a self-testing package. It marks an important step forward.

Case Study: How Do You Rate Charisma?

Test tested: Affective Communication Test
Example of questions: (i) Have you ever taken part in an acting class?
(ii) Ratings of expressive behaviour by friends
Form of answer: To (i) yes or no
(ii) 9-point scale
Our focus: An Unusual Topic

Most tests attempt to assess 'useful' traits in the individual. Scores on IQ and aptitude tests purport to reveal how well one will do in certain jobs. Even an esoteric test like the Intercollegiate Basketball Instrument tries to see how much teamwork basketball players are likely to reveal and how that will make them play. But some qualities would seem to defy paper-and-pencil testing. Charisma is one, though not quite a test of charisma, the Affective Communication Test (ACT) comes close to it. We include it among odder techniques for two reasons. First, it shows how testing can be applied to 'offbeat' aspects of personality; secondly, it has some impressive attempts at validation.

Charismatic men and women seem to be able to use non-verbal cues to move, lead and inspire others for good or evil. Churchill delivered his beautiful speeches with wit and passion. Harold Macmillan even at 90 has not lost the Supermac touch which allowed him to control the House of Commons. Hitler, too, had charisma because he could hold his audiences spell-bound even when mouthing nothing but evil rubbish. Psychologists argue that one aspect of charisma is expressiveness. Churchill, Hitler, De Gaulle, Charlie Chaplin could all mesmerise audiences and make them pay attention to the slightest quiver in the voice or movement in the moustache. Their personalities 'expressed' themselves not just verbally. Non-verbal cues function mostly without our being aware of them. If we see someone we fancy, for instance, our pupils get larger, but we aren't aware of it and can't control it. In devising the ACT, Friedman and his co-authors (1980) admitted this problem, but argued that most people receive feedback when they interact with others. It seemed reasonable to suppose, therefore, that people knew something about judging expressiveness in others.

As a first step, Friedman and his colleagues got a number of psychologists and psychology students to devise self-report items they thought would measure expressiveness. Some were weeded out, leaving 46 items. A self-report questionnaire was devised in a number of different forms so that the order in which items were presented was counterbalanced. Half the items were worded so that you had to answer 'no' to indicate expressiveness. As a result, some obvious pitfalls were avoided. From the 46 items, they refined the questionnaire to a short, 13-item scale.

The final items used a scale on which subjects could say how true a statement was about them from +4 to −4. To score the scale, first 5 was added to every score to eliminate negative numbers and so an answer of −4 became 1. Then, the scores for the six items where a 'no' indicated expressiveness were reversed. So if you said −4 to whether you liked making speeches, that became 9, since a liking for speechifying indicated expressiveness. All this jiggling was sensible, and the only question that seemed confusing was Question 11: 'I am terrible at pantomime as in games like charades'. This would not be very inteligible for those who did not know what charades were.

Friedman warned that the ACT was developed on, and expected to be used by, college students. 'Given no evidence that the ACT is not valid with other populations, researchers should not refrain from the cautious use of the ACT with other groups of people'. Beware the double negative, beware making too dogmatic use of the ACT with non-collegiates!

The first validity study was done through ratings by friends. Each of the 68 undergraduates who completed the ACT was given three rating forms with stamped envelopes and instructed to distribute the forms to three friends. The form asked the friend to complete the ratings in private and mail them directly back to the experimenter.

The rating form was also had 9-point scales on which the friend judged the extent to which he or she is expressive with face, with body and with voice. A fourth item asked the friend to rate whether he or she would make a good actor. The four questions were positively intercorrelated. At least one rating form was returned for 61 of the 68 subjects; 56 subjects had two or three forms returned. The correlation between ACT scores and ratings by friends was 0.39. The ACT also turned out to be internally consistent and its test/re-test reliability was good.

Nine of the 13 items used related to activities.

Question 1: lecturing: Had they volunteered or been asked to give a lecture?
Question 2: political charisma: Had they ever been an elected official of any organisation?
Question 3: theatrical experience: Had they ever had a major part in a stage play or show?
Question 4: Had they ever taken an acting class?
Question 5: To what extent had they been involved in acting or drama? (on a 9-point scale from 'never' to 'constantly involved').
Question 6: social interaction in occupation: Did their present work involve working with and influencing people?
Question 7: What job did they plan to do after leaving college?
Question 8: salespersons: Had they worked as a salesperson whose job it was to convince people to buy something?
Question 9: labworkers: it was thought that students who spend a lot of time in scientific laboratories or interacting with a computer would tend to be relatively low on expressiveness.

Expressiveness, as measured by the ACT, was significantly related to lecturing, political charisma, stage acting, acting class, acting experience, occupation, future occupation and sales, but no association was found with time spent working in scientific laboratories.

Expressive people should interact with lots of people or have many followers. In a family-practice clinic setting where each doctor is responsible for certain families, the number of patients seen by a doctor can be considered a measure of the doctor's popularity — accepting that there may be other reasons too. Twenty-five family-practice doctors were given the ACT. Each doctor's patient load was measured as the sum over six months of the number of patient visits per month, corrected by the number of days assigned to clinic work.

The correlation between the ACT and popularity (patient visits) was 0.52 (0.01 significant).

Friedman makes a strong case that expressiveness is about communication rather than traits or needs, but he does correlate the ACT with some of the traditional personality measures in the quest for validation and clarification. The Personality Research Form showed that individuals scoring highly on the ACT also were high on exhibition and tended to be affiliative, dominant, somewhat achieving, playful, and not socially proper. ACT scores were not related to impulsivity. ACT and extraversion (Eysenck's EPQ) were positively correlated, but ACT and neuroticism were slightly negatively correlated. Expressiveness does not seem to be due to emotional responsibility. There was a zero correlation with the lie scale.

Since charisma involves pleasing people, scores were correlated with the Marlowe-Crowne Social Desirability Scale, and the ACT does contain a small element of social desirability. Machiavellianism — the tendency to manipulate others for selfish reasons — is not socially desirable, but there may seem a parallel between expressiveness and the confidence trickster. The correlation between ACT and Machiavellianism was 0.08, implying no relationship between the two.

On Rotter's Internal-external locus of control — an individual's belief that he or she is or is not master of his or her own fate — there was a tendency for individuals with an internal locus of control to be more expressive. Additionally, there was also a tendency for individuals with a high self-esteem — as measured by Coopersmith's Self-Esteem Scale — to be more expressive.

Not the Right Expression

The paper-and-pencil Self-Monitoring Scale attempts to distinguish people who are concerned with how socially appropriate their emotional behaviours are, and whether they can tell what behaviours are appropriate in a social situation, as well as expressing appropriate responses and concealing inappropriate feelings. A big-mouthed bore might be low in self-monitoring but high in expressiveness, while a shy person could be sensitive to what he or she does and what others think but unable to communicate effectively. In one sample there was a very small positive correlation between ACT and self-monitoring, but non-significant correlations in another. This is consistent with the finding on the Personality Research Form where expressive people were not 'socially proper'. It seems that 'propriety' can be distinguished from 'genuineness'. Expressive people may be able to be enthusiastic but uncontrolled, express their feelings comfortably, effectively and with disregard for social conventions.

The last validity study was particularly ingenious, and interesting sex differences emerged. Subjects were to imagine that they were communicating an emotion to another person and to then try to express that emotion while being filmed on videotape. As non-verbal expression was the main interest, the verbal message was held constant. On some trials the subjects tried to communicate emotion while saying one of two verbally neutral sentences: 'I haven't seen you for a while' and 'Do you really want to do this?'. On other trials the subjects tried to express emotion while saying part of the alphabet. Seven categories of emotion were used: happiness, sadness, anger, disgust, surprise, fear and neutral. The videotape was divided into segments, and judges were instructed to decide which of the seven emotions the person on the videotape was expressing.

If, as implied by previous results, the ACT is measuring emotional expressiveness rather than self-control, people low on the ACT should score high on expressing neutral emotions since they are generally more neutral. But highly expressive people will show their feelings even when asked to be neutral. This was so: expressive people had a relatively difficult time appearing neutral. Overall, the ACT is positively correlated with acting ability, but the effects are very small.

For women, a strong relationship, even stronger than expected, emerged between acting ability and the ACT, but for males the correlation was either zero or even slightly negative. The major question as to whether expressiveness is related to the ability to show false emotion must, for the present, be 'yes' for females but apparently 'no' for males.

Taking the results as a whole, it seems that expressiveness is not synonymous with acting ability, and those who make the routine, socially acceptable, stereotypical response to a social situation are expressing nothing and impressing nobody. Expressiveness is more closely related to exciting others rather than manipulating others: dictators don't have to have charisma. An incidental finding was that judging sessions — judges were all given the ACT — were heavily influenced by the feelings (positive or negative) of the high ACT person in the group. This has tremendous implications for the whole of society. What effect could one juror have upon a verdict that is supposedly a collective decision? When 'expectancy' effects on a student's performance are found — and, sometimes, not found — is it due to the teacher's charisma rather than to the student's abilities?

In assessing the ACT, Friedman and his co-authors have been ingenious and cautious. The ACT is only a start in capturing that elusive quality we call expressiveness or charisma. The extravert may be the Aries fiery type, but what of the Brando-like type who sits, smoulders and conquers. It's not what you do but the way that you do it that captures attention.

Odd Conclusions

The collection of case studies in this chapter have been deliberately chosen to highlight areas where testing has had some interesting new ideas. Do-it-yourself testing, testing on the job to see how well trainees learn, and testing for unlikely attributes such as charisma do not resolve many of the problems of testing we have focused on; but these are all examples that show what can be done if you don't get too obsessed with classic modes of testing.

9 POPULAR TESTING

All the tests examined in this book so far have been serious psychological efforts. For all their deficiencies, much research went into their creation, and we presume that few of them were made up in an afternoon. In addition to these academic tests, each year also sees the publication of many popular tests in books, newspapers and magazines. One of the authors of this critique has, in his own time, provided tests of 'How Ambitious Are You?' for glossy magazines and a St Valentine's Day quiz for *The Sun*. The latter, predictably, asked 'How Romantic Are You?'. Since such 'fun' tests are often published, it seemed interesting to add to this study of serious testing by studying the way the media use tests.

Most of the data in this chapter come from a survey of the British media published between 20 November and 15 December 1984. We do not claim that this survey is a complete analysis of everything that was published, but we did read all the national daily papers, all the Sunday national papers, a large selection of mass-market and special-interest magazines. We made no attempt to test for tests on the radio and television. Our survey of the press was affected by two special factors. First, since the period was close to Christmas many magazines did run quizzes especially in the issues published around 15 December. Most of these quizzes were not psychological tests but tests of general, or esoteric, knowledge. The one exception to this was a quiz in *My Weekly* 'the magazine for women everywhere', which asked: 'Are You Coping with the Festive Season?'. The second special factor was the publication of two books of popular testing. One by Nathanson, *The Book of Tests*, included some hundred tests that covered everything from intelligence and creativity to how snobbish you were. Rather more glossy was de Carlo's *Psychological Games* (1984), which included some of the best-laid-out IQ tests we have ever seen. De Carlo had much fun organising questions about distorted shapes to tease out the level of intelligence of its consumers. Both these books fall into a well-established tradition of books of tests for the lay audience. One of the first popular successes of Hans Eysenck was his do-it-yourself guide *Know Your Own IQ*, and in the 1940s Penguin issued a slim volume of psychological tests which offered the reader a complete kit of measures of attitudes and aptitudes. The publication of two books of popular tests within a month of each other shows, if nothing else, that publishers think there is a market for them.

Our analysis of the press suggests they were right. Despite the current craze for bingo, portfolio and other newspaper competitions, quizzes continue to be a regular feature of two kinds of papers — the down-market tabloids and the middle-range Sunday papers. Tests which are linked to health issues such as 'What would motivate you to jog?' surface even in the quality press.

During the period surveyed we found the following tests in national papers:

23 November: *Daily Star* 'Are You a Show Off?'
26 November: *Daily Star* 'How To Be a Perfect Party Person'
3 December: *The Sun* '6 questions from the new game, 'Trivial Pursuit''
4 December: *The Sun* 'Six more such trivial questions'
Daily Star 'What Do You Know About Princess Di?'
5 December: *Daily Express* 'What Do You Know about American Express?'
9 December: The *Mail on Sunday* 'How Big a Snob Are You?'
9 December: *Sunday Times* 'Do You Seriously Want to be Slim?'

These tests ranged from a few questions like the *Daily Star*'s asking whether you are a show-off to quite detailed tests like the *Sunday Times*, which certainly would claim to have some form of validity. The questions in the *Daily Star*'s test were all too obvious. They included; 'Has a friend ever told you to stop showing off?', 'When you are playing a team game, are you usually looking for a chance to show off?' There were only six questions in all. There was no warning to readers not to take the test too seriously.

In introducing its test on 'How Big A Snob Are You?', the *Mail on Sunday* adopted a middle-of-the-road posture. It warned: 'Although this test is only a bit of fun, it might get under your skin'. More bizarrely, the paper then added: 'Sweeping generalisations and valued judgements about people are actually based on *your* personal tastes. The basis for all casual criticism is the total sum of your own personal conditioning, your parents, friends, education, social encounters, etc. . . . .'.

If you did turn out to be a big snob, then that was OK since it was your taste. The other interesting thing about the introduction was its casual assumption that readers would understand psychologically complex terms like *conditioning* without any explanation.

The *Sunday Times* offered readers the most heavyweight of tests. It was part of a three-page feature on health and slimming. The paper emphasised the credentials of the test deviser, Dr Glenn Wilson of the Institute of Psychiatry. Wilson had collaborated with the *Sunday Times* medical correspondent, Dr Oliver Gillie, in creating it. Gillie is as aware of the pitfalls of psychological tests as any other commentator in Britain since he was instrumental in exposing Sir Cyril Burt. The test stemmed from a survey that the *Sunday Times* did when it invited readers to write in about their experiences of eating and slimming, or failing to slim. Two thousand readers wrote in, and Wilson factor-analysed their answers. Despite its concern to be serious, the article never once mentioned the possibility that the eating habits of those who write to newspapers about their eating habits might differ importantly from eating habits of the rest of the population that prefers to keep quiet about them. Wilson extracted different kinds of eaters. There were the 'Gourmet', the 'Binger', the 'Emotional Eater' and the 'Sugar Sweetie'. More mind-breaking analysis suggested to Wilson that those most liable to be overweight were the 'Lazybones', the 'Emotional Eater', 'Nibbler' and 'Guzzler'. There is nothing wrong, of course, in scientific work using entertaining names; still, the emphasis on these jolly names does warn perhaps that the test ought to be treated with a measure of caution. Wilson found that laziness was an important factor in overweight. Heavy men were three times more likely to agree with the statement 'I'd get a taxi home rather than take a 15-minute walk' than were thin men. With this background well explained, the *Sunday Times* went on to offer a rather short 12-item quiz, 'Do you seriously want to be slim?'. Unlike the *Mail*, which had warned that their test was both a bit of fun, and actually revealing, the *Sunday Times* was convinced of the value of its test. The scoring grid divided readers into those who had *abandoned*, those *set in your ways*, those *on course* and decadent *backsliders* who would soon balloon grotesquely if not forced back on the thin and narrow by the *Sunday Times*.

As we have argued, the questions in the *Daily Star*'s show-off test were so transparent as to be hard to take seriously. Most of the other tests in the daily papers were a mixture of attitude test and information test. The *Daily Express* test on the American Express card had two questions about attitudes to credit; the *Daily Star*'s interrogation about Princess Diana also asked about attitudes to Princess Diana, but these were minor features. What was really being tested was if the reader remembered the day Prince Charles and Princess Diana had had their first date and what dress she wore on what occasion. The *Daily Star* nicely spoofed this form of quiz with their own 'Do You Know Dallas from Dynasty?'. This was published on 28 November and constructed by a learned professor of soapology! The paper also used this format at times to broaden their readers' horizons with one improbable quiz on what they knew about arranged marriages. For no clear reason, the *Daily Star* was the only tabloid to put such an emphasis on publishing tests that were either straight personality tests of a mixture of informational and attitude tests. *The Sun* carried almost no such tests nor did the *Daily Mirror*. One possible reason is that bingo and nudes have replaced them.

The problems that popular tests present differ in many ways from the more professional ones. Both the *Mail on Sunday* and the *Sunday Times* sacrifice much for entertainment value. Nearly all the questions are set in a cheery way as one might expect of a measure aimed at 'Lazybones' or the 'Sugar Sweetie'. The *Sunday Times*, for example, starts off with a statement to which there are four possible responses:

We'll start early in the morning and you have a day off; hooray, no need to get up.

1. I'll probably have a lie in.
2. I'll still get up at my usual time (more or less).
3. I'm quite likely to skip breakfast.
4. I'm likely to have breakfast whatever time I get up.

It all sounds jolly-hooray. However, the questions are full of contradictions. What is getting up at my usual time *more or less*? To the diabolically idle, and the self-deceiving 'more or less' could be two hours later. Is there a difference between 8 and 10? To the exercising classes, two hours abed is almost certainly a deliciously decadent lie-in. Statement 3 is also confusing. The really lazy who don't get up till two certainly skip breakfast but have lunch the moment they rise.

Question 3 is also rampant with jollity. 'The free morning leaves plenty of time for a healthy walk jog or brisk walk but, oh dear, it's raining.' Alternatives are:

(a) Out with the trusty brolly and waterproofs.
(b) It's more sensible to wait till it clears up.

The adjective, *healthy* for jog suggests that to be a socially desirable answer, while 'oh dear' belongs to that fake cheeriness of which 'hooray' and the 'trusty brolly' are other signs.

Question 10 also leaves no doubt as to what is the right answer. It says: 'You are rescued by a dinner invitation which is too good to decline; you eat a huge and excellent meal.' The options facing the unexpected guest are:

(a) 'I'd write it off, accepting that an occasional aberration is not the end of the world.'
(b) 'I'd make sure I ate lightly at the next meal to compensate.'

The word *aberration* suggests that alternative (a) is that of the wicked glutton, while rounding off alternative (b) with 'to compensate' hints that this is the way the conscientious slimmers prove themselves.

Such flaws in the design of questions would matter less if the test did not take itself quite so seriously. It offers those who take it a scoring grid where choosing alternative (a) on question 10 marks you out as *abandoned*, while alternative (b) is not even *on course* but *set in your ways*. There is no answer the motivated slimmer could give to Question 10. We can only presume he never gets invited to dinner because he refused everything other than raw cabbage without salad dressing. One of the best-respected nutrition experts, however, Gaylord Heuser, used to advise those who followed his diets that if they had a lapse, they ought to compensate at the next meal. For him, that was more than acceptable. Question 10 is full of assumptions which wouldn't matter in a 'fun' quiz, but do matter in one that aspires to be authoritative.

The whole of the *Sunday Times* test suggests, in fact, that it is very difficult for a popular test to achieve the minimum standards one would expect of a serious test. Far more is wrong with the *Mail on*

Sunday test, which admits it is only a bit of fun though with a dash of insight. The snobbish test demands a vast amount of specialised knowledge, but also assumes that its authors are proper arbiters of what is, and is not, snobbish behaviour. The authority they have for this is never disclosed.

Question 1 commits more psychometric mistakes per word than most. It asks: 'Have you ever been contemptuous of any of the following?' Note the words *been* and *ever*. We are not sure whether we are being asked if we ever did anything to express our contempt, or whether we merely felt contemptuous. For example, I might think that Marks and Spencers is a dowdy shop for the middle classes because I couldn't find the trousers I wanted there and bought a different pair instead. On the other hand, my contempt might determine my behaviour and I would refuse to visit Marks and Spencers. Arguably, most people feel the occasional twinge of contempt for many things. Question 1, if answered truthfully, requires us to tick any of the following if just once in a lifetime, for a fleeting instant, we didn't like it. To compound matters, the question then lists 15 items. A tick against any of these gives you a score of 2 on the snobbishness scale so you can score a total of 30 snob points.

The questions reveal as much about the authors of the test as anything else. The 15 items that follow are: (our comments in italics and vitriol)

Music centres:
'Spitting Image': *Does everyone know it is a TV show?*
Neasden: *Do they mean the real place or the satirised place as in* Private Eye?
Private Eye: *Can you hold Neasden and* Private Eye *in contempt, or do different kinds of snobs sneer at* Private Eye's *Neasden and the real Neasden?*
Artificial Fibres: *misread first time as a kind of wholefood.*
Effete southerners:
The 3-2-1 TV programme: *Are those who have never heard of it less snobbish or more snobbish?*
Heavy metal music:
Macrobiotics:
Marks and Spencers:
Digital watches:
Polish film directors: *There are intellectual snobs who adore any*

Polish film, particularly those they don't understand.
Computer dating:
Ballroom dancing:
'Love is . . .'
The Ecology Party: *Ecologists have their own snobbisms.*

The test requires much specialised knowledge. There are also people who we might regard as snobbish who are besotted by The Ecology Party, macrobiotics, Polish films and heavy metal music. The question is so riddled with the authors' assumptions that it passes nicely as fun but not as much else.

Question 5 asks subjects about their attitudes to cults and whether they are (i) exciting, vital and new; (ii) mindless trendiness; (iii) significant social movements and (iv) pitiful. For some reason (iii) scores a zero, even though it could again be argued that one species of snobs, the supreme intellectual pseud, sees them as significantly revealing of contemporary contradictions! Question 13 asks which of the following is most offensive at a party (i) name-dropping; (ii) bad dancing, (iii) ugly people and (iv) enforced party games. The test tells us that to despise 'ugly people' is the most snobbish! It may well be the most cruel, but that is not the same thing. Our proper snob *sine nobilitate magno* would despise name-dropping far more, and has never been at any gathering where there are enforced party games other than roulette for high stakes. We deem the 'How Big a Snob' a test as lamentably inferior and fit only for the lowest classes. Its only redeeming quality is that it does not take itself too seriously.

Women's Magazines and Health

The *Sunday Times*, the *Mail on Sunday* and the *Daily Star* are not specialised media. We surveyed 17 women's and health magazines and found that four of them carried quizzes and tests. One in *Slimming* was essentially an information test asking how much readers knew about what made a balanced diet. The more interesting quizzes were in *Woman*, *My Weekly* and *Company*. The trendy magazine *Cosmopolitan* also carried a kind of quiz about how to behave if you went away for a weekend with a lover during the Christmas season. It was not meant as a personality quiz of any kind but a sort of amusing feature on customs of our times, so we did not analyse it any further.

The most seasonal of the women's media tests was *My Weekly*'s 'Are You Coping with the Festive Season?'. It has twelve questions aimed at finding out how one would cope with such crises as forgetting the stuffing for the turkey, seeing 'across a teeming shop, exactly the gift your partner would love', and the Christmas tree falling down and spattering the turkey with pine needles. Each question had four options. Without the stuffing you could:

(a) Phone friends to see if they had any to spare. When they didn't, you served the meal anyway, apologising for the lack of stuffing and making jokes about how silly you were to forget it anyway.
(b) Worry about it vaguely at the time, but things were so hectic that come mealtime, you served up the goodies and quite forgot you'd forgotten to buy the stuffing anyway. There's so much to eat nobody notices anyway. It made you wonder what other things you could forget. Wouldn't it make life easier?
(c) Think there may be an abandoned half pound of sausages at the bottom of the freezer. Perhaps you could skin them and mash them up for meat for the stuffing. But you forgot to look for them.

One interesting aspect of the *My Weekly* quiz is that it offers some of the most comprehensive descriptions of reactions we have come across in any testing. There are many reactions you could have other than (a), (b) or (c) like blaming your husband/son for the disaster. But there is something original in the long sequence of realistic behaviours offered as options. The answers to what to do if your child wanted a pony and the other questions described were all as lengthy. The test was scored so that all those who picked mostly (a) or (b) or (c) were deemed to have different coping strategies. All the options were flattering. You were either a 'drift-along sort of "coper"' or (b) 'one of those enviable people who breeze through life' or (c) 'wise about Xmas' or (d) 'very efficient'. No one was a pathological wreck. Unlike the snob test (where it's not glamorous to be a snob) *My Weekly* did not condemn any of its readers as noncopers. The psychological test becomes, in effect, a way of reassuring people.

A similar process could be seen in the *Woman* feature, 'Personality Posers'. This consisted of five different tests which were described as 'intriguing'. The first was a test of numerology. Readers had to write down their dates of birth. Assume that it was 13/12/1944. You added each of the numbers $1+3+1+2+4+4+1+9 = 25$. You then added the two digits of the answer to produce 6. Six was then your number and *Woman* provided a short character profile for each number. They used a star, Mick Jagger, to illustrate how the test worked. Jagger's date of birth was 26/7/1943 so that his number was 32. This made him, according to the personality profile, typical of those who are 3+2, i.e. 5. *Woman* said:

> Number 5. What a capacity for giving you have — you often give of your money, talents and your affections and ask little in return. You're the first to fall for a hard luck story, and your extraordinary sense of humour can land you in hot water . . . You are a very friendly and cheerful personality and there are a lot of ways to your heart.

Others in the personality profile were different, but none of them were bad. Number 3, for example, wanted lots of friends, was an idealist and 'your intuition is excellent and you might be psychic'. As for Number 8, 'you are luxury-loving and with a terrific sense of fun but you do like a stable love life'. Number 9 appears to let his head rule his heart, but watch out, 'underneath there's a lot of sensuality once you let go'.

The other series tests in the feature were an animal test, a doodle test and a bumps test. There may be no truth in phrenology, but there is certainly plenty of stamina. In the animal test, readers had to choose three animals that were their favourites. The characteristics of the first animal revealed 'what you would like to be'; those of the second 'what you thought others see you as'; those of the third 'what you were really like'. The feature gave no rationale for any of this nor any guidance on what different animals signified. If I chose lion, bear and owl, presumably one wanted to be strong, was perceived as cuddly and, in reality, was wise! The bumps mentioned were, again, reassuring. A high forehead meant brains; other bumps meant talent at love or creativity. There were no bumps which indicated you were a devious half-wit with the sensitivity of a hyena. Even as sheer entertainment, the *Woman* feature was spectacularly second rate.

A much more serious feature appeared in *Company*. It consisted of four tests from Nathanson's *Book of Tests*. One was a simple vocabulary test giving one four and a-half minutes to say which of our words was closest in meaning to a given word. The feature argued that vocabulary was a mark of intelligence. In fact, of course, it is only a mark of verbal intelligence. A second test was just a list of things that annoyed you. They included not being listened to, loud noises, being in a room with the TV being on, people being late for appointment. There were 45 items in all, and subjects had to tick each one that made them annoyed. The analysis of the test said that those who had ticked less than 10 items did not easily get annoyed, while those who ticked more than 20 items did get annoyed perhaps a shade too easily. It advised they should discuss with their partners things that annoyed them too much. We were rather annoyed by this annoying test.

The third test was again a simple test. It asked if you were eating the wrong kinds of foods. It listed 45 foods from avocados to not, alas, zabaglione, but to roast beef. Subjects had to tick which of these foods they ate more than three times a week. A scoring chart then divided the foods into those that were acid and those that were alkali. Nuts, meat, fish and eggs especially were acid. Leading nutritionists, we were assured, said that a healthy diet was 20 per cent acid and 80 per cent alkali as this reflected the acid/alkali balance in the body. If one ate too many of the acid foods one's diet was faulty. Since the test gave a chart mentioning this next to the actual list of foods readers had to tick, any worried reader could quickly adjust his or her memory and tick less of the 'bad' foods. Assuming that the magazine wanted readers to learn something about their eating habits, the lay-out sabotaged any such hopes. If you see the 'right' answers while you do the questions, you are likely to fiddle your responses a little to come out as a healthy eater.

The fourth test was aimed at aspiring executives and titled 'Would You Make a Manager?'. It began with a claim for authority. The test was based on one developed by the University of Southern California to help select good managers. Readers were given a series of statements like:

Money talks
The race is always to the swift
Trust men but not too much

Readers then had to indicate whether they usually agreed, always agreed, usually disagreed, usually always disagreed! If you usually always disagree with the statement, does that mean that you sometimes (i.e. unusually for you) disagreed? The test then gave readers a series of boxes in which to mark their responses. They then had to match their responses with the 'correct' ones for the good manager. The test had the merit of being surprising. The good manager did not agree that money talked or that the race was always to the swift. In summing up the test, *Company* noted:

> In some cases, the answers are what you might expect. The manager tends to always agree with the following:
>
> Discontent is the first step in progress
> He who hesitates is lost
> Nothing under the sun is accidental
>
> and always usually to disagree with the following:
>
> What will be, will be
> Everyone finds fault with his own trade
>
> But, rather more surprisingly, good managers disagree also with the following:
>
> Life is a battle
> Every man has his price
> There is nothing better than being on the safe side.

The test is surprising — which is a merit — though *Company* do not provide either a rationale for its findings or information as to whether it differentiates managers from non-managers or good managers from bad managers. We do not also know what managing here refers to — a middle job in a competitive firm like IBM or running the local fish and chip shop or its Californian equivalent. Still, the test does at least make one wonder when it transpires that managers agree with 'easy come, easy go'. If we were running a highly competitive business we might not wish to hire those who believed that, however good the studies to back it up.

This survey of personality testing in the media leads to four observations. First, the use of tests in the media is relatively frequent, but it is limited to certain kinds of media and certain kinds of issues. Almost all the tests we found were in women's magazines. Even the *Mail on Sunday* feature appeared in *Femail*, a part of the paper aimed at women readers. The one exception was the *Sunday Times* test. This reflected, however, fashionable concern with health and exercise issues. *Slimming*, the acid/alkali test and the *Sunday Times*, one and all argue that the media see tests as a useful way of putting over information about good eating habits.

The second fact to emerge is that the standards of test used are deplorable. There are almost no *caveats* about not taking tests too seriously. The most basic issues of test design are ignored so that questions do not alternate 'yes/no' answers. In some cases the right answers are given on the same page and not even upside down, so that readers can't use the tests properly even given their limits. You can see what you are supposed to say. The *Mail on Sunday* ran the answers to the snob test on a different page, but otherwise there was no attempt to conceal the results. The preambles to tests often lay claim to much authority, but usually give not the slightest reference to work on which it is based nor the cautions the original test designers pointed to.

Thirdly, there is a growing trend to informational or 'puzzle' testing. What is being tested is not attitudes or personality but knowledge. Someone who had read a good diet book would be able to pass the acid/alkali test with flying colours. This trend to informational testing may well be due to the fact that the media see tests as an easy way of passing on knowledge. You inform readers without it being too heavy or too preachy.

Finally, in the more down-market media, tests seem to be used to reassure readers. There are never any truly negative options. It would have been novel if the *My Weekly* test, for example, had included behaviours which suggested that people hated Christmas and really could not cope with the pressures. Since there is evidence of an increase in domestic tensions and disputes over all holidays, there would have been good reasons for including some such items. They could have warned readers on what stressful situations to guard against. But, we suppose, that was thought of as too risky.

It is a pity that the media tests are so poor. We have argued throughout that one reason why psychology is interested in tests is that people do like to find out about themselves. There is no reason why popular media should not have useful tests with interesting questions, using basic principles of test design and scoring guides that have some meaning. Our survey showed that in over a month we could not find one such example. That in turn shows that while our culture is full of psychology and psychologese — words like neurosis, complex and insight certainly abound in women's magazines — the media do not really bother to provide their readers with tests that begin to pass muster.

10 PLAYFUL CRITERIA

We have so far avoided giving psychologists any test in this book. Though what follows is not a test, they are three problems and problems with a purpose.

'I've never bothered to find out my own IQ because I don't know what I could do with it if I knew it.' The author of these defiant words turns out to be Arthur Jensen, advocate of intelligence testing. The quote has been used to show that Jensen is human after all, and even a bit of a sceptic. We want to focus on a more telling detail. Imagining taking a test, Jensen at once sees himself in control of the situation. Why should he bother to take his own IQ if he does not know 'what I could do with it if I knew it'. Usually, subjects who take tests do not know what to do with their score on the Lie Scale, or the F Scale, or on the Intercollegiate Basketball Cohesion Instrument. Still, they have to tick on.

Imagine, therefore, the kind of test that Jensen might find it worth his while to take.

The tortoise and the hare are admittedly old hat and have even been revived in *Gödel Escher and Bach* (Hofstadter 1981). Still, even they can find their uses in a book of tests. After the original result, the tortoise decided it would be better manners to hibernate and not to gloat; the hare went on an extended drinking spree. Now, after much effort, they have been re-matched in what has been called 'The Race of the Centuries'. Personality tests have determined that the hare is well motivated and very determined; perceptual tests have determined that the hare sees far better, and motor tests have determined that the hare is much faster. The hare is not going to repeat his mistake and be overconfident. The tortoise has had a bad attack of muscle cramp because it hibernated in too tight a shell.

Explain how the tortoise wins yet again.

Next problem:

Real love or just an image?

Source: *Psychology News*

Explain how you improve on this.

Did you expect the answers to come next?

Ah, those who set the puzzles and control the puzzling environment have a big advantage.

We hope the ambiguities of these problems — including the notion of improving on real love — will nudge readers into an open, playful frame of mind. It is easier to criticise old criteria than to evolve new ones, but having used tests as 'case histories', we want to imagine some rather different versions of testing. Levy (1981) recently argued that psychology was in danger of being enslaved by its methods, psychologists were becoming so subservient to statistics and methods that they were forgetting their subject was people, not numbers. We want to argue now both for tougher and less tough criteria for testing. We do not propose to engage in a statistics-bashing exercise, but researchers need to be much more careful about the meanings they attribute to numbers.

In this chapter we have divided our topics into:

(i) historical background to the control of testing,
(ii) who sets the norms for tests,

(iii)   issues of sampling,
(iv)   the treatment of error scores,
(v)   test/re-test reliability,
(vi)   validity,
(vii)   collaborative prediction,
(viii) the construction of factors,
(ix)   a different agenda for testing,
(x)   some ethical guidelines.

We try throughout to be constructive, pointing the way forward to meaningful testing. Our tougher criteria often involve appeals for realism; our less tough criteria are an attempt to open up testing so that it can take into account some of the ideas developed by critics of conventional scientific psychology. Radford and Reason (1981) argue that subjects and experts ought to collaborate in research as equals; Henriques, Holloway, Urwin, Venn and Walkerdine (1984) claim that psychology has ignored large-scale social processes and tended to reinforce the *status quo*. *Models of Man* (1981), an enlightening collection of different views by leading psychologists, had many who wanted to see a far less rigid discipline. Our proposals for 'less tough' criteria are an attempt to see how such ideas can be useful for those involved in creating tests.

The Control of Tests

The debates about the value of intelligence testing were very much debates *between* psychologists. No one, until 1981, studied what ordinary people thought intelligence was. Historically, psychologists have been jealous of their control of tests. The problem was first debated in 1923 when the American Psychological Association set up a committee to monitor the use of tests by non-psychologists. At the time, American psychologists were worried by their status, especially their status relative to doctors. It could be argued that in setting up this Committee the Association had double-edged motives. Altruistically, some members fretted that American industry, full of enthusiasm for the new-fangled science, would make irresponsible use of tests; selfishly, some members saw a chance to boost the status of psychology. Only doctors could prescribe drugs; therefore only psychologists should prescribe tests.

The pretensions of psychologists to control tests were challenged early. In the 1920s the American columnist Walter Lippman derided psychologists who used IQ results to suggest that the average American had the wit of a 14-year-old. Terman replied to this accusation and was worsted in the debate because Lippman took a 'muck-raking tone' and made 'irreverent pinpricks', according to one of the doyens of testing, Cronbach. Though testing continued to grow — the Scholastic Aptitude Test (SAT) was introduced in America as early as 1926 — there was less criticism of testing in the 1930s and 40s. After the Russians launched their Sputnik in 1957, American education came under pressure to compete and achieve. Tests enjoyed a new vogue since they held out the promise of selecting an intellectual elite that would do battle with the Reds. By 1962 there were questions being raised. Hoffman in *The Tyranny of Testing* (1962) warned that they were far from infallible: another book, *The Brainwatchers* (1962) had the same flavour. Like Lippman, journalists mocked some psychological pretensions. The columnist Art Buchwald produced his own Personality Inventory which asked subjects to tick their feelings about statements such as: 'A wide necktie is a sign of disease'.

The questioning of tests led the *American Psychologist* to devote a whole issue to it in 1965. Throughout the 1970s, after Jensen had published his article on IQ in 1969, political pressure urged guidelines for the use of tests. In America there were three major sets of guidelines published — by the Federal Equal Employment Opportunity Agency (1970), by the Justice Department (1976) and by the Government Accounting Office (1978). In 1978 a set of 'uniform' guidelines was created out of all these. For all the debate, the actual guidelines were fairly anodyne. They required that 'a test user should understand the literature pertaining to the test he uses and the testing problems he deals with it'. When scores on tests were used to select those who scored above a certain cut-off point, there had to be a rationale for that. Furthermore, the guidelines warned test results 'should be interpreted as an estimate of performance under a given set of circumstances. They should not be interpreted as some absolute characteristic'.

The preamble to the guidelines also took note of some apparent contradictions. Tests were better validated by 1978 than they had been previously — for example, Wechsler IQ scales had been restandardised on a population that included black school children — but still they had 'adverse effects' in terms of ethnic minorities. For all that, it was claimed tests did provide less biased information than other procedures. Minorities were more likely to be hired by employers who relied on tests and interviews than by employers who relied on interviews alone.

In America psychologists have lost their role as the final arbiters of the value of tests. A series of legal decisions in the 1970s has left the status of tests somewhat confused. A further crisis was reached in 1981 when Ralph Nader, the consumer champion, attacked the prestigious Educational Testing Service (ETS). Nader claimed that the SAT which ETS used to select high school graduates for university places was a poor predictor of subsequent achievement. The ETS defended itself vigorously. Nader was then himself attacked for misunderstanding the nature of the statistics which, it was claimed, showed SAT scores and school grades were excellent predictors of university performance.

There has been no conclusion to these debates in America, but what has emerged is a sense of change. American psychologists are better organised than psychologists in any other country; the American Psychological Association makes for a powerful lobby in Washington. But despite that, psychologists have had to concede that tests are politically too sensitive to be left just to them. Lee Cronbach (1980) noted: 'All of us have entered a new world . . . if you thrive on uncertainty, you live in the right times'. He repeated that 'change is in the air and no one can regret that there is an awakening of industrial, social, political, scientific and professional concern'.

The implication of both the legal decisions and of Cronbach's view is that people should be much less the victims of tests. They ought to have more rights and they ought to have more say both in the way that tests are used to make choices, and perhaps even in the kinds of tests that are developed. For all the change in the air, there is little sign of that, even in the United States. Individuals have a few more safeguards, but that is all.

In Britain tests have never provoked the same sort of controversy since the demise of the 11-plus. The only court case in which tests have been a central issue has been a bizarre one in which an accused was charged with sophisticated fraud. There was a complex argument between psychologists about whether his scores on a variety of tests suggested that he was too dumb ever to execute the fraud or not. A number of pained articles (Tunstall, Gudjudsson and Hayward 1983; Heim 1983) bemoaned the fact that courts of law did not treat psychological tests with sufficient respect, and one learned judge was berated for reading the test items out loud and scoffing at them. What lese-psychology!

The relative lack of political controversy here about the use of tests since the end of the 11-plus led many to suppose that educationalists hardly ever used tests. Steadman and Gipps (1984), however, found that 82 out of 104 education authorities still had a testing programme though they were often ambivalent about its value. They interviewed headmasters and teachers involved in the schools', or the local education authorities' standardised testing programme.

The researchers' initial survey revealed widespread, school-based testing. Only 7 per cent of the primary schools used no standardised tests at all. Eighty-six per cent used standardised tests as part of the school policy with whole age groups (usually two or more), and a further 7 per cent used tests with individuals though they did not test whole age groups. Local authority testing has little effect on the volume of testing in the classroom: the fact that LEAs test a particular subject and age does not mean schools will not. The most popular topic and age testing is reading at the age of 7 plus, both in LEAs and schools.

At primary level, the major use of both LEA and school test scores was for record-keeping, both for the primary school itself and for passing on to secondary schools at transfer. Twenty-five per cent of headteachers and 19 per cent of teachers thought LEA tests were of little or no use, but defended school-initiated tests. School tests monitored children's progress and determined their reading ages. At secondary level, the main use of test scores was to assign children to teaching groups and to keep records. Nearly all secondary schools used tests in the remedial departments to diagnose individual difficulties and check progress.

The two reasons why primary schools make limited use of LEA test results are that they come at the wrong time of year or are not the ones the school would have chosen. Despite this, only 12 per cent of primary headteachers and a small number of secondary teachers wanted to do away with the whole or part of the LEA testing programmes. The main reason few objections were raised to LEA testing is that, while they may do no good, 68 per cent of primary headteachers did not think there were any adverse side-effects. Further, most accepted the need for higher authorities to monitor standards as part of an accountability procedure.

For local educational authorities, the symbolic ritual of setting up a testing programme is what satisfies, rather than the rigorous use of test results. Steadman and Gipps note that 'the testing programme is acting as a safety net in the event of questions about standards'.

Standardised tests are a means of calibration of what is achieved within an individual school. Particularly at primary school level, where there are no public-exam results, there is a lack of comparative yardsticks by which schools may judge themselves against others. As far as headteachers are concerned, as their day-to-day contact with individual pupils is minimal, the neutrality of standardised test scores is one basis for discussing pupils with teachers and parents. Providing 'objectivity' is also very important for individual teachers.

Local authorities use standardised tests broadly for the same reasons as above. An impartial and precise measurement tool points to managerial efficiency, and can be used to support decisions which might be more strongly challenged if the evidence was subjective. The other major attraction is the simplicity of communicating a test score, often in terms of a simple figure, which is much easier, and less open to direct criticism, than if long screeds had to be written about an individual child's ability.

Who Sets the Norms?

A professional joke notes that if a person asked a friend to perform 50 press-ups, the response would be 'Why?'. If, however, the same person said, 'This is a psychological experiment and I would like you to do 50 press-ups', the response would be 'Where?'. If psychology is to have any credibility, then the bizarre use of testing in British schools needs to be discussed. Tests should not be hidden away in school records to be used by local education authorities when it suits them to bring out some hard, scientific-looking fact to support their monitoring of standards. Steadman and Gipps (1984) argued that testing could be used effectively, especially in guiding individual children rather than selecting children against each other. In this they echo Sandra Scarr, a leading American developmental psychologist, who has wanted to see testing developed for the child rather than for selection. The reality of educational testing in Britain is that it continues to be used but in an unnecessarily mysterious way. In America the kind of closet testing Steadman and Gipps identified would, by now, be challenged in the courts, especially if it were shown that test scores affected a headmaster's recommendations for further education.

There has, of course, been much debate on whether intelligence tests are fair to ethnic minorities. In continuously emphasising this issue, writers have tended to forget that tests may be unfair to minorities in quite different ways. Consider a test of adjustment to growing up. The psychologist constructing such a test may well frame it in terms of Anglo-Saxon Western culture. The test may then be used on Jews, Sikhs and Chinese, who may score poorly on it not because they are not growing up 'properly', but because they are growing up properly in the terms of their own culture. Spence (1982) attempted to remedy this situation by bringing out a manual for social skills training. The manual included many tests for adolescents including a test of perception of Emotions from Facial Expression. Spence warned that her manual was not a test, and suggested a variety of additional techniques to assess and refine social skills. These included role-playing, interviews, discussions. What was most interesting was that Spence felt obliged to caution

> The manual should NOT [her capitals] be used as a test as such. There are no norms available and to provide them would be meaningless as the criteria for socially acceptable behaviour varies immensely according to the type of clients and the type of situation involved.

Spence added that the general aim of the testing and the training should be to benefit the trainee rather than to oil the smooth running of the institution. Submission should not score extra marks. In one of her role-playing tests/games, she offers 'sessions which focus on police encounters', and stresses that these should discuss individual rights and methods rather than teaching the need to accept, without question, authority.

Spence's manual accepts that there are no norms to judge social behaviour by. In that, it is rare. A much more typical test is Youngman's test for Assessing Behavioural Adjustment to School (1979). Youngman first culled 40 items to describe typical school behaviour, but he culled these exclusively from teachers. Not surprisingly, teachers stressed studiousness, compliance and teacher contact. There were questions like 'Do you always ask the teacher before you leave your place?' and 'Do you always ask for help if you get stuck with your work?'. The latter was taken to mean help from the teacher. Apart from problems of test/re-test reliability, the test is politically interesting in that it takes adjustment to school as something to be judged entirely in terms of the values, and views, of the teachers. Not surprisingly, perhaps, Youngman then found that *compliance* correlated with measures of academic achievement which, given that the children were aged between 9 and 13, meant academic achievement as rated by the teachers. Comply well and you'll do well.

Youngman's test leads to a subversive thought: 'What would a test of adjustment to school devised by the children be like?' Would the same qualities matter to them? Goffman (1963) suggests that people in different positions of power in institutions experience those institutions very differently. Your role shapes your behaviour and your views. Youngman perceives adjustment to school totally in terms of the powerful group. In his original assessment, Shelley sniped: 'This test measures aspects of the *status quo* in schools but should not be seen as a justification of what is currently the *status quo*'. Youngman's test illustrates a key problem in the construction of tests. They are devised from a particular expert's point of view. Youngman ignored the consumers of education almost totally. His research highlights one of the conventions we think ought to change — that of imposing on subjects the tests psychologists believe ought to work for them.

Democratic Samples

Too many samples rely on college students. In a witty note to the *Bulletin of the BPS*, Ray (1981) commented:

> Authors may possibly have the proper reservations in the back of their minds but the findings are generally presented as telling us something about processes of quite a general kind. People talk as if they were studying (for example) 'attribution' — not just 'attribution among students'.

Ray wanted to see more use of random samples, even random samples gathered on the doorstep. Opinion polls had long made use of such opportunistic sampling, he claimed. There is much merit in Ray's points, but we should take them further.

There certainly are problems where doorstep samples have their value. Ray is, however, a little inexact in the description of polls. In Britain, at least, organisations like MORI go to great lengths to provide a representative quota sample. Their two-weekly polls question some 2,000 individuals in 157 constituencies. The sample is selected to be nationally representative in terms of class, jobs, house ownership and education. Data are presented at the end of each poll about all these factors. Few psychology departments have the financial resources of MORI, who, of course, sell their research expertise, but there is something to be admired in the thoroughness of their sampling.

Conservative psychologists may say that it is easy to ask for an end to using students as experimental fodder, but who would replace them? At present, of course, students in American universities often get course credits for being subjects in tests. Why not, instead, make students give the particular test to five individuals (not other students) to obtain that credit. That would not make for representative sampling on the scale that MORI can afford, but it would mark a step away from conventionally narrow sampling.

If students had to give tests to a small number of people, they might also be asked to include questions that would give feedback on what the subjects thought of the test. This is a suggestion we develop later. In areas of psychology where data have to be gathered from non-students, professors seem able to send their students forth to observe and interview. Research on how mothers and babies interact is no longer marooned in the laboratory. Sroufe and Wunsch (1972) sent their students out to see what made babies laugh in the first year of life, getting them to tick off a checklist and interview the mother. Using a checklist rather than just observing the interactions meant psychologists still controlled the situation, but at least they did go outside the confines of the lab and campus. Carrying paper-and-pencil tests off the campus to give to friends or strangers ought not to tax the undergraduate unbearably. Psychologists could give some basic training in how to give tests as part of psychology courses. Students would have to be warned not to give all their tests to friends, and particularly friends of the same age group. The procedure, for all its imperfections, would open up sampling. The notion that psychology has to settle for student samples is not so much defeatist as lazy.

Class bias is a second sampling problem. When Kinsey was framing his investigations into sex, he wrote to a friend:

> We have had suggestions from a number of psychologists of Terman's generation that we should confine ourselves to a good

normal, middle-class group, such as college professors. In actuality, the histories of this group represent one of the widest departures from anything that is typical of the mass of the population. (Pomeroy 1982, p. 293)

Tests still seem to be created by the middle class about the middle class, with interesting exceptions. We have argued that tests tend to reinforce the *status quo*. The very names of tests like the Hospital *Adjustment* Scales hint at the bias. Adjustment becomes the ability to fit in with the needs of a particular group. If West Indian children are voluble at school, then they have a problem in failing to 'adjust'; if Asian children are little restrained, then they too have an adjustment problem. One nice illustration of this class bias is the examples used by Rathus in his scale of assertiveness and aggression. Here is the kind of behaviour indulged in by the macho-virile super-toughs: 'If a famed and respected lecturer makes a statement which I think is incorrect, I will have the audience hear my point of view as well'.

This was just the kind of aggressive behaviour that made Al Capone, Mohammed Ali, Ronnie Kray and Humphrey Bogart famous. In the pubs of the East End, the assertive are always insisting on famed and respected lecturers hearing their point of view.

Class bias becomes most manifest in intelligence testing. Sternberg found that ordinary lay persons and academics had rather different ideas both about the nature of intelligence and, curiously, about what made an ideal person. Both saw the ideal person as intelligent. For the academics such intelligence meant abstract skills; for the ordinary people intelligence went with unlikely qualities such as being on time, being sensitive to others, being frank and open, admitting mistakes and having a social conscience. Intelligence was part of social life. It could be argued that intelligence could also be defined as being able to mend a fuse, wire up an electric plug, do simple car repairs, cook a cheap meal, shop wisely, or being able to write books about intelligence testing. Usually, intelligence test items are abstract, abstruse and not very relevant to the ordinary person. Kinsey may have been talking about sex but his point is general. Psychologists should be careful about imposing their ideas and values. What they take to be erotic may not be erotic for the rest of the population; what they take to be intelligence may equally be unrepresentative. Psychologists, however, have always controlled the agenda for tests and devised the constructs used in interpreting results.

Our drift is clear: psychologists need to work against the bias in tests. We would claim they need to do much more than make tests more accessible to working-class subjects or those from minorities. More radically, the discipline needs to do some market research and see what help can be got from ordinary subjects in devising less narrow tests. The Practical Intelligence Test (PITS) might be one. Academics may dismiss this idea as idealistic; the masses would never be interested in such an exercise. Yet magazines like *Logic Problems* and *Puzzler* publish nothing but entertaining puzzles and tests; each has a circulation of over 100,000. The London *Evening Standard* includes the following 'quizzes' each day: a Quick Crossword, a Cryptic Crossword, a word game in which you see how many words you can fashion out of RIDICULE or ANAGRAM, a chess problem and a bridge problem. The Cryptic Crossword has 'easy' or 'difficult' clues. We did not include such tests in our survey of the media because they make no psychological claims, but in playful mood, people enjoy testing their wits and finding out about themselves. Psychologists who ought to have harnessed this enthusiasm have managed instead to make most tests rather dull and a source of 'test anxiety'.

Using wider samples would, in itself, be an initial corrective. In order to devise tests which depend less on academic preconceptions, psychologists need to involve ordinary people in the construction of tests and ask them what tests they want. Sternberg's work on different ideas on intelligence is a step in that direction.

We would also propose that each test should include a clear statement of what samples it has been validated on, not hidden away among the complicated-looking statistics which non-specialists may skip, but prominently displayed. A warning that this test was only validated on 37 psychology students might inspire psychologists not to make too grand claims about human nature on its behalf. Such a warning will not deal with a further statistical problem — that if you use a small sample, vast differences are needed to push results of tests to statistical significance, while if you use large samples, small differences will register as highly significant. But wider sampling ought to help here somewhat too. None of these warnings should discourage people from making use of samples as they find them, but there should be a conscious effort on the part of psychologists to broaden their sampling.

The Treatment of Error Scores

Error variance has been used too much as a means of dumping pertinent questions. Mistakes are made in the administration and marking of tests. Kendrick admitted, in a letter to the *Bulletin of the BPS* in 1981, that the reproduction of his Object Learning Test is so poor the objects are barely decipherable. Scores can be added up wrongly. It is proper to label these as 'error variance'. However, if the reliability of a test is being assessed, is it sensible to call any changes in people between the two administrations the 'error variance'? We would argue this practice needs to be revised. One might just as well label environmental effects as 'error score' or talk of the 'ability error score'. If we are focusing on individual differences, we must not discard differences as 'errors'.

Test/Re-test Reliability

This has long been one of the classic criteria. If people produce wildly different scores on two occasions, then the test must be unreliable. The criterion clearly is important, but it leaves out one possibility. Have individuals changed in between the two takings of a test? In Chapter 2 we focused on the problem of consistency and the general assumption that people are consistent. As with error scores, psychologists seem to think their subjects exist in suspended animation between tests. (In fact, psychologists don't think that at all, but find it convenient to assume it for the purposes of testing.)

We would propose, therefore, that when a test is taken again, the subject be asked a number of questions about any changes in his or her life that have occurred. This would involve getting the subjects to reflect on being tested. They should be asked if they had different reactions to some items, what bits of the test they remembered, if they felt differently about the exercise. It need not be a long addendum to the test, say 5 to 10 minutes at the most. There are obvious difficulties with such a proposal. First, it involves more work. Secondly, it opens up the way to contradictions. On the one hand, such procedures might put low test/re-test reliabilities in perspective; on the other hand, consider this scenario with PITS. Subject A returns the same score at a 2-month interval showing high practical intelligence with distinctions in fuse mending and cookery on the cheap. Subject A has during the last 2 months been divorced, lost his job and was run over, leaving him with some brain damage! The test may be reliable, but its very reliability begs questions. The scenario is not fanciful. Mandelburg and Brooks (1976) found that a year after they had sustained brain injuries in road accidents subjects had normal IQ scores (and their previous occupations suggested that, before the trauma, they were not exceptionally bright or stupid). Since Mandelburg and Brooks were not studying the use of intelligence tests but recovery after road accidents, they did not comment on the reliability of the tests directly. They were amazed by the rate of recovery, but also puzzled as to why with their brain in shape again, patients were failing to get their lives together again. Few were being re-employed, for instance.

Despite such problems, we would argue that while tests do need to be tested for reliability, these procedures should incorporate questions that would attempt to explain any changes. The environment should not be discarded as 'error variance', and if the test/re-test reliability is not good, why not question the people as well as questioning the test?

Constructing Validities

Our suggestions with regard to sampling and test/re-test reliability both involve less narrow criteria, and also applying some of the criteria more rigorously. The proposals we want to make about validity and interpreting validity studies also have this Janus-like quality of facing both ways.

Our case histories often revealed a situation in which tests were judged not by their ability to predict or correlate with real life but with other tests. There certainly are interesting questions that can be asked about scores on two sets of tests. Do people who score highly on spatial intelligence also score highly on neuroticism, for example? Such questions can be asked when correlating well-proven tests like the Wechsler and the Eysenck Personality Inventory, but even then psychologists ought to specify just what is going on.

Since this is meant to be a lucid chapter, we shall now return to the philosopher's favourite, Wittgenstein's language game. Wittgenstein noted that language was a matter of conventions. The meaning of the word 'slab' depended on how it was used in a particular community. He argued, and Gilbert Ryle followed him, that many philosophical puzzles were due to a confusion of categories. In one example, Ryle commiserated with a Frenchman who, on coming to Oxford, asked where the university was. Was it in the colleges? At the Bodleian? The university could not be located in one place. Equally, if the Frenchman, observing *le cricket*, asked where the 'team spirit' was, he would have to be treated to a donnish lecture on the fact that team spirit just was not that kind of thing. Scientists have been reluctant to admit that their activity, too, is like a game, though Peters and Ceci's work on what papers get accepted show only too clearly that it often is. When dealing with validity, psychologists must begin to decide what kind of psychology game, they are playing. Students, and the public, clearly believe that quite definite claims are being made. Those who score high on intelligence tests will do better at school, in work and, perhaps, in other areas of life. If criteria are to be used to make decisions about individuals, they need to be interpreted more rigorously.

Messick (1981) has accused psychologists of neglecting to look for alternative explanations of test scores. A high score for extraversion assumes the person does go to parties and makes dirty jokes, not that he is pretending to. Messick says that psychologists should make sure that a low score on an intelligence test means that subject was incompetent, not that he was worried about his girlfriend, could not read, was badly motivated or angry. Parents of clever children who do not do well at school understand the dilemma. Little Freddie will concentrate on his homework if supervised, pushed or bribed; left to his own devices, he'll be sloppy because he wants to watch television. Focusing just on the one behaviour, attitude or aptitude in question is, Messick argues, deliberately ignoring other aspects of the personality that may be material. Messick's point is particularly apt because test tasks are often so boring. We are told that many people can't even add up a single column of figures until their wages are wrong or they want to work out how much they make on a triple accumulator bet. Then they become unexpectedly numerate. The need to discount rival interpretations is important when tests are used for selection, and also, theoretically. There are two ways of checking why the subject did not do well — talk to him about his feelings about the test or give him further tests. (The Japanese even use a Fear of Success scale with underachieving students!) Both of these seem useful options. They may not lead to an idiographic assessment of the person, but they ought to lead to a more rounded one. An effort to use interviews and tests to see why someone may not have done well also opens the door for collaborative prediction, which we discuss later.

However, since this is also meant to be playful chapter, we need to fantasise about validity. Imagine the following. Both the American Psychological Association and the British Psychological Society recognise that testers often use a cut-off point. Above 51, you pass; under 50, you fail. If these tests are about attaching numbers to people, why not attach numbers to tests? If someone with an IQ of under 110 cannot go to college, why should a test with a predictive power of less than X be used? Equal treatment for tests and people!

Cronbach (1970) has suggested that those tests whose field re-test reliability rating was less than 0.9 should not be used in making decision about individuals. Odams and Smithers (1973) counter that hardly any test comes up to this rating. Nevertheless, the principle is sound. If we are to play the serious psychology game, then we need a serious cut-off point telling us what tests to hire and what tests to fire.

Put like this, the problem becomes all too clear. What validity coefficient (i.e. what correlation between scores on a test and performance in real life jobs or education) would be acceptable? Psychologists are usually ecstatic with a coefficient of 0.7, but even these only mean that that factor accounts for 0.7^2 of the variance — i.e. less than half, 0.49. Ghiselli was criticised by Toplis for his quite conventional claim that even 0.3 was a useful correlation coefficient; 0.3^2, however, equals 0.09. In other words, that factor accounts for less than one tenth of the variance. Such a test might hardly be worth administering. If you had to decide between candidates, you might as well take pot luck or the one with blue eyes. The implications of all this for the use of tests in selection are important, and some political aspects of it are covered in this chapter.

Wittgenstein's language-game analogy alerts us to different uses of validity. We say a passport is valid if it shows us to be British citizens if it has been properly issued and is not out of date. A valid bus pass will allow you to travel on the buses without paying a fare. An argument is valid if it is true, or leads to true conclusions. Often, it is hard to know if arguments are valid or not, but it is never hard to know if a passport is valid or not. Psychologists trade on the rigorous sense of valid when discussing tests. A test is said to be valid and reliable — two copper-bottomed adjectives. We would argue that this use of words obscures the reality of the situation and helps lend tests an overscientific appearance. One device for foregrounding a different emphasis is to set a word in a different way typographically. It can be done as a joke. For 'pheasant' read 'peasant' throughout as it is noted in *1066 and All That*. Or for validity read VALidity throughout. We have two 'tough' proposals concerning testing for validity.

(1) Tests should be tested not against other tests but against some real-life task. People expect tests to predict real behaviour, not paper-and-pencil behaviour. In exceptional cases it should be made very clear that the validation has been carried out on other tests.

(2) That we learn to rewrite validity as, we suggest, VALidity. This will not require too much effort on the part of psychologists or their word processors, but it will draw attention to the fact that we are using the word in a special technical sense. Non-professionals who use the test will, we would hope, be made more aware of the fact that saying a test has VALidity is not quite the same as saying that my passport is valid. For a passport either is, or is not, valid. Tests are in a different category, as Ryle might have observed.

These two proposals are serious, and also deliberately playful because we hope to show that there are different ways of approaching the validity game.

Thinking About the VALidity Game in Real Life

Psychologists have not been unaware of the issues we have raised above, of course. Many who research attitudes have wondered why, when individuals endorsed certain items on attitude scales, that did not predict their future behaviour. In this section we want to examine the implications of subjects not being naïve, and being able to think through the consequences of their behaviour.

Traditionally, there have been three components to attitudes — affective (feelings), cognitive, and conative (actions). A racist waiter at a luxury hotel might dearly love to tell the wealthy sheik, 'Get out of my country and don't come back, you inferior wog'. The waiter is realistic, though; he knows that the hotel will sack him to keep the sheik's business. So the waiter keeps his feelings to himself, ladles out the caviar and bitches to his girlfriend. Psychologists are suspicious of getting subjects to evaluate the questions because of the research on social desirability. People might give the answers they believed were wanted, projecting what they would wish to be rather than what they were like. This is a problem, but it is a problem that can be confronted. Psychologists are aware of it and can probe subjects to see if their answers, when questioned about tests, are being fatally undermined by playing good. We believe there is a less flattering reason why psychologists do not usually seek a dialogue about the process of testing. Jensen may see no point in testing himself, but Jensen is not likely to have an IQ test offered him at a job interview. A leading British occupational psychologist, MacKenzie Davey (1983), in a guide on how to interview well, advised candidates: 'Many companies now use psychological tests in their selection procedures. You may not always be told in advance about this but, in any case, there is no homework you can sensibly do to prepare yourself'. In Davey's world tests are done to subjects who have no choice but to comply. What counts is whether the tests predict what the employer wants to predict.

Writing critically of the many assumptions tests make, Sternberg (1984) warns sternly against the myth that to be fast is to be smart. In the hard, science-prediction game, scores on tests do often depend on speed. Candidates are told they have 20 minutes for 50 items. This leaves out the crucial question of how much people are prepared to devote to a task. Imagine a situation where you do not do as well on a test as your rival for a job. The rival, however, says clearly that for him the job ends at five o'clock. You say you badly want the job and will work till whatever needs to be done is done. The rival may be more intelligent, but will it matter? It is a problem that Sternberg began to address in 1981.

There is some support for the view that visions of intelligence reflect our own values. Sternberg and colleagues (1981) asked three groups of people — 61 studying at Yale Library, 62 waiting for trains in New Haven station, and 62 at a local supermarket to list behaviours characteristic of intelligence, academic intelligence, everyday intelligence or unintelligence. Subjects were also asked to rate themselves on the first three items but not, tactfully, asked to rate themselves on unintelligence.

Those in the college library rated associated items of intelligence with academic intelligence, not everyday intelligence. If you are concerned with whether Calvin was caused by economic forces, mending a plug doesn't seem very critical. In the railway and the supermarket, the main associations were between intelligence and everyday intelligence. Calvinism is of little concern to those who want to get the best buy in frozen peas. Self-concepts, not surprisingly, reflected the previous findings. Bookworms preferred the academic image; railway persons the everyday one; supermarket people were in between.

In a second survey, 122 lay persons who answered advertisements were compared with 140 experts in the field of intelligence. Students were (for once) excluded. Three of the findings were especially interesting. Experts in intelligence see intelligence as closely related both to academic and everyday intelligence; lay persons see more of a rupture between the two, seeing academic intelligence as something slightly remote and abstract. Secondly, both intelligence experts and lay persons perceived intelligence as being rather more than is measured by intelligence tests. Motivation mattered for experts but no motivational factor emerged in lay persons' ratings. Even academics admitted that intelligence was not 'pure', but that much depended on how eager subjects were to use it. Sternberg's refreshing work, and Messick's stress on rival interpretations, points to far more collaboration between psychologists and subjects.

Collaborative Prediction

We want to urge two different kinds of collaboration. The survey of intelligence emphasises that psychology has much to gain by asking people what they take various attitudes and aptitudes to be. Is the ordinary view of 'leadership' or 'assertiveness' or 'sensitivity' different from the expert view? Our analysis of Bem's (1974) work pointed out that she had, perhaps deliberately, polarised visions of the ideal male and female. Asking people what kinds of tests they would like to see developed — hardly an impossibility given that market research constantly does that about products — would open up testing. Collaboration between experts and 'subjects' might lead to the creation of more relevant and subtler tests. Psychologists would have to be willing to abandon some of their power to set the agenda and devise the constructs, but would that necessarily be such a bad thing?

Collaboration could also be far more individual. Collaborative prediction refers to a process by which the psychologists and subject could do a test, discuss the results, see what the person wanted to do as a consequence, and then collaborate to make that prediction happen. Take the following sequence. Harry is tested for a job. At 19 his profile shows good-to-average verbal skills, poor number skills, poor spatial skills. Harry wants to be a photographer. Having discovered what his results (and weaknesses) were, he decides not to abandon his photographic ambitions but to work on his spatial skills. He goes to exhibitions, borrows money to take pictures, works at it. Two months later he does much better at spatial skills, and convinces the photographic course to take him on. Taking the test has worked for him because it gave him something to work with and work at. From a predictive point of view, the test could be said not to have functioned too well. Those with poor spatial skills should not make photographers. For the individual, though, the test was a success. In this scenario people use tests to make choices for themselves rather than allowing their scores on tests to be final arbiters of what they can, and can't, do. Giving subjects detailed feedback on their performances becomes vital in such a situation, as does analysing their results in a way that they become important information the person can use. This way of working gives primacy to different interests than those of employers or educational establishments, who generally want to be reassured that the person is good for the role they have on offer.

At present few psychologists employ tests like that. Two interesting exceptions are Fransella (1981) and Hawton and Catalan (1981). Fransella used Kelly's Repertory Grid to help establish the kinds of situation in which a stutterer felt most anxious and stuttered most, and those in which he coped best. She felt able, then, to build upon his strengths to offer therapy. Even more interesting is the use of tests with attempted suicide patients. Hawton and Catalan (1981) recommend interviewing patients as soon as they regain consciousness. They are also given some tests often including the General Health Questionnaire and the Beck Inventory Depression. Discussing their answers in detail allows patients and social workers and psychologists to pinpoint what areas need work. The tests complement the interviews and help describe the patient's present feelings. They are used to start a therapeutic dialogue. Many clinics deal rather less imaginatively with attempted suicide patients, but Hawton and Catalan offer a good model. Results on tests are predictively useful; to some extent, they help identify the person who is at most risk of repeating an overdose. But that is not the main use of the tests. They become a tool to use with, and for, the patient. The fact that this may well make the patient knowledgeable about the purposes of the test make the question of prediction harder and the test less 'scientific'. But it is not, therefore, less useful either to the subject or the experts. Such collaborative prediction implies that both those who take and those who give tests are on the same side. In fact, they are not. The interests of subjects and experts in industrial tests differ. The company wants to know who to hire; the applicant wants the job.

Too radical criticism of industrial tests is likely to be greeted with howls of outrage. Consider the reaction when Odams and Smithers

(1973) examined the Morrisby Differential Test Battery (DTB), created by Mr Morrisby and sold with 'relevant' manuals to companies all over the world. Odams and Smithers found the Morrisby distinctly flawed. They took particular exception to the 'typical profiles' the manuals included. One point was that one item involved subjects writing backwards. One might imagine that being dextrous and perceptually sharp might be a bonus. Not so. Morrisby claimed that writing backwards too well was part of the delinquent profile. Well, they were both proof of deviance, weren't they? Morrisby did not present, Odams and Smithers noted, 'any evidence of effectiveness', which did not stop him exuding confidence. Odams and Smithers found that in one northern town, many companies used the Morrisby DTB. Prospective apprentices went to so many sessions their backwards writing got rather good, whereupon they were promptly labelled delinquent. The assessment was critical of test/re-test reliabilities and urged scepticism. Morrisby thundered that many of the criticisms could have 'no validity whatsoever' because Odams and Smithers had not been on a training course approved by him! Morrisby went on:

> Research in this, as in any other field, can be undertaken only by competent qualified persons, thoroughly experienced in the ordinary practical use of the techniques they propose to study . . .. It is a matter of great regret that while this principle is accepted without question in every scientific field, it is so often disregarded in what is called 'psychology'.

The editor of *Occupational Psychology* added acidly that he hoped Morrisby would follow with publication of the evidence for the reliability and validity of the DTB.

This episode suggests that it will not be comfortable for many test constructors to abandon ancient claims about how well tests predict behaviour. Yet at present, the evidence for 'tough' prediction is poor, and psychologists often miss opportunities for attempting different kinds of prediction. Elaborating proposals on VALidity, we would suggest:

(1) The development of the kinds of procedures for collaborative prediction briefly outlined.
(2) Much greater use of critical feedback about both tests and test items. Psychologists really ought o listen to their subjects more than

they do. Such feedback need not mean that one must always accept the 'common sense' of subjects, even if the common sense of psychologists seems rather erratic. The subject's view should not become absolute, but we stress it as a corrective to the total power of the psychologists.

(3) Collaborative prediction implies that we need to develop trainability testing much more, involving a mixture of abstract and 'real' skills. Here, subjects could get feedback about their performance and, from test results, decide what to work on. There is nothing new in all this. Sports coaches offer it as a service and so, instinctively, do good trainers in management. But psychologists have rarely maximised the potential of tests in this kind of diagnostic way largely, we would argue, because they have remained bound by the laboratory origins of tests.

(4) We are not proposing the abandonment of predictive VALidity as a criterion, but asking for it to be applied more rigorously and imaginatively. There are many ways of playing psychology; but, as we shall see in the next section, it is hard for psychologists (who are only human) to admit it.

Factors of Interpretation

Our new criteria urge psychologists to be cautious in interpreting data. This is nowhere more true than in factor analysis. A factor is a dimension, trait or characteristic that has been determined by a mathematical procedure of factor analysis. A factor is not a thing or, even an attribute of individuals. A personality trait theorist, for example, might give a large number of trait questions to people and the factors will be the questions that tend to cluster together. If 'going to parties', 'eating exotic food', 'being the centre of attention' are intercorrelated, the set of questions as a whole, or factor, might be labelled extraversion. It is clear that psychologists can only get out of factor analysis what they put in. It is also clear that people are not always sure what questions really mean (Nowakowska 1971).

Psychologists trying to interpret factor analysis are nearly always faced with a problem of deciding what things go together and what things are separate. Cattell (1965), a personality trait theorist, favours an oblique rotation in factor analysis and produces 16 personality factors (16PF). Hans Eysenck (1970) is also a personality trait theorist, but he favours an orthogonal rotation in factor analysis. Eysenck (1970) claims that Cattell's factors are not independent, and the intercorrelations in turn 'require to be submitted to factor analytic studies' (p. 137), and that these 16 personality factors can be reduced to 3. Therefore, even when researchers have a common, theoretical approach ('personality traits' rather than 'environmental situations'), they cannot always agree what method to use and how to interpret findings.

Thurstone has been credited for devising the oblique method of rotation in factor analysis (Radford and Govier 1980; Aiken 1982) and used it to identify seven factors or primary mental abilities, but Guilford (1966), who favours orthogonal rotation in factor analysis, insists there are at least 120 distinct intellectual abilities. Aiken (1982) observes:

> The (Guilford) structure-of-intellect model, which is basically an extension of Thurstone's theory of primary mental abilities restricted to orthogonal factors, is of course, not the only contemporary factor-analytic approach to the definition of intelligence. (pp. 193–4)

Eysenck can use a method (orthogonal rotation) to *reduce* Cattell's personality factors, while Guilford can use the same method to *increase* Thurstone's primary mental abilities. Therefore, neither a common theory nor a common method is any guide as to what the results of factor analysis will be. Eleanor Willemsen (1974) explains that for her reader, the important fact is that there is no unique factor solution for any given intercorrelation table. Further, for any given correlation factor matrix, there are several equally defensible interpretations and 'the reader's own should be one' (p. 167).

Factor analysis is a useful tool, but it has now achieved such pre-eminence that it is being used to replace theory. Once again, method has been confused with substance. It is a convention in factor analysis that answers correlating 0.33 or higher with each other are kept while others are discarded. Block and Dworkin (1977) quote Terman and Merrill, who said: 'Tests that had low correlation with the total were dropped even though they were satisfactory in other respects'. There should be good reasons for both including and excluding test items, but a statistical criterion alone is inadequate. Factor analysis is another example where statistical significance has been confused with significance. If none, or a few people, answer a question in a particular way, what are the reasons and what do they signify? In the psychologists' land of verification and positive correlations these questions are never asked, but are dismissed as 'error variance'.

A Different Agenda for Testing

It is worth attempting perhaps a short summary of our proposals so far. We have criticised the fact that psychologists have controlled testing so much that they have nearly always imposed their own ideas of what issues are important and what constructs matter. We have urged not the abandonment of 'tough' criteria like test/re-test reliability and construct validity, but more realistic use of them. We have offered the outline of a model in which testers and test-takers work together, so that those who are subject to tests can use the results to help themselves. We also echo Messick's (1981) demand for rival explanations of poor test scores, especially where people's careers may depend on the outcome. These proposals would be the start of a rather different use of testing which would still have many pitfalls and limitations, but which would be more rounded and more relevant than much of what currently prevails.

New Ethical Guidelines — Some Suggestions

The British Psychological Society has issued guidelines for the use of testing, but rather like the American guidelines, these offer a few more safeguards for test-takers within the traditional context in which expert psychologists give tests to inexpert people. Though there are useful suggestions for making tests less discriminatory against both minorities and women, the guidelines remain a rather orthodox document. We believe rather more radical ideas are called for:

(1) Access is the first essential issue. Subjects ought to have access to tests and better access to a proper interpretation of their results. At present, psychologists tolerate (and many may secretly cherish) the secrecy that surrounds tests. The National Foundation for Educational Research (NFER) continues to refuse to sell most of its tests to individuals who are not on its qualified list. Anyone can buy a textbook on surgery, but it seems not everyone can buy a test. In a

recent letter to *Bulletin of the BPS*, Karle (1981) wondered if, as the principal psychologist at Guy's Hospital, he had the right to communicate to teachers the scores of some children on NFER tests. He doubted that he had that right. He was also worried that teachers might treat these results as totally reliable, and that to give them 'would lend them spurious reliability and validity'. The parents and children would seem to have no right to these results.

While the 11-plus was used to select children against each other, there might have been a case for denying access to tests. The wise parents could train his child by getting hold of tests; the lazy one wouldn't bother. But now that tests are not used in this way, it is hard to see what justification there is for making them as hard to obtain as state secrets.

(2) As well as allowing tests to be freely available, publishers ought to be encouraged to include a preamble to all their tests. The widespread use of opinion polls (even in papers like *The Sun*) has made people more aware than ever before of the frailty of statistics. The preamble should include an independent assessment of the limits of the test. It should note, for example, that when re-tested, test A achieved only 60 per cent reliability, it should include examples of studies used to validate it. All those taking the test should be allowed to read this preamble. Alerting subjects to the limitations of the test might well reduce anxiety about it. To give subjects an informed account of what the test is meant to do and its own record may occasionally hinder an experimental design which depends on deception. In that case, as soon as possible, subjects should be given exactly that information and an explanation of why it was necessary to deceive them.

(3) We have suggested a few qualifications to free access to all tests. There ought to be no reservations about total access to results. Individuals should be entitled to feedback about their performances. We argued earlier that one problem with many psychometric tests was that they tended just to tot up errors and correct answers and errors. Such quantitative scoring may be useful for psychologists, but people are often curious to know where they failed or why they succeeded. The shift to computerised testing should make it possible for test-takers to receive detailed feedback, especially about their mistakes. The Japanese Productivity Centre in their annual stress test of 130,000 Japanese, provide personalised feedback to each subject and, if necessary, advice on any counselling they might need. Taking the test becomes not just a form of being

evaluated for the sake of the company but a source of useful information for the individual. Results can become the start of a process by which a person changes. Imagine that detailed feedback of your performance on a series of intelligence tests showed that you were poor at spatial ability. You could then use the test scores as a diagnostic tool and decide to work on spatial skills. Tests would become a tool for people to use for, and with, themselves rather than a device experts used on others.

Medical education has long been criticised for taking human beings as machines. In response to much criticism, doctors have begun to explain far more to their patients both about diagnoses and possible treatments. Making patients aware has become an issue it was not 20 years ago. Psychologists need to move in the same direction. Sharing the meaning of tests ought to become routine, not an esoteric exercise in 'democracy'.

(4) The use of tests to select people for jobs and educational courses ought to be examined. Tests ought not to be used just in isolation. If people who fail to get a certain score on a test are rejected then they ought to be told this openly, and the rejecting company or institution ought to be able to justify why this cut-off score was so crucial. The preamble we propose to every test used ought to be useful here.

(5) Great stress ought to be placed on improving well-validated tests so that norms do not discriminate against ethnic minorities or women. The re-standardisation of the Wechsler IQ scales to include black schoolchildren was an important step in that direction. In Britain the Commission for Racial Equality has not raised the issue of the fairness of testing very loudly. We would argue that it ought to. Some countries, Kenya for instance, have tried to adapt intelligence tests to local conditions. Bali, Drenth, van der Flier and Young (1984) claim that the tests can be used in Keyna to select which children should have higher education. Even where much effort has been devoted to making tests culture-free, many factors other than sheer ability affect performance. Institutions ought to be conservative and not rely too much on the tests that exist at present.

(6) Tests-users should understand the implications of research on anxiety about taking tests. They should read instructions out loud and ask if subjects have understood them and know what they have to do. Creating an informal atmosphere as unlike academic examinations as possible might help.

(7) Test-givers should encourage subjects to ask questions about what they are doing and its meaning.

(8) We would suggest, serious attention should be given to asking people what kinds of tests they would like to see. Creators of psychological tests should be more willing to discuss how they create them so that the public might feel less intimidated by the whole enterprise. Discussion of how psychologists devise tests ought to help make a climate where individuals and groups can discuss the kinds of tests they want. Why shouldn't a self-help group for depressives commission a test of the attitudes of psychiatric nurses to depression?

These recommendations are not panaceas, but we believe they all have their uses. More access would make test-givers and test-takers more equal; our proposed preamble, with its caution of how valid, reliable and useful a test was, would make it harder for people to give, as Karle (1981) feared, 'a spurious reliability' to test results. Encouraging subjects to discuss and question the exercise is not a radical pipedream, but is some acknowledgement of the fact that many psychologists want the subject to become more democratic and participatory. Just because rats can't enter into a dialogue about testing the design of mazes is no reason to deal with human subjects on the same level.

Tests are here to stay and will continue to be a central part of psychology. Psychologists need to be more flexible in their attitudes to them. Some who shun them as psychometric absurdities need to reconsider that dogma; others, especially devotees of testing, need to broaden the criteria on which they judge the tests. The exercise we have engaged in, testing a number of tests, has led us not merely to see the flaws and problems of testing but also their potential, both for psychologists and subjects. In 1918 Watson argued that all psychology students ought to use tests to analyse themselves drawing up 'a balance sheet of the self' before they practised on others. Given the present state of testing, how many psychologists would trust tests to reveal what they were good at and what they were like? We need tests psychologists are happy to use on themselves! Only then will we have tests fit for the general public.

Having struggled so far, readers are entitled to the answers to our original playful puzzles.

One way to improve on our cartoon of real love is to draw our attention to the difference between images and the real thing. It is of little use to someone who wants a kiss. Real lips would be an improvement. If, on the other hand, you are in the mood for riddles and puns, then the following punch line in *Psychology News* is, perhaps, an improvement.

The lovers were drawn together by Matthew Cullerne-Bown

Source: *Psychology News*

It's a kind of meta-image, pointing up even more the irony of images of images.

The hare was, you may recall, determined not to fail. He got to within a yard of the finishing line when he decided that really he had made his point and ought not to rob the tortoise. He preferred, having now become wise, to win a moral victory, so he waited patiently for the tortoise to turn up and then let him go through first. The writers of many children's textbooks had also appealed to the hare not to reverse the course of history because who knew what might happen then? Altruistic, but not over confident, the hare this time let the tortoise triumph.

As for Arthur Jensen, it is clear that we are some way to devising the right test for him. Obviously, his IQ does not concern him. We would collaborate with him to find out what he does want to discover about himself. Bearing in mind that he would be a rather knowing subject, we would construct measures (some based on existing tests, some on interviews) that would begin to satisfy his curiosity, and ours.

Testing is a central issue in psychology. It will continue to be controversial, and while we would argue both for more rigour and more imagination, we would hope it could also be more fun.

BIBLIOGRAPHY

Adams-Webber, J. R. (1979) *Personal Construct Theory; Concepts and Application*, Wiley, New York
Aiken, L. R. (1982) *Psychological Testing and Assessment* (4th edn), Allyn & Bacon, London
Anastasi, A. (1976) *Psychological Testing* (4th edn), Macmillan, New York
Apter, M. J. (1982) *The Experience of Motivation*, Academic Press, London
Baldwin J. M. (1942) 'Personal Structure Analysis', *Journal of Abnormal and Social Psychology*, 37, 163–83
Bali, S. K., Drenth, P. J., van der Flier, H. and Young, W. (1984) *Contribution of Aptitude Tests to the Prediction of School Performances in Kenya*, Swets & Zeitlinger, Lisse
Bannister, D. (1981) 'Personal Construct Theory and Research Method' in *Human Enquiry* (eds Reason, P. and Rowan, J.), Wiley, Chichester
——Adams-Webber, J., Penn, W.I. and Radley, A.R. (1975) 'Reversing the process of thought-disorder', *British Journal of Social and Clinical Psychology*, 14, 169–81
Barham, P. (1985) *Schizophrenia and Human Value*, Blackwell, Oxford
Bem, D. J. (1973) 'The Case for Nonconsistency' in *Contemporary Issues in Social Psychology* (eds Wrightman, L. S. and Brigham, J. C.), Brooks/Cole Publishing, Monterrey
Bem, S. L. (1974) 'The Measurement of Psychological Androgyny', *Journal of Consulting and Clinical Psychology*, 42, 155–62
——(1979) 'Theory and Measurement of Androgyny', *Journal of Personality and Social Psychology*, 37, 1047–54
——(1981) Interview in *Psychology News*, no. 29
Benney, M. (1950) *How People Vote*, University of London Press, London
——(1981) *Low Company*, Caliban Books, London
Binet, A. (1911) *L'Étude Experimentale de l'Intelligence*, Schleicher Frères, Paris
Block, N. and Dworkin, G. (1977) *The IQ Controversy*, Quartet, London
Buros, O. K. (1978) *The Eighth Mental Measurement Yearbook*, Gryphon Press, Hyland Park, NJ
Cattell, J. M. (1896) 'Physical and Mental Measurement of Students at Columbia', *Psychology Review*, 3, 618–48
Cattell, R. B. (1965) *The Scientific Analysis of Personality*, Penguin, Harmondsworth
Chapman, T. and Foot, H. (1981) *Models of Man*, British Psychological Society, Leicester
Chein, I. (1972) *The Science of Behaviour and the Image of Man*, Tavistock, London
Chesney, M. A. and Testo, D. L. (1975) 'The Development of the Menstrual Symptom Questionnaire', *Research and Therapy*, 13, 137–44
Clare, A. (1976) *Psychiatry in Dissent*, Tavistock, London
Clarke, A. B. D. and Clarke A. M. (1975) 'Consistency and Variability in the Growth of Human Characteristics' in *Developmental Psychology* (eds Sants, J. and Butcher, H. J.), Penguin, Harmondsworth
Cohen, D. (1977) *Psychologists on Psychology*, Routledge & Kegan Paul, London
——(1981) *Broadmoor*, Psychology News Press, London
——(1983) *Piaget: Critique and Reassessment*, Croom Helm, London

——(1984) 'Japan's Image', *Psychology News*, no. 41
Cooper, J. (1970) 'The Leyton Obsessional Inventory', *Psychological Medicine, 1*, 48–64
Cronbach, L. J. (1970) *Essentials of Psychological Testing*, Harper & Row, New York
——(1980) 'Selection Theory for a Political World, *Public Personnel Management, 9*, 37–50
Czikszentmihalyi, M. (1982) 'Self-awareness and Aversive Experience in Everyday Life', *Journal of Personality, 50*, 1, 15–29
Dalton, K. (1969) *The Menstrual Cycle*, Penguin, Harmondsworth
Dearnley, E. J. (1980) 'Experimental Self-monitoring', paper to the annual BPS conference
De Carlo, N. (1984) *Psychological Games*, Macdonald, London
De Waele, J. P. and Harré, R. (1979) in *Emerging Strategies in Social and Psychological Research*, G. P. Ginsburg ed., Wiley, Chichester
Dicken, C. F. (1959) 'Simulated Patterns on the Edwards Personal Preference Scale, *Journal of Applied Psychology, 43*, 372–8
Dickson, H. J. and Rothlisberger, F. J. (1966) *Counselling in an Organisation*, Harvard Business School, Cambridge, Mass.
Dunnett, S., Koun, S. and Barber, P. J. (1981) 'Social Desirability in the Eysenck Personality Scale', *British Journal of Psychology, 72*, 19–26
Edwards, A. L. (1957) *The Social Desirability Variable in Personality Assessment and Research*, Dryden, New York
——(1959a) *Edwards Personal Preference Schedule*, The Psychological Corporation, New York
——(1959b) 'Social Desirabilty and Test Construction' in *Objective Approaches to Personality* (eds Bass, B. M. and Berg, I. A.), Van Nostrand, New York
Elithern, A. (1981) 'Psychological Testing; the Way Ahead', paper presented to the BPS conference
Elliott, A. G. P. (1981) 'Some Implications of Lie Score Scales in Real-life Selection', *Journal of Occupational Psychology, 54*, 9–16
Essen Moller, E. (1956) 'Individual Traits and Morbidity in a Swedish Rural Population', *Acta Psychiatrica Scandinavia*, supp. no. 100
Eysenck, H. J. (1966) *Know Your Own IQ*, Penguin, Harmondsworth
——(1968) *Psychology Is About People*, Penguin, Harmondsworth
——(1970) *The Structure of Human Personality*, Methuen, London
——and Eysenck, S. B. G. (1976) *Psychoticism as a Dimension of Personality*, University of London Press, London
Farley, F. H. (1966) 'Social Desirability, Extraversion and Neuroticism; a Learning Analysis', *Journal of Psychology, 64*, 113–18
Fine, J. L., Malfetti, J. L. and Shoben, E. J. Jr (1965) *The Columbia Driver Judgement Test*, Teachers College Press, Columbia University, New York
Foucault, M. (1973) *The Birth of the Clinic* (trans. Sheridan, A.), Tavistock, London
Frank, P. (1948) *Einstein; His Life and Times*, Cape, London
Fransella, F. (1981) *Personal Change and Reconstruction*, Academic Press, London
Franzoi, J. and Brewer, C. (1984) 'Self-conscious Awareness', *Journal of Experimental Research in Personality, 18*, 321–9
Friedman, H. S., Prince, L. M., Riggio, R. E. and DiMatteo, M. R. (1980) 'Understanding and Assessing Non-verbal Communication; Affective Communication Test', *Journal of Personal and Social Psychology, 59*, no. 2, (vol. 39) 333–51
Galton, F. (1892) *Hereditary Genius*, Macmillan, London
Ghiselli, E. E. (1966) *The Validity of Occupational Aptitude Tests*, Wiley, Chichester
Gibson, A. J. (1981) 'A Further Analysis of Memory Loss in Dementia and Depression in the Elderly', *British Journal of Social and Clinical Psychology, 20*, 179–85

Bibliography

—— and Kendrick, D. C. (1979) *The Kendrick Battery for the Detection of Dementia in the Elderly*, NFER, Windsor

Goffman, E. J. (1963) *The Presentation of Self in Everyday Life*, Penguin, Harmondsworth

Goldberg, D. P. (1972) *Detection of Psychiatric Illness by Questionnaire*, Oxford University Press, Oxford

Goodchild, M.E. and Duncan-Jones, P. (1985) 'Chronicity and the GHQ', *British Journal of Psychiatry, 146*, 55–61

Gordon, M. E. and Kleiman, L. S. (1976) 'The Prediction of Trainability', *Personnel Psychology, 29*, 243–53

Gorman, B. S. (1968), 'Social Desirability Factors and the Eysenck Personality Inventory', *Journal of Psychology, 69*, 8, 75–83

Gould, S. J. (1981) *The Mismeasurement of Man*, Norton, New York

Gross, M. (1962) *The Brainwatchers*, Random House, New York

Grunau, R. V. E., Purves, S. J., McBurney, A. K. and Low, M. D. (1978) 'Identifying Academic Aptitudes in Adolescent Children by Psychological Testing and EEG Spectral Analysis', *Neuropsychologia, 19*, 78–86

Guildford, J. P. (1959) 'Three Faces of Intellect', *American Psychologist, 14*, 469–79

Haley, J. (1964) 'Research on Family Patterns; an Instrument Measure', *Family Process, 3*, 1

Hall, J. A. and Halberstadt, A. (1980) 'Masculinity and Femininity in Children; Development of the Children's Personal Attribute Questionnaire', *Developmental Psychology, 16*, 270–80

Hardy, J. D., Wolff, H. G. and Goodell, H. (1940) 'Studies on Pain, a New Method for Measuring Pain Threshold', *Journal of Clinical Investigation, 19*, 649–57

——, ——, and —— (1952) *Pain Sensations and Reactions*, Williams & Wilkins, Baltimore, Md.

Harré, R. and Secord, P. F. (1972) *The Explanation of Social Behaviour*, Blackwell, Oxford

Hawton, K. and Catalan, J. (1981) *Attempted Suicide*, Oxford University Press, Oxford

Heim, A. (1983) 'Professional Issues Arising from Psychological Evidence Presented in Court, No. 2', *Bulletin of the BPS, 35*, 329–33

—— and Wallace, J. G. (1948) 'The Effects of Repeatedly Testing the Same Group on the Same Intelligence Test', *Quarterly Journal of Experimental Psychology, 1*, 151–9

Henriques, J., Holloway, W., Urwin, C., Venn, C. and Walkerdine, V. (1984) *Changing the Subject*, Methuen, London

Hoffman, B. (1962) *The Tyranny of Testing*, Collier, New York

Hofstadter, R. (1981) *Gödel, Escher and Bach*, Harvester Press, Brighton

Holland, J. L. (1973) *Making Vocational Choices; a Theory of Careers*, Prentice-Hall, Englewood Cliffs, NJ

Howarth, E. and Hoffman, M. S. (1984) 'A Multidimensional Approach to the Relationship Between Mood and the Weather', *British Journal of Psychology, 75*, 15–23

Jackson, P. (1981) 'Unemployment and Mental Health', paper presented to the BPS annual conference

Jensen, A. R. (1983) *Bias in Mental Testing*, Methuen, London

Kagan, J. (1966) 'Developmental Studies in Reflection' in *Perceptual Development in Children* (eds Kidd, A. H. and Rivoire, J. E.), International University Press, New York

Kamin, L. (1974) *The Science and Politics of IQ*, Erlbaum, Hillsdale, NJ

——(1982) *The IQ Controversy*, Temple Smith, London

Karle, W. (1981) Letter to *Bulletin of the BPS*

Bibliography 195

Kasl, S. V. (1980) 'The Impact of Retirement' in *Occupational Stress* (eds Cooper, C. L. and Payne, R.), Wiley, Chichester
Kelly, G. (1955) *The Psychology of Personal Constructs*, vols 1 and 2, Norton, New York
Kendler, H. (1982) *Psychology: A Science in Conflict*, Oxford Unviersity Press, Oxford
Kendrick, D. C. (1982a) 'Why Assess the Aged?', *British Journal of Clinical Psychology*, 21, 47–54
——(1982b) 'Administrative and Interpretive Problems with the Kendrick Battery for the Detection of Dementia in the Elderly', *British Journal of Clinical Psychology, 21*, 149–50
——(1982c) 'Psychometric and Neurological Models; a Reply to Dr Rabbitt', *British Journal of Clinical Psychology, 21*, 61–2
Kirchner, W. K., Dunnette, M. D. and Mousky, N. (1960) 'Use of the Edwards Personal Preference Scale in the Selection of Salesmen', *Personnel Psychology, 13*, 421–4
Labov, W. (1970) 'The Logic of Non-standard English' in *Language and Poverty* (ed. Williams, F.) Rand McNally, Chicago
Laing, R. D. (1971) *The Politics of the Family*, Tavistock, London
Lamiell, J.T. (1981) 'Towards an Idiothetic Psychology', *American Psychologist*, March, 279–87
Levy, P. (1981) Paper presented to the BPS annual conference
Lynn, R. (1982) 'IQ in Japan and the United States Shows a Growing Disparity', *Nature, 297*, 222–3
Mackenzie Davey, J. (1983) 'How to be Interviewed', TVS pamphlet
Mackinnon, D. W. (1964) 'The Nature and Nurture of Creative Talent' in *Readings in Learning and Human Abilities* (ed. Ripple, R. E.), Harper & Row, New York
Mandelburg, P. and Brooks, C. (1975) 'IQ After Traumatic Injury', *Journal of Neurology, Neurosurgery and Psychiatry, 38*, 1121–6
Matheson, D. W., Bruce, R. L. and Beauchamp, K. L. (1971) *Introduction to Experimental Psychology*, Holt, Rinehart & Winston, New York
McClelland, D. C. (1961) *The Achieving Society*, Van Nostrand, New York
——, Atkinson, J. W., Clark, R. A. and Lowell, E. L. (1953) *Achievement Motive*, Appleton Century Crofts, New York
—— and Winter, D. C. (1969) *Motivating Economic Achievement*, Free Press, New York
McKerracher, D.W., Watson R.A., (1968) 'The E.P.I. in Male and Female Subnormal Psychopaths in a Special Security Hospital', *British Journal of Social and Clinical Psychology, 7*, 295–302
Meehl, P. E. (1954) *Clinical Versus Statistical Prediction*, University of Minneapolis Press, Minneapolis
Melzack, R. (1975) 'The McGill Pain Questionnaire; Major Properties and Scoring Methods', *Pain*, 1, 277–99
—— (1977) *The Puzzle of Pain*, Penguin, Harmondsworth
—— and Torgerson, W. S. (1971) 'On the Language of Pain', *Anaesthesiology, 34*, 50–9
Merton, K. (1968) The Matthew Effect in Science', *Science, 159*, 56–63
Messick, S. (1981) 'Constructs and their Vicissitudes', *Psychological Bulletin, 89*, 575–8
Michaelis, W. and Eysenck, H. J. (1971) 'The Determination of Personality Inventory Factor Patterns and Interrelations by Changes in Real-life Motivation', *Journal of Genetic Psychology, 118*, 223–34
Miller, E. (1971) 'On the Nature of Memory Disorder in Presenile Dementia', *Neuropsychologica, 9*, 75–8

―― (1975) 'Impaired Recall and Memory Disturbance in Presenile Dementia', *British Journal of Social and Clinical Psychology, 14*, 73–9

Minton, H. L. (1984) 'Iowa Child Welfare Research Station — 1940 Debate on Intelligence', *Journal of the History of the Behavioural Sciences, XX*, 160–6

Mischel, W. (1973) 'Towards a Cognitive Social Learning Reconceptualisation of Personality', *Psychological Review, 80*, 252–83

Morss, J. (1981) 'Development in Normal and Down's Syndrome Infants', paper to BPS London conference

Murgatroyd, S. (1984) 'The Validity of the Telic Dominance Scale', unpublished MPhil. dissertation, Open University

Murray, H. (1938) *Explorations in Personality*, Oxford University Press, Oxford

Nathanson, N. (1984) *Book of Tests*, Fontana, London

Nemoff, R. D. (1954) 'A Study of Pain Sensitivity and its Relationship to Certain Manifestations of Anxiety', *Dissertation Abstracts, 14*, 874–5

Newson, J. and Newson, E. (1970) 'Changes in the Concept of Parenthood' in *The Sociology of Modern Britain* (eds Butterworth, E. and Weir, D.), Collins, Glasgow

Nowakowska, M. (1971) 'A Model for Answering Questionnaire Items', *Polish Psychological Bulletin*, vol. 2, no. 1

Odams, A. and Smithers, A. (1973) 'The Reliability of Some Psychological Tests', *Occupational Psychology, 47*, 167–75

Osgood, C. E. (1967) 'Semantic Differential Technique in the Comparative Study of Cultures' in *Readings in the Psychology of Language* (eds Jakobovits, L. A. and Miron, M. S.), Prentice Hall, Englewood Clifs, NJ

Packard, V. (1959) *The Hidden Persuaders*, Penguin, Harmondsworth

Parker, G., Tupling, H. and Brown, L. B. (1979) 'A Parental Bonding Instrument', *British Journal of Medical Psychology, 52*, 1–10

Pattie, A. J. and Gillard, C. J. (1979) *Clifton Assessment Procedure for the Elderly*, Hodder & Stoughton, London

Peters, D. P. and Ceci, S. J. (1981) in *The Behavioural and Brain Sciences (ed. Harnard, S.)*, vol. 5, no. 2, Cambridge University Press, Cambridge

Petrovich, D. V. (1958a) 'The Pain Apperception Test: Psychological Correlates of Pain Perception', *Journal of Clinical Psychology, XIV*, no. 4, 267–74

―― (1958b) 'A Survey of Painfulness Concepts', *Journal of Clinical Psychology, XIV*, no. 3, 288–91

―― (1959) 'The Pain Apperception Test: an Application to Sex Differences', *Journal of Clinical Psychology, XV*, no. 4, 412–14

―― (1960) 'Pain Apperception in Chronic Schizophrenics', *Journal of Projective Techniques, 24*, no. 1

Petty, M. F. and Field, C. J. (1980) 'Fluctuations in Mental Test Scores', *Educational Research, 22*, no. 3, 198–202

Pollock, L. (1983) *Forgotten Children*, Cambridge University Press, Cambridge

Pomeroy, W. B. (1982) *Dr Kinsey and the Institute for Sex Research*, Yale University Press, New Haven, Conn.

Rabbitt, P. (1982) 'How to Assess the Aged: Some Comments on Dr Kendrick's Paper', *British Journal of Clinical Psychology, 21*, 55–9

Radford, J. and Govier, E. (1980) *A Textbook of Psychology*, Sheldon Press, London

―― and Reason, P. (1981) *New Paradigm Research*, Wiley, Chichester

Rathus, S. A. (1973) 'A 30-item Schedule for Assessing Assertive Behaviour', *Behaviour Research and Therapy, 4*, 398–406

Raven, J. C. (1947) *Progressive Matrices*, H. K. Lewis, London

Ray, J. J. (1981) 'Is the Ideal Sample a Non-sample?', *Bulletin of the BPS, 34*, 128–9

Reimann, M., Raichele, H. E., Butler, F. K., Herscovitch, P. and Robins, E. (1984) 'A Focal Brain Abnormality in Panic Disorder', *Nature, 310*, 683–4

Reuman, D.A. (1982), 'Ipsative Behavioral Variability and the Quality of Thematic Apperceptive Measurement of the Achievement Motive', *J. Personality and Social Psychology*, 43, no. 5, 1098–110

Robertson, I. T. and Mindel, R. M. (1980) 'A Study of Trainability Testing', *Journal of Occupational Psychology*, 53, no. 2, 131–8

Rubenowitz, S. (1963) *Emotional Flexibility Rigidity as a Comprehensive Dimension of Mind*, Almquist & Wiksell, Stockholm

Runyan, W. M. (1984) *Life Histories and Psychobiography*, Oxford University Press, Oxford

Ryle, A. (1969) 'The Psychology and Psychiatry of Academic Difficulty in Students', *Proceedings of the Royal Society of Medicine*, 62, 1263ff

Scott Armstrong, (1980) 'Unintelligible Management Research and Academic Prestige', *Interfaces*, 10, 80–6

Scott, J. P. and Fuller, J. L. (1965) *Genetics and the Social Behaviour of the Dog*, University of Chicago Press, Chicago

Sheehey, G. (1979) *Passages*, Ballantyne, New York

Shelley, D. S. A. (1982) 'Children's Personal Attributes Questionaire', *Psychology News*, no. 24

Shipman, V. C. (1976) *Notable Early Characteristics of High and Low-achieving Black Low and SES Children*, Educational Testing Service, Princeton, NJ

Shotter, J. (1984) *Social Accountability and Selfhood*, Blackwell, Oxford

Smithers, A. (1984) Studies of the British official census, *The Guardian*, 19–23 March

Spence, J. T. and Helmreich, R. (1975) 'Ratings of Self and Peers on Sex-role Attributes', *Journal of Personality and Social Psychology*, 32, 29–39

—— and —— (1978) 'The Personal Attributes Questionaire' *JSAS Catalogue of Selected Documents in Psychology*, 4, 43, MS 617

Spence, S. (1982) *A Manual for Social Skills Training*, NFER, Windsor

Sroufe, L. A. and Wunsch, J. P., (1972) 'The Development of Laughter in the First Year of Life', *Child Development*, 43, 1326–44

Steadman, S. and Gipps, C. (1984) 'Teachers and Testing: Pluses and Minuses', *Educational Research*, 26, 2, 121–6

Sternberg, J. R. (1981) 'Testing Cognitive Intelligence', *American Psychologist*, 36, 1181–9

——(1985) *Beyond IQ: a Triarchic Theory of Human Intelligence*, Cambridge University Press, Cambridge

——, Conway, B. E. and Katron, J. L. (1981) 'People's Conceptions of Intelligence', *Journal of Personality and Social Psychology*, 41, 37–55

Stott, D. H. (1981) 'Behaviour Disturbance and Failure to Learn', *Educational Research*, 23, no. 3, 163–72

Svebak, S. (1980) 'The Significance of Effort as well as Serious-minded and Playful Motivational States for Task-induced Tonic Physiological Changes', paper presented to the annual meeting of the British Psychological Society, London

Taylor, M. C. and Hall, J. A. (1982) 'Psychological Androgyny: Series, Methods and Conclusions', *Psychological Bulletin*, 92, 347–67

Terman, L. M. (1925) *Genetic Studies of Genius*, Stanford University Press, Stanford, Calif.

—— and Oden, M. H. (1959) *The Gifted Group at Mid-life*, Stanford University Press, Stanford, Calif.

Thorndike, E. L. (1903) *Educational Psychology*, Scientific Press, New York

Toplis, J. (1981) 'Aptitude Tests and Negative Correlations', *Psychology News*, no. 19

—— and Bedford, F. D. (1980) 'Using Aptitude Tests in Vocational Guidance', paper presented to London Conference of British Psychological Society

Truax, C. B., Carkhuff, R. R. and Kodman, F., Jr (1965) 'Relationships between

Therapist-offered Conditons and Patient Change in Group Psychotherapy', *Journal of Social and Clinical Psychology, 21*, 327–9

Tunstall, O., Gudjunsson, H. J. and Hayward, L. (1983) 'Professional Issues Arising from Psychological Evidence Presented in Court, No. 1', *Bulletin of the BPS, 35*, 329–33

Walvins, J. (1984) *Passage to Britain*, Penguin, Harmondsworth

Warr, P., Cook, J. and Wall, T. (1979) 'Scales for the Measurement of Some Work Attitudes and Aspects of Psychological Well-being', *Journal of Occupational Psychology, 52*, 129–48

Watson, J.B. (1913) 'Psychology As the Behaviourist Views it', *Psychological Review, XX*, 158-78

Watson, J. B. (1919) *Psychology from the Standpoint of a Behaviourist*, Lippincott, Phil.

Weber, M. (1958) 'The Sociology of Charismatic Authority' *from Max Weber, Essays in Sociology* (eds Gerth, H. H. and Mills, C. W.), Oxford University Press, Oxford

Whitehead, A. (1973) 'Verbal Learning and Memory in Elderly Depressives', *British Journal of Psychiatry, 123*, 203–8

—— (1974) 'Factors in the Learning Deficit of Elderly Depressives', *British Journal of Social and Clinical Psychology, 13*, 201–8

Whyte, W. H. Jr (1956) *The Organisation Man*, Simon & Schuster, New York

Willemsen, E. (1974) *Understanding Statistical Reasoning*, W. H. Freeman, San Francisco

Wing, J. K. (1977) *Reasoning About Madness*, Blackwell, Oxford

Youngman, M. B. (1979) 'Assessing Behavioural Adjustment to School, *British Journal of Educational Psychology, 49*, 258–64

Yule, W., Gold, R. D. and Busch, C. (1982) 'Long-term Predictive Validity of the WPPSI; an 11-year Follow-up', *Personal, Individual Differences*, vol. 3, 65–71

AUTHOR INDEX

Adams Webber, J.R. 68
Aiken, L.R. 185
Allport, G. 65–6
Anastasi, A. 73
Apter, M.J. 101, 136–42
Atkinson, J. 31–4

Bali, S.K. 188
Bannister, D. 22, 68–70
Barber, P.J. 116
Barham, P. 38
Bedford, J. 92
Bem, S.L. 83, 93–100, 105, 181
Benney, M. 33
Binet, A. 5–6
Block, N. 185
Brewer, C. 36–7, 42
Brooks, C. 113, 176
Brown, L.B. 18–22
Buchwald Art, 167
Buros, O.K. 73
Busch, C. 113

Carkuff, R.R. 69
Catalan, J. 182
Cattell, J.M. 4
Cattell, R.B. 184
Ceci, S.J. 120–2, 177
Chein, I. 105
Chesney, M.A. 124–7
Clare, A. 39
Clark, R.A. 31
Clarke, A.B.D. 114
Clarke, A.M. 114
Cohen, D. 6, 105, 133
Cook, J. 123
Cooper, J. 43–5
Cronbach, L.J. 116, 166–7, 178
Cziksentmihalyi, M. 36, 46

Dalton, K. 124–7
Dearnley, E.J. 34–8, 46, 68, 79
De Carlo, N. 151
De Waele, J.P. 66
Dicken, C.F. 74
Drenth, P.J. 188
Duncan Jones, P. 43
Dunnett, S. 116–17

Dunnette, M.D. 73
Dworkin, G. 185

Edwards, A.L. 72–4, 115
Elithern, A. 108–10
Elliot, A.G.P. 116–17
Essen-Moller, E. 39
Eysenck, H.J. 40, 47, 118, 151, 187

Farley, F.H. 117
Field, C.J. 113–14
Foucault, M. 3
Fransella, F. 182
Franzoi, J. 36–7, 46
Freud, S. 5, 9
Friedman, H.S. 146–50
Fuller, J.L. 13–15, 27–30

Gall, F.J. 3
Galton, F. 4
Gevins, A. 102
Ghiselli, E.E. 91–2, 178
Gibbs, C. 168–70
Gibson, A.J. 57–8
Gilbert, J.A. 4
Gilliard, C.J. 62–4
Gillie, O. 153
Gold, R.D. 113
Goldberg, D. 39–43
Goodchild, M. 43
Goodell, H. 52
Gordon, M.E. 134
Gorman, B.S. 116
Gould, S.J. 2, 5
Govier, E. 185
Grunau, R.V.E. 101–4, 113
Gudjudsson, G. 167
Guilford, J.P. 185
Gustad, A. 73

Halberstadt, A. 98–100
Haley, J. 123, 130–3
Hall, J.A. 97–100
Hardy, J.D. 52
Harnad, S. 121
Harre, R. 66, 105
Hawton, K. 182
Hayward, E. 167

Heim, A. 107, 113, 167
Heimreich, R. 95
Henriques, J. 165
Henry, V. 5
Hoffman, B. 166
Hoffman, M.S. 22
Hofstadter, R. 163
Holloway, W. 165
Howarth, I. 22

Jackson, P. 42
Jastrow, J. 4
James, W. 46
Jensen, A.R. 6, 91, 163, 166, 180, 190

Kagan, J. 17
Kamin, L. 5
Karle, W. 187
Kasl, S.V. 145
Kelly, G. 8, 67–72, 80
Kendler, H. 105
Kendrick, D.C. 48, 57–60, 175
Kinsey, A. 172–3
Kirchner, W.K. 73
Kleiman, L.S. 134
Kobuta, H. 133
Kodman, F. 69
Koun, S. 116

Lamiell, J.T. 74–80
Lazarus, D. 120–1
Levy, P. 164
Lippman, W. 166
Low, M.D. 101–4
Lowell, E.L. 31
Lynn, R. 79, 111–12

Mackenzie Davey, J. 180
Mandleburg P. 113, 176
McBurney, A.K. 101–4
McClelland, D.C. 31–4, 105
McKerracher, 116
Melzack, R. 49–53, 56
Merton, K. 120
Messick, S. 177, 181, 186
Michaelis, W. 118
Miller, E. 58
Mindel, R.M. 134–6
Minton, H.L. 6
Morrisby, D. 183
Morss, J. 110
Mousky N. 73
Munsterberg, H. 4
Murgatroyd, S. 139
Murray, H. 3, 65, 72–3, 80

Nader, R. 167
Nathanson, N. 151, 159
Nelson, K. 121
Nemoff, R.D. 52–3
Newson, E. 20, 21
Newson, J. 20–1
Nowakowska, M. 23–7, 30, 184

Odams, A. 178, 183

Packard, V. 13
Parker, G. 18–22
Pattie, A.J. 62–4
Penn, W.I. 68
Peters, D.P. 120–2, 177
Petrovich, D.V. 48, 52–7
Petty, M.F. 113
Piaget, J. 6, 63, 110, 114
Pollock, L. 19
Pomeroy, W.B. 172
Purves, S.J. 101–4

Rabbitt, P. 48, 57, 60
Radford, J. 165
Rathus, S.A. 84–7, 173
Ray, J.J. 171
Reason, P. 165
Reimann, M. 106
Reuman, D. 37–8
Robertson, I.T. 135–6
Rosenthal, R. 120
Rubenowitz, S. 73
Runyan, W.M. 8, 66, 79–80
Ryle, A. 68–9, 71
Ryle, G. 176

Scott Armstrong, 120
Scott, J.P. 13–16, 27–30
Secord, P. 105
Sheehey, G. 142
Shelley, D. 7, 99, 129, 139–40
Shipman, V.C. 17
Shotter, J. 105
Simon, T. 5
Smithers, A. 133, 178, 183
Spence, J.T. 170–1
Spence, S. 95, 98
Spurzheim, G. 3
Sroufe, A.L.A. 172
Stapp, J. 95
Steadman, S. 168–70
Sternberg, J.R. 10, 173–4, 180, 189
Stott, D.J. 15–17
Sveback, S. 139–40

Taylor, M.C: 97
Terman, L.M. 5–6, 12
Testo, D.L. 124
Thorndike, E.L. 3, 5
Thurstone, L. 185
Toplis, J. 90–2, 178
Torgerson, W.S. 49
Truax, C.B. 69
Tunstall, O. 167
Tupling, H. 19

Urwin, C. 165

van der Flier, H. 188
Venn, C. 165

Walkerdine, V. 165
Wall, T. 123

Wallace, J.G. 113
Walvins, J. 4
Warr, P. 123, 127–30
Watson, J.B. 5–6, 36, 83, 189
Watson, R.A. 116
Whyte, W.H. Jr 13
Willemsen, E. 185
Wilson, G. 153
Wing, J.K. 39
Winter, D.C. 32
Wolff, H.G. 52
Wundt, W. 4
Wunsch, J.P. 172

Yerkes, R. 5–6
Young, W. 188
Youngman, M.B. 170–1
Yule, W. 113–14

SUBJECT INDEX

Academic Promise Test 100–4
Affective Communication Test (ACT) 145–50
Australian Junior Non Verbal Test 114
Automated Testing 107, 108–10

Beck Depression Inventory 182
Behaviorpak 142–5
Bem's Sex-Role Inventory 83, 93–8

California Personality Inventory 142–3
(CAT) 106
(CATEGO) 39
Cattell's Sixteen Personality Factor Questionnaire (16-PF) 24, 117, 184–5
Children's Educational Coping Styles 15–18
Children's Personal Attributes Questionnaire 98–100
Clifton Assessment Procedures for the Elderly (CAPE) 48, 60–2
Columbia Driver Judgement Test (CDJT) 83, 87–90
Coopersmith's Self-Esteem Scale 148
Cornell Health Questionnaire 44

Department of Employment Vocational Assessment Tests (DEVAT) 83, 90–2, 104, 134
Digit Span 108
Dogs, Comparing Performance of, 13–15, 27–30
Down's Syndrome 110

Edwards Personal Preference Schedule (EPPS) 72–4
Electroencephalograms (EEGs) 101–4
Experiential Self-Monitoring (ESM) 34–8, 46
Eysenck Personality Inventory (EPI) 11, 83, 101, 105, 115–19, 176

Family Interaction Analyser 130–3
Fear of Success Scale 177

Gallup-Thorndike Vocabulary Test 88
General Health Questionnaire (GHQ) 38–43, 46, 82, 182

Hospital Adjustment Scales 71, 173

Idiothetic Testing 75–8
Incomplete Sentences 47
Intercollegiate Basketball Instrument 7, 145, 163

Japanese Productivity Centre Stress Test 129–30, 187–8

Kagan's Reflectivity-Impulsivity Dimension 17
Kelly's Repertory Grid Test 11, 26, 66–72, 182, 184–5
Kendrick Battery for Detection of Dementia in the Elderly 48, 57–60, 61, 175

Leyton Obsessional Inventory (LOI) 43–5, 46
Likert Scale 20

Machiavellianism Scale 148
Marlowe-Crowne Social Desirability Scale 148
McGill Pain Questionnaire 48, 49–52
Medical Questionnaire 54
Menstrual Symptom Questionnaire (MSQ) 124–7
Mental Health Scale (MHS) 42, 82
Minnesota Multiphasic Personality Inventory (MMPI) 115
Morrisby Differential Test Battery 183

Pain Apperception Test (PAT) 52–6, 63
Parental Bonding Instrument (PBI) 13, 18–22
Perceptual Mays Test 108–9
Personality Research Form 148, 149
Physiological Testing 136, 139–42
Present State Examination 39

Index

Questionnaire Item, Model for Answering a 23–7
Quick Tests 7

Rathus Assertiveness Scale (RAS) 83, 84–7, 123, 173
Raven's Progressive Matrices 111, 113–14
Rorschach Ink Blot Test 8, 10, 11, 47, 56
Rotter's Internal-External Locus of Control 148

Scholastic Aptitude Test (SAT) 166, 167
Self-Monitoring Scale 148
Self-Testing (Behaviorpak) 142–5
Social Skills Training, Manual of 170
Stephenson's Q Sort 66
Strong-Campbell Interest Inventory 142–4

Taylor Manifest Anxiety Scale 54
Telic Dominance Scale (TDS) 101, 136–42
Thematic Apperception Test (TAT) 8, 11, 20, 31–4, 37, 38, 47, 48, 52, 71, 81, 82, 130, 132
Trainability Tests 134–5, 142

Wechsler Intelligence Scales 59, 166, 176, 188
Wechsler Intelligence Scales for Children – Revised (WISC-R) 101, 103, 104, 111–13
Word Speech Samples 71
Work, Scales for Attitude to, and Aspects of Psychological Well-Being 127–9

Youngman's Test for Assessing Behavioural Adjustment to School 170–1